J. Morrison

Russia under Alexander III

And in the Preceding Period

J. Morrison

Russia under Alexander III
And in the Preceding Period

ISBN/EAN: 9783743454590

Printed in Europe, USA, Canada, Australia, Japan

Cover: Foto ©ninafisch / pixelio.de

More available books at **www.hansebooks.com**

RUSSIA

UNDER ALEXANDER III.

AND IN THE PRECEDING PERIOD

TRANSLATED FROM THE GERMAN OF H. VON SAMSON-HIMMELSTIERNA

BY

J. MORRISON, M.A.

EDITED, WITH EXPLANATORY NOTES AND AN INTRODUCTION,

BY

FELIX VOLKHOVSKY

London

T. FISHER UNWIN
PATERNOSTER SQUARE
MDCCCXCIII

CONTENTS.

I.
ALEXANDER III. AS TSAREVICH 1

II.
ALEXANDER III. AS ABSOLUTE RULER . . . 12

III.
THE EMPRESS AND HER SURROUNDINGS 21

IV.
THE SMALL COURTS 29

V.
PERSONALITIES OF THE COURT AND THE STATE . . 37

VI.
VON GIERS 43

VII.
POBYEDONOSTSEV AS MINISTER 52

VIII.
SECRET POLICE 62

IX.
THE NECESSITY OF KNOWING RUSSIA . . . 74

X.
MISDOINGS OF THE CLERGY 86

XI.
FINLAND 95

XII.
THE AKSAKOV FAMILY 133

XIII.
M. N. KATKOV 182

XIV.
ALEXANDER KOSHELEV'S MEMOIRS 191

XV.
KRAYEEVSKY AND BYELINSKY 250

XVI.
RUSSIAN PIONEERS 277

APPENDIX 287

INTRODUCTION.

THE amount of information circulating among the English about the phenomena of Russian life is so sparse and so out of proportion to the increasing interest in the subject, that every new book concerning Russia should call forth special attention from the English public, especially if it gives information which cannot be derived from any other source. And so it is, undoubtedly, with the present volume. Characters —both official and unofficial—of the most different types, positions, and activity, pass before the reader in vivid pictures. The Tsar with his surroundings; Pobyedonostsev, that evil spirit of the present Russian Government; the original Aksakov family, together with other old Slavophils; the Liberal land-owner, statesman, and agitator Koshelev; the founder of Russian Radicalism Byelinsky, who, though dead, is still living; Krayeevsky, the typical representative of business abilities, a figure without which Russian life of our day would be not fully represented,—all these profiles, so strikingly different from one another, show to the foreigner the variety of Russian life. The author touches among other matters upon clerical misdoings and the secret police, and gives a very good sketch of Finland. In many cases we cannot share his point of view. Yet it is perhaps as well that he holds those views, as they spur him to get hold of facts not generally known, and to make some interesting revelations, while on the other hand his attitude towards the burning question of Panslavism furnishes us with the opportunity of discussing it at some length on a basis which, we believe, is not usual in the English press.

The present volume is not a full translation of von Samson-Himmelstierna's book, but a collection of sketches selected from it, a large part of the original work being of no value to the English reader. For from that part no knowledge of Russian life or history is to be gained, and if it is characteristic of anything, it is of the author himself, who is a curiously pronounced specimen of an "Ostsee Junker," a devout Roman Catholic who sees only the brilliant side of Catholicism, and a "patriot" of the type that would have nothing to say of the whole world if there were no Germans on earth. As for the Russians — mind, not only for Russian imperialism, not for Russian officialdom, but for the whole Russian people, the Russian race—they are in the author's estimation nothing else than a horde of barbarians, fit for nothing but for being crushed down by the united forces of civilised Europe, if Europe does not wish to be invaded by cossacks and brutalised by "Nihilism"—which in the author's mouth means the same as barbarism. Spurred on by these ideas, the author has written whole chapters which would pass muster as practical jokes, but hardly as serious matter. The English reader could not, however, appreciate their comic character. When a Russian reads, for example, the chapters upon the great Russian painter Alexander Ivánov, or the present Minister of Justice Manasséïn, who both are proclaimed by the German writer most atrocious "nihilists"—the former in art and the latter in statesmanship,—he is most pleasantly amused and cannot help bursting into laughter outright. He has read about Ivánov and perhaps seen his great work —Christ coming to be baptized—in the "Ermitage" in St. Petersburg; so he knows that the painter was simply an advocate of truthfulness to nature in art, and rather a creator than a destroyer. He understands, also, why Mr. Manasséïn is called by the *Ostsee Junker* "a destroyer" and "a nihilist." He destroyed the feudal jurisdiction of the Ostsee nobility over the peasants by introducing a better system of law courts in the Ostsee provinces. The present writer is, certainly, not an admirer of any of the Tsar's ministers, who are, in the whole of their activity, only tools of the Russian bureaucratic absolutism, while he is the bitterest enemy of the latter. Still, it would be absurd and unfair not to see that the reform mentioned was in the interest of the overwhelming majority of the population. The bulk of that population consists of Esthonians, Lievs (both of Finnish origin), and Letts (of Lithuanian origin),—tribes having their own languages and literature, but kept in subjugation by the Germans (forming the nobility and the greater part of the town population), who introduced their language in the law courts as the official one, and still retained many mediæval privileges in jurisdiction. On the other hand, it is ridiculous to call the minister who effected that reform a demagogue and a revolutionist in uniform, as his motives were not at all of a democratic and revolutionary character. It was in the interest of Russian imperialism to weaken the strong in the Ostsee provinces, and this he did without really re-establishing all the rights of the weak, as, abolishing the privileges of the German language in the courts, he did not think of acknowledging the equal rights of the native ones, but introduced, as the official language —the Russian. Thus the system of jurisdiction was bettered, some former injustices replaced by new ones, and the whole was done in the interest of Russification. On the whole, Mr. Manasséïn acted only as an official of the present reign.

All these facts, however, are unknown to the English reader. He, therefore, is unarmed for a criticism of von Himmelstierna's assertions; he cannot follow his polemics in other parts of the book, and to present the English reader with chapters of such character would only mean to waste his time, to bore him, and sometimes to mystify him. That is why they were omitted altogether.

If we have indulged in these explanations at some length, it is because the author's personality, his peculiar point of view, tendencies and ways of dealing with his material, must be always kept in mind even when reading that part of his book which is valuable as a statement of facts and which is given in this volume.

Those facts are of different origin, of different character and of different value. Some of the chapters now given in English—as, for example, those about Byelinsky, Katkov, the Aksakovs and Koshelev—are simply compilations from Russian sources, which the German author follows completely, though they are sometimes not quite consistent with his low opinion of the Russian people. Whenever the standpoint of the Russian writers he followed was right—as, say, about Byelinsky, the Aksakovs and Katkov—his own versions are correct. On other points, however, he had no such guidance. Koshelev in his memoirs is, very naturally, defending his own policy in favour of the Polish landowners when a minister in Poland, and blaming Nicholas Milyutin, who was on the side of the Polish peasantry.

The peasants' interests were, very naturally, opposed to those of the nobility, and either the first or the second had to be sacrificed. The great misfortune of Milyutin and all the Russian statesmen who were inclined to act democratically in Poland, was that they had to act in the capacity of delegates and representatives of an arbitrary, foreign power, which had just put down a national rising and trampled under foot the just claims of the Poles for national liberty and independence. They had to enforce beneficial measures by hateful means, as they acted as conquerors and tyrants, and it must be acknowledged that the most beneficial (to the working majority) of their measures were only details in a whole system of weakening the national Polish element in Poland, of making of Poland a province of the Empire, and of rendering a new rising in it, if not altogether impossible, at least impossible for many years. To that should be added that the best men, like Milyutin, had to work through a legion of officials of which an overwhelming majority had absolutely nothing to do with any democratic and beneficial ideas, but had come at the time to Poland simply for the sake of double salaries and of the expectation that in a recently conquered land they could easily have their own way and fill their pockets.

No just and reasonable man would blame the Government of Alexander II. for having provided the Polish peasant with land in a proportion, and generally having raised his economic position to a level unknown to the average Russian peasant. The sin of that Government (but not of N. Milyutin personally) was that it was not sincere in its resolution to act according to the interests of the overwhelming majority of the Polish people at the expense of the oppressing class, and that in that direction it stopped halfway. The Polish peasant wanted, besides a good economic position, also justice, personal liberty, liberty of conscience, some education, and the undisturbed use of his native language. But these wants clashed with the levelling tendencies of the Russian autocratic and bureaucratic imperialism. The Russian Government therefore introduced the Russian language instead of the Polish in the proceedings of the courts, and in the educational system, and it began to persecute the Roman Catholics as such. Thus, while supporting the peasants against the nobility so far as it was necessary for the purposes of conquest, the Russian Government acted utterly against their interest outside those limits.

For all that Nicholas Milyutin is not to be made responsible. His position was not that of one who directed the whole policy of the Imperial Government in Poland. He was allowed a certain position in a government composed of the most different elements, partly altogether opposed to one another, and headed by an insincere trimmer (Alexander II.), and of that position he availed himself as best he could to endow the peasant with land. Brutes like the Count Michael Mouraviyóv wanted to crush down all the classes of the Polish people, to extirpate the nation itself, if possible. Bureaucrats *pure-sang*, like Count Valuev, then Minister of Internal Affairs, opposed Milyutin's plans for peasant communal self-government. High-placed representatives of the official routine, like Count Berg, and some Russian Liberal landowners like Koshelev, thought it "impossible" to sacrifice altogether the interests of the Polish nobility. Nationalists of the semi-democratic type, like Prince Cherkasky, again, wanted in the first place to Russianise the Poles. And besides all that, a clique of greedy, intriguing courtiers and lacqueys in high uniform, caring for no principle at all, but trying to undermine every one of high standing for the mere purpose of taking his place—such were the surroundings in which N. Milyutin had to carry out his problem. In such a position he had to shut his eyes to what was done outside the limits of this problem, and even to compromise within its limits, inasmuch as the whole scheme was entirely dependent upon the good- or ill-will of a potentate who had not much faith in his own plans, and was open to the most contradictory influences, and could never be relied upon. It would be a great injustice to put N. Milyutin—a sincere Radical—on a level with Prince Cherkasky or any of his supporters (as the German author does), simply because they worked side by side at the same work, pursuing each his own line.

Not all the information given by the German author is derived from Russian literature. There are spheres of Russian life which are strictly interdicted to literature—indeed, to the eye and ear of the whole Russian people. Such is, among others, the sphere of government. The Russian people are allowed to be informed now and then (*post factum*, as it is not safe for the adored sovereign to expose his sacred person to *some* manifestations of the feelings he arouses among his people) at what reviews the Tsar has made his appearance; they get regular intelligence about all the births and deaths occurring in the innumerable royal family, as they must know the proper time both for rejoicing and sorrowing. But it is not expected that these feelings of admiration, love, and sympathy should be based upon the people's acquaintance with the Tsar's and his relatives' personal character and activity, but simply upon the fact that he is an hereditary potentate. Besides, as the reader will see even from the most moderate accounts given of that point by the German author, it is safer for the imperial halo if the earthly particulars of the reigning dynasty's life and "activity" are kept under a veil. Consequently, the Russian Tsar, the Tsarina, their kinsmen and helpers, the good and evil spirits surrounding and influencing them—that whole sphere is kept almost an utter mystery, an enigma, both to foreigners and to Russians themselves. That sphere is, however, one which awakens not only the deepest curiosity, but also a just, legitimate interest. These men—whether good or bad, whether first-class minds or the poorest mediocrities—enforce certain laws, take certain practical measures, which, whether they will leave any trace in history or not, may inflict suffering on millions of living men, or may relieve their misery for the time being. In this volume the reader will find some most interesting characteristics of different personages of that mysterious Russian Olympus of which the centre is now the Anichkov, now the Gatchina Palace. These sketches cannot fully enlighten him upon the subject, but they will certainly add a good deal to the scanty material which is to be found in the press by one who would like to form some idea of the personages upon whom Russian politics — internal and external — depend nowadays.

It is a sad dependence. For a Russian who has a man's heart—more than that: it makes his heart bleed.

Even in the outlines given by an eulogist, what is really the present head of the Russian Government? An obstinate, narrow-minded man, who with the pertinacity of strong conviction clings to the idea that it is good to do evil. (We must not forget that Mr. Stead, who interviewed the Tsar personally, and is his most enthusiastic admirer, says plainly that in Alexander III.'s opinion it is good to persecute five millions of Jews, harass and tyrannise several millions of Russian dissenters, &c.) He is a hot-tempered person who has to keep himself in check by means of reason, which he unfortunately is not very abundantly provided with. He is supposed to be very kind at heart, yet all around him tremble, as he is convinced that to be independent he must be stern. He is supposed to be honest, and so in a certain way he is; and yet he does things which are not easily reconciled with honesty, simply understood. Our author tells us that as early as the Turkish war Alexander III. lost all belief in the honesty of Russian bureaucracy, and in the efficacy of the control exercised over it at present. He had many opportunities later on to see clearly how grossly he was cheated by his own agents. For him personally the possibility of controlling it is made still narrower, as he is so afraid of committing some blunder in personal relations that he avoids discussions, and does not permit his ministers to go into the details of the subject. Under such circumstances, a monarch of the honesty of Peter the Great would certainly come to the conclusion that if the present system of control fails, another must be tried. There are only two such systems: either the control is in the hands of the head of the State, who entrusts his power into the hands of special agents, who are supposed to be responsible before him and his representatives (the present Russian system); or it is entrusted into the hands of the whole population, who watch, Argus-eyed, incessantly and unremittingly, wherever any human breast is breathing. Such a control could be easily and gradually developed by only giving fair play to the local elective bodies (*Zémstvos*), instituted in Alexander II.'s reign, by abolishing the preventive censorship, and by instituting reforms by which every official should be open to a prosecution by any private citizen — in other words, by making the *chinovniks* directly responsible before independent tribunals. This, however, the present Tsar does not like to do. He curtailed the microscopic amount of independence from bureaucratic control the *Zémstvos* had; the evil activity of the censorship is harsher than ever, and the fraudulent and tyrannical official is protected in his misdoings by a law according to which no private person can prosecute him in law courts for any offence committed when on duty, but has instead to apply to the offender's chief, that is, to one of the bureaucratic caste, which is always either purposely or instinctively trying to keep its power out of reach of the citizens. As all this tyranny cannot be easily endured, it creates an enormous amount of, so to say, artificial offences —offences which would never either exist, or be regarded as offences, if certain tyrannical restrictions of useful activity were not imposed by bad laws. "Offences" lead to punishment, to imprisonment, exile, material ruin, and spiritual misery. All this the Russian potentate knows, as he is yearly presented with the reports of the Minister of Justice, the Chief of the Prison Department, the Chief of the Administration of the Press, and so on. And yet he prefers the existence of all this misery, side by side with his impotence to put an effective check on the ill-doings of the bureaucracy, rather than to try the system of control of the people by the people. And why? Because Pobyedonostsev whispers in his ear that in case national control of justice and public life comes into existence, it may finally come to inquire into the rights and doings of the Tsar himself. Now Alexander III.'s honesty comes out in its unmistakable character—the honesty of a good householder and shopkeeper, but certainly not that of the sovereign of a great state. He feels himself entrusted by fate, history, or the orthodox Almighty, with a certain position, a certain power; this power he must transmit undiminished to his children and grandchildren. And so he will, at any cost. He is too good a father, and too honest in filling the duties of his position, not to "honestly" torture over a hundred millions of men, women, and children, provided his "duty" towards the dynasty and the principle of autocratic bureaucracy be done!

One of his predecessors, Peter I., was not such a good father. He had put to the rack, tried, and secretly executed (those were cruel, brutal times) his own son Alexis, because he considered him a traitor to the Russian nation. He was not a very good father, no; but he was undoubtedly *a really honest sovereign*. I am afraid Alexander III. is not much like him. Even not going, in our standard of a ruler's honesty, so far as that, one may feel very disappointed when looking into some particulars of the present Tsar's personality and activity.

A vile crime against the nation was committed under the Minister of State Domains, Count Lieven : 1,358,148 acres of national land, including a virgin oak forest which had been taken away from the peasants for State shipbuilding purposes, were feloniously appropriated by Lieven himself, Mákov, the then Minister of Internal Affairs, the Governor-General of the Orenbóurg and Oufá provinces (where the lands were situated) Krizhanóvsky, the governors of these provinces, and a number of officials from the highest rank in the central government down to the humblest of the locality. When the scandal came to light, Alexander III. became aware of all the particulars of that revolting theft. Now what steps did he take to expose and punish the crimes that had been committed, and to restore to the nation its stolen property? He issued (through Ignatiev, then Minister of the Interior) a circular which condemns "plunder" altogether, and dismissed from their official positions *four* persons—the already-mentioned Minister Lieven, Governor-General Krizhanóvsky, and two local officials. But all the stolen property remained in the hands of the robbers, and not one of them was brought to trial. Nor is this all; that very Lieven, whose dishonesty in his quality of Minister was formally recognised by the fact of his dismissal, now sits in the Council of State as a member. A certain high official, Perfíliev, who took part in the land robbery, and who was afterwards convicted of stealing public money, and condemned for it by a lawcourt, has been pardoned by the Tsar, and now continues his prosperous career of "usefulness" by serving in the Senate. Lióvshin, the Governor of Oufá (after receiving a public reprimand from the Emperor), has been transferred to the Governorship of Yaroslavl, &c., &c. . . .

Is it not clear from all this that whatever be the ideas of the present head of the Russian Empire on honesty in other matters, he in any case regards the plundering of the nation not as a great crime, but as a sort of "delinquency" for which a reprimand or some other "disciplinary measure" is punishment enough? Indeed, after his Imperial

Majesty proclaimed the best part of the Merv oasis, acquired at the cost of the nation's blood and money, his private property, he has to be indulgent towards his faithful servants when they try to snap up here and there a little bit for their own benefit.

Around this autocrat, who is more afraid of being supposed to be influenced by any one than of anything else, are arrayed the most hopeless mediocrities, bigots or mere seekers of wealth and position,[1] as his helpers and servants, who command an innumerable army of minor officials, of whom many are good, intelligent, honest men, who, however, are compelled by the acting *system* of government to act mostly in the capacity of tyrants, of stiflers of every token of personal independence and intellectual life, and agents for pressing taxes out of the economically exhausted population. The better part of these officials try to avoid doing, so far as they possibly can, what the system forces them to do; the worse part try to turn their power into a means for personal profit; and this creates a most unnatural position of things in the country: both parts practically (though silently) teach the population that laws are created in order not to be

---

[1] Although the German author says that the present Russian Government consists of "honourable" men, the reader will notice that so long as the Lievens, the Lióvshins, and the like are in office, the statement of von Samson-Himmelstierna cannot be taken literally.

observed, and it must be confessed that the respect for law is at a very low level in Russia. The last famine, with its ghastly train of evils—the typhus, the scurvy and the cholera, and the latest news about the Imperial Minister of Finance planning to re-establish the salt-tax and the farming of the spirits monopoly—those two scourges of the unfortunate nation, that contributed so much to its impoverishment and demoralisation—speak for themselves of what is the present Tsar's government from the economic point of view.

On such a government is dependent a population of over 110,000,000, consisting of several young, fresh nationalities, which have already proved their possessing a certain originality, a genius of their own. We will not speak here of the Poles, of the Finns; nor will we touch upon nationalities of minor importance, like the Caucasian Georgians, though this race shows itself to be a very promising one. Let us confine ourselves only to the bulk of the population of the Empire, consisting of three large tribes of the same Slavonic root: the Great Russians, the Oukraïniens (or Little Russians), and the White Russians. These tribes, generally known under the common name of "Russians," are the predominant ones both in number, in the dimensions of the territory they occupy, and also in the part they have played in Russian history, and now play in Russian life.

The Russians who, a few centuries ago, occupied only a small territory round the Lake of I'lmen, on the Dviná, and all along the Dnépr river and its tributaries, gradually spread over the half of Europe and one-third of Asia, notwithstanding the fact that they were all the time pressed from all sides by other nationalities, especially by Barbarian hordes from the east, and the south,—hordes that were numerous, warlike, and powerful at that time. This fact is generally attributed to the greediness of the Muscovite Princes and Tsars, and later on of the Russian Emperors, and the explanation is true so far as concerns territorial acquisitions by force of arms. But it is not generally known in Western Europe, that side by side with that official extension of the boundaries of the State there has existed, ever since the Russian people has existed, a system of peaceful extension of the territory occupied by that people, by means of colonisation carried on by the Russian peasant (who sometimes called himself, and was called by others, *kozák*—cossack), on his own account and at his own risk. Without any warlike intentions, thousands upon thousands of settlers set out "to get some land" for tilling among some neighbouring tribe with whom they lived on friendly terms as regards their religion and customs—whether they were Christians or not. Thus, for example, before Siberia came into the possession of the Russian

INTRODUCTION.

Tsars in the sixteenth century, there existed there a number of Russian immigrants. It was only owing to that settled population, scarce though it might be, that the Muscovite troops could be successful in their operations. The same process is going on nowadays as well, along the whole Asiatic frontier of Russia.

Thus the conspicuous abilities of the Russian peasant as a colonist were proved by centuries of practice. For centuries he has been steadily extending the territory of the plough among the nomads, without violating what they consider sacred, without embittering them against the approach of civilisation. If after that comes the soldier with his bayonet, and the *chinovnik* with his bureaucratic tyranny and pressure for taxes, it is not the peasant's fault. He tried himself to escape Muscovite or imperial officialdom, with which he has nothing in common, by the very act of emigrating. And were not his historic past so hard, did not that past create for him the fetters in which he is moving about now—the fetters of *bureaucratic autocracy*—he would have brought long ago to the nomads of the East other blessings besides the plough. The Russian peasant created his popular song and his popular tale, and the same spirit that created them has gradually developed into the music of Michael Glínka, of Alyábïev, of Dargomízhsky, of Tchaykóvsky, and of Seróv, the poetry of Pushkin, of

Lermontov, of Nekrassov, of Shevchénko, the humour and satire of Gogol, Griboyédov, and of Saltikóv, and in the Russian novel represented by Turgenev, Dostoëvsky, Leo Tolstoi, Goncharóv, Korolénko, and others.

Hardly any man of taste and critical insight will deny nowadays that the Russian novel is a real and honourable contribution to the treasures of universal civilisation. Russian music has already made its way among other nations, and has been received with much admiration. There can be no doubt that when Russian art, especially painting, becomes known in Western Europe, it will show still more strikingly the powers of the Russian genius. Men of science know that Mendeléëv in some way remodelled the science of chemistry; that Pirogóv, Botkin, Sechénov, Pashóutin, and others contributed much to physiology and medical science; while a number of Russian names are most honourably associated with other branches of knowledge. In this very volume the reader will find, among others, an account of V. Byelinsky which will give him an idea both of the moral height a Russian can attain when animated with lofty ideals, and of the amazing power he can display when gifted by nature with the talent of a critic and publicist. Another German (Alexander Reinhold) says[1] that Byelinsky did for the

---

[1] *Das Magazin für die Literatur des In-und Auslandes*, 1884 —"Die Kritik in Russland," von A. Reinhold.

Russians the same as Lessing did for the Germans, with the difference that while Lessing had to address an educated public, who were ripe for understanding him, Byelinsky had first to educate his readers, to teach them to understand him. And all that he contrived to do, notwithstanding the unimaginable pressure of the censorship which forced him to speak only in a very veiled language.

These few hints as to what the Russian people could contribute to the rich stock of universal civilisation if free from the stifling plague—Imperialism with its bureaucratic system—are given here intentionally to contrast the Russian people with official Russia, a contrast which is but little understood by foreigners, the author of these sketches included. At the close of chap. ix. and the beginning of chap. x., and in some other places in his book, von Samson-Himmelstierna treats with derision " Russian civilisation." He is as bitter against the " Russian pioneers " among the Balkan and Austrian Slavs as one can be, and he cannot speak of " Russians " and " Russia " in other terms than those of contempt and irritation. If he would speak only of " official civilisation," " official or semi-official pioneers," and " official Russia," every true and reasonable Russian patriot would subscribe to all the bitterness with which he treats " Panslavism." Unfortunately our author is himself one of those curious living specimens of patriotism of a different type, who would like to see the whole world German, blessed with "good" *Junkerthum*, "good" capitalism, and "good" Catholicism. So whether the Balkan or Austrian Slavs are assisted in their endeavours to preserve their nationality and their personal and political rights by official and semi-official Russia, or by the Russian people, its best educated class included—it is all equally hateful to him. Here, however, our points of agreement with the German end, and here is the explanation why.

It is quite true that official Panslavism, as represented on the one side by Count Ignatiev, with his Slav Society, and on the other by Alexander III. and Mr. Pobyedonostsev, is dangerous to Europe. But why is it so? First, because it is associated with "Autocracy, Orthodoxy, and (narrow) Nationalism" —principles which are in bitter opposition to progress and civilisation; and, secondly, because it is backed by a standing army of over 2,000,000, which can be put in the field at the first sign from an autocrat, who cannot be checked either by any representative body (or bodies), or by the will of the nation expressed through the press, petitions, or manifestations. The reports about Alexander III. being the most peaceful man personally, may be true. But on the other hand we know that he is a hot-tempered and self-willed man, and that he would not shrink from war if he imagined it to be his duty. Now the tricks played by him on Prince Alexander of Battenberg, the mission of Koulbars, and other more recent tricks performed in Bulgaria, as well as his persecution of the Jews and Russian dissenters, show how impossible it is to reckon on the Autocrat's ideas about his duties. Besides, whatever be the personal character of an autocrat, such is his very position that—for dynastic reasons or otherwise—he is far more easily induced to wage war than any responsible and democratic body of people's representatives.

Official Panslavism—the Panslavism that would like to see *imperial* Russia absorbing, or at least leading, the different Slav nations in the name of "Autocracy, Orthodoxy, Nationalism"—was never popular in Russia. Originated by a handful of men who were always sitting between two chairs—autocracy and democracy,—who opposed Western ideas, and thus, practically, were on that point at one with the hated officialdom of Nicholas I., which persecuted and suppressed those ideas, Slavophilism and its child Orthodox Panslavism, could not gain ground among the educated class. That class suffered too much from official tyranny. As a matter of fact, the educated class, except that part which was altogether indifferent to any ideas and politics at all, was always led by Byelinsky, Herzen, Granovsky, and later on by Chernishévsky, Dobrolúbov, Kostomárov, Kavélin, Stassulévich, Mikhailovsky—the representatives of progress and Western ideas. The German author does not give in his book any sketch at all of the great Russian Liberal movement which followed immediately after the Sebastopol war, of the revolutionary movement of the 'seventies, and of the vigorous leading part the Liberal and Radical literature, beginning with the time of Nicholas, played in Russian life. For this he is not to be blamed, as it simply did not enter into his intentions to give a full history of modern Russia. On the other hand, his main purpose being to trace the origin of the now reigning official Panslavism, he had to devote to Slavophilism more attention and space than would be justifiable were it treated from the point of view of its real popularity and importance among the Russians as a school of thought. The English reader must be cautioned therefore against imagining that because the sway of Liberalism and Radicalism is very insufficiently represented in the present volume, they are less popular in Russia than Slavophilism in any form. Quite the contrary. Liberalism and Radicalism may be in vogue and in power, as at one time under Alexander II., or they may be suppressed and smarting, as under Alexander III., but they always remain the dominant mode of thinking and acting — either openly or secretly — of the overwhelming majority of the enlightened Russian class.

There can be no talk of conscious Panslavism in any form among the Russian peasants, who are eighty-five per cent. of the whole population.

International politics, they most earnestly believe, "are not their business." As for their instincts, they are certainly not such as to favour any warlike enterprise of the officially Panslavistic character. On page 80, our author acknowledges the peacefulness of the mass of the Russian people. Nor has the Russian peasant any inclination to force his religious opinions upon any one. An orthodox Russian peasant believes—so long as his orthodoxy is not shaken by some new doctrine—that it is his duty to remain orthodox because his forefathers were so, and because he was born so. But at the same time he would tell you with the deepest conviction that "every man can be saved according to *his* religion." He will fight against any nation as a matter of obedience, if ordered by the Tsar to do so; but he would not assault any nation so long as he can keep peace with it.

It is evident now, we hope, that if the Russian government were changed from an autocratic and irresponsible into a democratic and representative government, all danger for Europe, proceeding from "Panslavism," would be at an end. The will of the people—a peaceful, tolerant, and open-minded people—would put a check on the now artificially cultivated jingoism of a few conceited nationalists and many fortune-seekers, and on a policy which, though perhaps in the interests of the dynasty, would be injurious to the bulk of the nation. The

Liberal and Progressive elements of the educated class would acquire their natural predominance in national life and national affairs. And the permanently threatening ghost of "Panslavism," invading Europe in the name of "Autocracy, Orthodoxy, and Nationalism," would vanish from sight for ever.

This does not mean that *all* Panslavism would vanish. Quite the contrary; and those who are burning with *racial* hatred towards the Slavs should prefer the present position of things, however dangerous, because if the Russians liberated themselves from their present bondage and developed their welfare and their national genius without hindrance, all the other Slav nations would feel themselves stronger, and instead of keeping cautiously aloof from that scarecrow the Russian imperialism, would lean towards Russian democracy; then the forcible Germanisation and Magyarisation of the Slavs would be made as impossible as would be any Russification of the Poles or Finns. But that is just what people blinded by racial hatred do not like at all. We are not addressing blind men, however. We are addressing those who have eyes to see and ears to hear; who have a feeling of justice and humanity in their hearts and reason in their minds; who will readily understand that "Panslavism" of which we are talking now is nothing more than a tendency preserving the national genius of any Slav nationality from being violated by any other, securing to the Slav genius fair play, and thus enabling the Slav race to attain a similar position in the civilisation of the world to that which is already held by the Anglo-Saxon, the Teutonic and Franco-Roman races. Every reasonable and just man must acknowledge that this would be nothing but a gain for the whole of mankind; while those who think that no good can come out of the Slav Nazareth must at least admit that, in any case, there would be no harm and much justice in letting the Slavs have their chance.

It is self-evident that all that has been said above can be supported by facts. The history of Bulgaria since its enfranchisement furnishes a splendid opportunity to contrast the working and effect of both the " Panslavisms "—the official and the radical. The level of civilisation in Bulgaria is even lower than it is in Russia. Thus, taking into consideration the nearness of both languages, which enables a Bulgarian to pretty fairly understand a Russian talking his own tongue, Russia could do an enormous good to Bulgaria that no other country could do. Merely making the Russian language popular in Bulgaria (certainly without a fantastic effort to replace by it the Bulgarian) would mean to throw open to the Bulgarians the gates leading to the whole of Russian literature. Now what was done by official Russia for the Bulgarians? The vile intrigues and common crimes perpetrated upon the poor, young, helpless country by Russian *official* Panslavism are in every one's memory. To recall a few details and also to show the work of *unofficial* Russian Panslavism, we will quote M. P. Dragománov, a man of deep knowledge and great intellectual power, who left Russia because of his Radicalism, and is now Professor of History at the Sofia University in Bulgaria :—

"The Russian diplomatic agents in Bulgaria showed a peculiar combination of insolence and want of ability; churlishness and immorality reigned among the army officers, who seemed to have been purposely badly selected for the young country from the whole Russian army; and the central Russian Government, for its part, displayed an unbecoming eagerness to deprive Bulgaria of her independence. The result of all this was that the Bulgarians were beginning to hate everything Russian.

"It is difficult for any one who is not familiar with the matter to realise, yet it is the fact that this hatred began to diminish, while respect for the Russians began to increase in Bulgaria exactly from the time that the Imperial officers and diplomatists left the country. In this very direction are working, among others, those physicians, technical engineers, and teachers, of whom the well-known note of the Imperial Government to the Bulgarian complains. These men, in their own persons, show to the Bulgarians examples of Russian knowledge, skill, and diligence on the one hand, and of respect to the

Bulgarian spirit of independence on the other. Such Russians—whether refugees or not—maintain the use of the Russian language in Bulgaria and spread the knowledge of Russian literature. In this matter such Russians move in the same direction with the Bulgarian Government, which energetically defends the independence of the country against both open and secret foes, yet at the same time preserves in the high schools the teaching of the Russian language, as obligatory, supplies the schools and public libraries with Russian periodicals and hundreds of Russian books, allows lectures in the Sofia University in Russian, side by side with lectures in Bulgarian, and so on."[1]

The good that was done on a small scale in Bulgaria can be done on a large one for the whole of mankind when the Russian contrives to shake off the fetters that tie him hand and foot. Let us hope the blessed day is not far off. If the Russian people could survive the Mongol yoke, the atrocities of John the Terrible (in the North), and of the Polish magnates (in the South and West), preserving their national genius and finally triumphing over their oppressors, —it will certainly triumph over the evils that are the last legacy of its unfortunate past. Mankind generally reaches good only through great evils, and this seems to be the fate of all the Russians—the

[1] *Free Russia* (a monthly magazine), for April, 1891. Truelove, Holborn, London.

Great Russians, the Oukraïniëns, the White Russians —more than of any other nationality. The last black years were so horrible that one cannot believe that all the miseries brought by them were in vain. Indeed the whole system of bureaucratic imperialism is shaken to its very foundation, and the thunder of popular despair is heard in the distance, not yet distinctly. Let us hope the night is coming to its end; and after the dark of the night comes the dawn.

December 1, 1892.   FELIX VOLKHOVSKY.

RUSSIA UNDER ALEXANDER III.

I.

ALEXANDER III. AS TSAREVICH.

"AUTOCRACY became again its special aim, as it had been before, from the death of Peter the Great to the time of Alexander I. The maintenance of its own existence was once more the vital question with the Government; all else was subordinate and conditional."

In these words the most competent of Russian historians sums up the history of his country during the three decades which followed the discovery of the military conspiracy of 1825. "That is," he continues, "what Russia has to thank her secret societies and conspirators for."[1]

Were it not in the nature of historical comparisons and parallels to be somewhat halting, the same thing might be said of the Government that followed the

[1] See Appendix, Note 1.

reign of Alexander II. The accession of this ruler was welcomed with the same acclamation as had been the change of sovereignty which raised the first Alexander to the throne fifty-five years before. Both reigns ended in blood, and as the memory of December 12th (24th) influenced the whole reign of the Emperor Nicholas, so does the policy of Alexander III., up to the present time, bear the impress of the atrocious and insane crime of March 1 (13), 1881. Alexander, too, like his grandfather, is dominated by the thought that "autocracy" alone is capable of saving both people and ruler from collapse and destruction.

Here, however, the parallel ends. Never did there exist men so different as the father and the son of Alexander II.

The Emperor Nicholas never presented more than the exterior of a great man. His natural capacity was as strictly limited as his education, but as a compensation for this he possessed the immense advantage of simple self-contained natures — he believed in himself. This was all the less to be wondered at, for Nicholas had developed under circumstances in which doubts were never entertained with regard to the justification and expediency of absolute power. Nicholas was twenty years younger than his brother and predecessor; he had never shared his political and military cares, and he never looked beyond the dazzling ceremonial of his brother's most popular Government. Although not born heir to the throne, he knew from his early years that the succession would in all probability fall to him, as both his brothers were childless. He was handsome and healthy, and of an essentially cheerful disposition: limitation of intellect and a knowledge of his own powers were so happily joined in him that he was even less given to distrust himself than to distrust others. The third son of Paul I. accepted the doctrine of the Divine mission of kings so simply and literally that he never doubted for a moment that God in granting him a ruler's position had likewise granted him a ruler's understanding.

He possessed in a high degree the *external* qualities requisite for his high office, for he was handsome, imposing, and captivating in his manners. But the strength of his character and the intensity of his belief in himself caused him to deceive himself and others in questions which were beyond his powers. Nicholas was affable, persuasive, and winning when he liked, but when it was necessary he knew how to conceal the narrowness of his vision and the superficiality of his intellect behind a reserve which barred the way once for all to unwelcome influences, and which in the course of years grew from a mask to a second nature. Favoured for a quarter of a century by unexampled good fortune, and surrounded for the most part by men of inferior intelligence and character, the ruler of the most extensive empire in the world came to regard himself as infallible, and to be looked upon in the same light by those who surrounded him. In private life he was cheerful and simple; he was fond of pleasantry and of jests which, in spite of being constantly repeated, produced the impression of heartiness. He thought it his duty when once he had adopted a course of action to follow it out with a fearlessness and severity which cost him no effort precisely because of the narrowness of his vision and the coldness of his nature.

Not a trace of his grandfather's qualities has descended to his grandson. Alexander III. grew up under the influence of the great agitation which attended the abolition of serfdom, when all existing institutions were called in question. When eleven years old he was impressed by the total collapse of the institutions set up by his grandfather, and by the wholesale desertion of the men who had been looked upon as the pillars of the old system. One after another the fundamental institutions of Nicholas crumbled to dust as soon as the breath of the new time began to touch them. What was previously regarded as sacred and venerable lost its significance in a night, and we need not wonder that the boy who had been brought up in the Winter Palace failed to understand the new condition of things.

Until his twentieth year Alexander Alexandrovich had no prospect of succeeding to the throne. He was brought up as a soldier, as exclusively as his grandfather had been before him; it was natural, therefore, when his brother died, that he should have found himself totally unprepared for the fulfilment of his future duties. But it was impossible for him to shut his eyes to his destiny with all the *naïveté* of former times, and to consider a ruler's calling and a ruler's capacity as convertible terms. For he had been a witness of the terrible crises of 1860 and 1861—the first "students' disturbances," the abolition of serfdom, the rebellious outbreaks of the peasantry, the hostile demonstrations of the nobility; in 1862—the revolutionary May fires,[1] the issue of the statutes of the new judicial and provincial administration; and in 1863—the Polish-Lithuanian revolution. But the task of remedying the defects of the past appeared enormously difficult to one who had formerly considered it sufficient to fulfil the ordinary duties pertaining to his office. Nevertheless he was not daunted. He applied himself assiduously to his studies, and it was while he was in the midst of these that the first of the attempts directed against his father's life was made. The event shook the very foundations of his existence; he felt himself on the verge of an abyss whose yawning depth was not dreamt of by the wisest men of the time.

The events which followed this criminal attempt were accompanied by a vexatious party warfare, which continued during the following year, and was

[1] See Appendix, Note 2.

never completely settled. This was the year of Alexander Alexandrovich's marriage with the intended bride of his deceased brother. The malcontents, as always happens, tried to ingratiate themselves with the heir to the throne, and to perplex and entangle his straightforward nature in the meshes of their interminable intrigues. It was known that the Emperor had betrayed a certain amount of sympathy with European Liberals, even when their influence was on the decline, and that he took an interest in the successes of Prussia, which had come to the front since 1866. This was gall and wormwood to the fanatics of the national party. It enabled the supporters of Aksakov and Katkov to play upon the Tsarevich, and by pointing to a return of dangers which were only apparently allayed to inspire him with fears of impending dangers: it also sufficed to cast suspicion on the ministers Valuev and Shuvalov, who favoured a European policy.

Tschikalov, a discharged provincial governor, had attacked Valuev with singular virulence since the winter of 1867–1868, the year of famine. He was a base intriguer, who, as a member of the committee of distress, of which the Tsarevich was president, tried to establish a party hostile to the Minister of the Interior; and he managed to entangle his august patron in a correspondence with Aksakov, which fell at last into the hands of the secret police, and involved the Grand Duke in angry disputes with Count Shuvalov. Subsequently Bogolyubov, a painter, succeeded in becoming one of the confidants of the Tsarevich. He made skilful use of the general discontent with Alexander II.'s friendship for Prussia in 1870, and raised against the Tsarevich the suspicion of carrying on a systematic opposition to his father's policy. At that time certain radical worshippers of Gambetta were momentarily successful in gaining the ear of the Tsarevich, and of obtaining for him the reputation of entertaining ideas of a decidedly constitutional character. The Commune and the events of May, 1871, quickly dispelled these foolish notions; but the Tsarevich never retreated from the position into which he had been driven.

These velleities, which were so little in keeping with the transparent honesty of his character, and which had been forced upon him, were only brought to a close by the outbreak of the Turkish war. What this war brought in its train was worse than anything that had been seen before. After a promising beginning, disappointment followed upon disappointment; one authority after another crumbled into dust, and the Tsarevich was once more forced into opposition with his father. The Tsarevich knew better than the Tsar that the charges of embezzlement and dishonesty made against the commander-in-chief were only too well founded, that the impression produced by the defeats before Plevna had caused a threatening agitation in the minds of the soldiers, and that the retirement of the Tsar to Gorny-Stjuden, and his disappearance for weeks from the eyes of the people, were fraught with serious dangers. The memorial forwarded through Vorontsov to the seat of war was addressed not to the Emperor, but to the Tsarevich. In this memorial Aksakov proposed the appointment of a central committee consisting of delegates of all the *zémstvos* (provincial elective boards), which should take the business in hand, and find out more capable men than those who were formerly army captains; and it was not the fault of the Tsarevich that this document was disregarded. Deeply moved by the horrors of the war, which, as a conscientious commander of an army corps, he had become acquainted with in all their terrible details, the Tsarevich on his return from the seat of war produced on all those who happened to see him the impression of a thorough pessimist. And how this pessimism was nourished by subsequent events! The Berlin Congress tore up the Treaty of San Stefano, and gave a terrible *dementi* to the policy of his friend Count Ignatiev. Some months later the era of uninterrupted outrages set in, causing panic in the Court, the town, and the provinces, and shattering the nerves of the threatened. And as if that were not enough, the scandal which Alexander II. had caused by his double marriage began to be generally known, and wounded the strictly moral heir to the throne in his tenderest feelings. It was only with difficulty that he succeeded in preventing the projected publication (1880) of his father's second marriage.

Experiences of so staggering a nature might have disturbed the balance of the strongest and most resolute character. But such a character the second son of Alexander II. had never been, and could not have been under the given circumstances. Naturally severe and simple-minded, the Tsarevich, from his twentieth year, had stood under the weight of a task whose magnitude was above his powers and his education. He was torn hither and thither by impressions of the most contradictory kind. He was deceived in everything which he had accepted as fixed and authoritative. He was excluded from all participation in the business which should form the work of his life, and from the nature of his position he was prevented from sharing with trusted friends the burden imposed upon him. The consequence of all this was that he lost confidence in himself and in his powers. His grandfather had tried one system, his father the opposite, and both were baffled—both had found out that the instrument of war had failed at the critical moment, just as the painfully elaborated civil order had done, and that a desertion had followed the failure, making the professions of the most loyal people in the earth appear a mockery and a lie. Where should belief in the future and confidence in oneself be found, in the midst of a chaos which seemed incomparably worse than anything which had ever been experienced in the so-called " pagan " lands of the West?

The catastrophe of March 1st (13th) happened, as is well known, on the day on which Alexander II. had resolved to call an assembly composed of representatives of all the provincial *zémstvos*. He acted on the advice of three of his most prominent ministers—Loris Melikov, Milyutin, and Abaza, the Minister of Finance. It was only when the horrified son stood before the shockingly mutilated corpse of his father that he became acquainted with the particulars of the resolution which had been taken.[1]

Its authors had stood aloof from the new Emperor, and did their best to keep him in as complete ignorance of the important measure as he had been of all that had been proposed and undertaken during the last stormy years. Could it be wondered at, then, that the opposite policy which had always been powerful at the Court, amongst the generals and the bureaucracy, should in the hour of universal panic prevail? The phrase used in the time of the Commune, "C'est là que mènent les idées," expressed the feeling in men's minds, and by implication the future course of action. Liberal ideas had been powerless to avert crime and confusion: consequently the alternative was Absolutism—abso-

[1] See Appendix, Note 3.

lute power as the absolute end. Modern ideas were responsible for the Nihilistic corruption of the rising generation: by this was meant that the "orthodox" Church — the immaculate-Byzantine patriarchal Church—was the only salvation for society. The objection that a systematic war against modern ideas would tend to the same disastrous results as had been experienced under Nicholas, was met by the most effective cry of modern times—Nationalism. Nationalism, pure and simple, that is, the absolute elimination of every Western European element, had not been tried as a solution of the problem, either under Alexander II. or Nicholas: no disaster had at any rate followed from its application. It might be that this talisman at once old and new would prove an efficacious remedy.[1]

The simplicity of this logic corresponded in every respect to the mode of thought of the young ruler, who had remained untouched by Western culture. The only question was, and is, how far the character of Alexander III. was fitted to undertake such an enormous task. Agitated by a hundred doubts, fundamentally at variance with the contradictions of modern life, naturally uncertain, filled with the deepest distrust of himself, this son of the reformer Alexander II. felt himself constrained to pursue a line of policy which had brought the strong-willed Nicholas to grief.

[1] See Appendix, Note 4.

II.

ALEXANDER III. AS ABSOLUTE RULER.

FRIENDS and foes are agreed that the present absolute ruler of all the Russians possesses in an unusual degree the virtues of an estimable private man. He is an excellent husband, a loving father, an economical and conscientious master of his house. He has an antipathy to all kinds of untruthfulness, immorality, and frivolity, and he is distinguished for the industry and punctuality with which he fulfils the duties of his high calling. Disinclined to every kind of coquetry, he goes his own way without courting the favour and applause of the people, and without using any of those little arts by which men in his station are wont to ingratiate themselves. When one sees him for the first time he looks as severe and imperious as his grandfather. Like him, too, Alexander III. is firm, resolute, averse to all concessions, and so completely penetrated with the right of his personality and his exceptional position, that inaccessibility to foreign influences and to considerations of doubt or apprehension can be easily understood.

If direction of the will and peculiarity of character were synonymous, and if it were possible for any man so to mould his character as he chose, then this conception of Alexander III. would be accurate. But it is not so. And because no man can be otherwise than as he has been formed by nature, so Alexander is not the man he would wish to be and to seem, but entirely different. These words of the poet apply to him:—

> "Wie an dem Tag, der dich der Welt verliehen,
> Die Sonne stand zum Grusse der Planeten
> Bist alsobald nur fort und fort gediehen,
> Nach dem Gesetz, wonach du angetreten,
> So *musst* du sein, *dir* kannst du nicht entfliehen."

The present Emperor's innate nature is impressionable, and ever prone to be at variance with itself; his contact with the world (as we have seen) has driven him to distrust and doubt both himself and others: in spite of his most strenuous endeavours to become a self-sufficient autocrat, he has never succeeded in the process. His characteristic reserve arises partly from an inborn and invincible shyness, partly from a want of self-confidence. The undeviating persistence in following out a given line of action represents a sense of duty which has been painfully acquired; it does not proceed from an inner necessity. The Emperor is almost impervious to the counsel and opinions of other people — not because he always has his own private opinion in which he puts implicit trust, but because he holds it as a duty to be and to appear incapable of being influenced, and because he fears the appearance of dependence still more than dependence itself. Von Manteuffel, the Prussian minister's much-ridiculed saying "that a strong man can afford to take one step backwards," applies to the Emperor *e contrario*. If he were stronger than he is, he would be more yielding, and if he had greater reliance in his own powers and a stronger will, the appearance of yielding would not trouble him. It cannot be disputed that life has taught him distrust of others; but the source from which this springs is distrust of himself and of his capacity. He arrives at a decision with a certain vehemence, because all decisions are troublesome to him. "Lorsqu'il prend une fois un parti, il veut avec fougue pour n'être pas obligé de vouloir longtemps." Alexander III.'s repugnance to the Western European system is closely bound up with this inner instability of his nature. It is in part founded upon the wish of the Emperor, at least in this one point, to possess a bond of union with the instinct of the people, and a reserve power in case of need, but more especially upon the thought that the Western development is, in his eyes, an uncanny and incommensurable quantity, which must be introduced as little as possible, and reckoned with as quickly as possible. The peculiarities so often mentioned in the daily life of the Tsar are explained by this contradiction between his own real nature and the nature of his duties, which excludes all dependence on others. He prefers to transact business with his ministers and generals rather by writing than by word of mouth, as he wishes to avoid the discussion of subjects with which he is unacquainted. As a matter of duty he receives hundreds of his subjects from all parts of his enormous Empire; but he never allows them to discuss minute points, because he fears explanations which may lead to difficulties. He avoids as far as possible direct and lengthy transactions with foreign diplomatists, because he has no confidence in his power of estimating them at their proper value, and because he has less facility in expressing himself in French than he would like to avow. Conscientious and industrious, he has gradually learnt to master the little round of his official duties : what lies outside this is carefully avoided, and for this reason meetings and intercourse with foreign monarchs are limited to the utmost (his friendly and unpretentious father-in-law naturally excepted). The fear of being forced to play a second part follows the grandson of the "infallible" Nicholas like a phantom. As is natural, the depression of the Tsar, who is constantly preoccupied in fulfilling the duties of his position, communicates itself to his *entourage*, and this depression produces a feeling of discomfort in the life of the Court which cannot be disputed by the most friendly witnesses. Although personally courageous he feels the prudential considerations that have to be taken with regard to the thousand dangers that surround him so galling as to deprive life of all its joy. Crushed by his official position, and compelled to constant repression of his true nature, he rises above the contradiction between *being* and *seeming* most of all during those periodical visits which he makes to the Court of Denmark. Here, where the feeling of responsibility is cast aside, he can give free play to his frank, pleasant, robust nature, but in the ordinary course of things he represses his feelings with a painful conscientiousness. Still the inner discord betrays itself to the attentive observer everywhere — in the salon, on parade, and even in the midst of festivities. The appearance of the tall, stately, vigorous man with the fine broad forehead betokens a mixture of strength and weakness, disdainful pride and invincible shyness, a mind constantly occupied with itself. This explains how he, who as a prince was merely unsociable,[1] has arrived at a degree of isolation within the last few years which surpasses anything ever shown by his predecessors.

Intercourse with his so-called intimate friends is strictly limited. Relations with persons standing outside the usual circle are almost excluded, and in

[1] See Appendix, Note 5.

the place of a personal exchange of views with the advisers of the throne there has arisen more and more a preference for documentary work and written intercourse, which, according to the views of the initiated, works very successfully.

From what has been said there will be no difficulty in drawing a conclusion. If the strange saying that private morality vitiates political morality were not a hundred years old, it would be easy to imagine that the phrase had been coined specially for the present Emperor and his mode of government. Since the failure of the ministry of that "man of genius," Count Ignatiev, in 1881, Alexander III. has preferred to surround himself with ministers whose blamelessness in private relations shall serve as a guarantee for their political trustworthiness and professional usefulness. That "honourable mediocrity leads to no difficulties" has been so abundantly proved by one part of the gentlemen appointed that nothing further need be said on this point. But the other part consists of the most dangerous of all classes of statesmen, namely, of the "conspicuously upright" fanatics of reflection, men whose uprightness is exceeded by a still more conspicuous narrowness and shortsightedness.[1] To make matters worse, these are the only high functionaries to whom the Emperor (always anxious about his independence) occasionally allows a predominating influence. The

[1] See Appendix, Note 6.

power of recognising capacity and ability and superior talents, and of making use of them, is limited to strong, self-confident natures: where these qualities fail, talent is opposed by a distrust which fails to assert itself in the presence of a fanaticism which is and appears honourable. That strong convictions make an incomparably greater impression on Alexander III. than well-reasoned-out opinions may be honourable to his moral character; the gain to Europe and to Russia would be incomparably greater if the contrary were the case. Perhaps the greatest part of our troubles in international questions is to be traced back to the apprehension of the Emperor with regard to foreign and especially German influences.[1]

The more the opinions and proposals, which had penetrated from the West of Europe, were unimpeachable, the more suspiciously were they received; while it was the custom to look upon the productions of the national and ecclesiastical fanaticism of races as a special advantage, inasmuch as "they spoke not to the head, but to the heart." As if the convictions of the heart possessed a privilege of infallibility which has been denied to the intellectual judgments, and as if subordination on rational grounds were less honourable than subordination to the strong impulses of others![2] There are indeed

[1] See Appendix, Note 7.
[2] And are there stronger impulses than those of envy, which is the mainspring of Russian Chauvinism?

instincts which are more certain than carefully elaborated reasonings, but such instincts are not found among "the conspicuously upright" or fanatical natures, but only among "gifted natures." Men of genius are to be found in the *entourage* of Alexander III. as rarely as they were under his predecessors, and, if they ever should be discovered, their fate would be very little different to that of the philosopher's stone :—

> "Und fänden sie den Stein der Weisen
> Die Weisen mangelten dem Stein."

But this will be treated more fully afterwards. Here nothing but the personality of the Tsar comes under consideration, and this has given rise to many false criticisms. Of these only one need be mentioned. Alexander, in contradistinction to his father, whose nervous, emotional, and weak nature was alloyed with a considerable element of internal frigidity, is in his disposition violent and passionate. Accustomed to keep his inner nature in check and under the control of reason, he can, when once he breaks loose, storm and rave with as little heed to consequences as his dreaded grandfather ever did. The reports which are current on this point are not without foundation, but they are for the most part greatly exaggerated. The atmosphere of painful restraint which pervades the Court shows that these outbursts of passion are not infrequently directed against intimate and dear friends (at times the dearest), but it proves at the same time that these explosions arise from physical causes, and that they have nothing in common with the strictly estimable moral nature of the man.

III.

THE EMPRESS AND HER SURROUNDINGS.

MORE female sovereigns have reigned in Russia than in any other modern State, and for this reason nowhere have the wives of the ruling monarchs exercised so small an influence on the Government as they have in Russia. So it was under Paul, under Nicholas, under the first and second Alexander, and so it has remained under Alexander III. It is even of greater importance, as the marriage of the present Emperor has turned out happier and more untroubled than that of any of his predecessors. It has contributed to this happiness that the absolute ruler has never felt himself obliged to offer any opposition to the influence of his wife. Whether a correct appreciation of her husband's character, or an innate lack of self-assertion, has had the chief share in the habitual self-effacement of the daughter of Christian IX., is an open question. As a matter of fact Maria Feodorovna always showed herself satisfied with her position as wife of the Tsar, and in this way laid the foundation for the happiness of her house and her married life: it is for this reason that she has obtained immense popularity in Russia.[1] It may be incidentally remarked that the Danish-Russian marriage had been since the beginning of the 'sixties a project which was regarded with favour by both Courts, and that the removal of the obstacles which had repeatedly come in the way was a source of real satisfaction to the Russian people, inasmuch as they desired that the next Empress should not be a *German*. The first obstacle presented itself in the winter of 1863-1864. Democratic Denmark's friendly demonstrations in favour of Poland in 1863 were still rankling in Gorchakov's breast when the outbreak of the Schleswig-Holstein war, and the insults heaped in consequence by the Copenhagen mob on the ladies of the Glucksburg dynasty, caused uneasiness to the friends of this marriage project. A year later the eldest son of Alexander II., who had been betrothed to the Princess Dagmar, died, and it appeared questionable whether the same intimate relations could be maintained between the two houses. That this was practicable has materially contributed to the favourable reception the Empress has received from the very first, and her winning ways have since ingratiated her in the hearts of the people.

[1] See Appendix, Note 8.

Natural vivacity and an optimistic temperament have enabled her, in spite of a nervous excitability, to cheer her husband in the midst of his incessant conflicts with himself and the world. The Emperor has nothing to fear from female influence, for it is never directed to subjects of a political nature. It has been occasionally rumoured that the Empress's sympathies are with the Finns, but it has never been suggested that these sympathies would be translated into acts, as it well might have been when the question of the exceptional position of the northern province arose. Maria Feodorovna's aspirations are the most moderate possible. If the Empress now and again takes a womanly interest in the "lions" of the Court balls or the admirers of her favourite ladies, it is done in so naïve and simple a way that no one can well be angry with the high go-between even in cases of failure.

It is precisely because the Emperor has become unsociable, and because his participation in Court festivities gives him pleasure only in exceptional cases, that he is glad that his wife finds inexhaustible joy in dancing and amusements, even though she runs up bills to the goddess of Fashion, which are not seldom as long as those of Josephine, the first wife of Napoleon, who spent half her life in her dressing-room.

The Empress has the virtue of living peaceably with everybody (including her brother-in-law and sister-in-law) and in threading her way with equal cleverness through the cliques and intrigues which are simply unavoidable at Courts. That she meets the Emperor's occasional outbreaks of violence with extraordinary tact can be easily understood in the case of a woman of so happy and discreet a nature.

Maria Feodorovna's buoyancy and cheerfulness have, it must be confessed, already received *one* shock. Although the Empress was able to overcome the heavy trials and dangers of the last year of the former reign and the first years of Alexander III.'s reign with apparent lightness of heart, yet the railway catastrophe at Borki unhinged her completely. For weeks her highly-strung nerves were unable to recover from the impression of those terrible pictures of destruction, and for a considerable time a regimen of care and rest had to be observed—a striking contrast to her former habits at Court. The fear that the terrible day would leave permanent traces behind, and necessitate the entrance of the Empress into a hospital, has, however, not been realised, and the imperial Court has almost regained its former appearance.

In the palace of Anichkov, as well as at Gatchina, the old breathless rush of society prevails: this is regarded by its devotees as desirable and pleasant, as it leaves no spare time for quiet contemplation and reflection. Montenegrin and Greek, Hessian and Mecklenburgian visits, betrothals, marriage schemes, travels and projects of travel, have pressed thick on one another for the last few years, as if to show that considerations for the physical and moral health of the Empress were no longer necessary.

A change in the *personnel* of the Empress's household was effected in the year of the catastrophe at Borki which deserves casual notice. The position of chief mistress of the Court (*grande maitresse de la maison*) became vacant through the decease of the Princess Helena Kochubei. The place was filled by the Countess Stroganov, widowed Princess Byeloseliskaya, *née* Bibikov. The well-known Princess Helena was regarded by exclusive society as the chief and most prominent representative of the best aristocratic traditions of the "good old times." She was the daughter-in-law of Victor Pavlovich Kochubei (formerly Minister of the Interior, and afterwards Chancellor of the Empire), who died in 1834, and who was loaded with decorations and distinctions by Alexander I. and Nicholas. Coming to the Court at an early age, and being as intimately acquainted with its traditions, customs, and prejudices as with distinguished society abroad (especially the Courts of Prussia and Baden), she rendered very important service to the Empress for many years; she exercised an extensive and beneficial influence upon her demeanour, and played a part which has been compared to that assigned to the Countess Voss at the Court of Queen Louisa of

Prussia. Naturally these services were limited to such questions as the strict and conscientious observance of etiquette and advice in personal questions. The old princess, known to everybody by her grave outward appearance, was looked upon by society as a *grande dame* who was distinguished from the rest of her class only by reason of her greater pretensions and the sharpness of her tongue. The priests and devotees of etiquette maintain that it would be impossible to find another *grande maîtresse de la maison* either in Russia or elsewhere equally prominent and equally well fitted to all the duties of her office. Sober-minded people, on the other hand, are of opinion that the Empress who has been the centre of society for a decade is no longer in need of a *grande maîtresse* to act at once as her *duenna* and adviser. Antonina Bludov, maid of honour to the Empress, has no influence with her. She belongs to the fanatical ecclesiastical school of Tolstoi and Pobyedonostsev; she was regarded in her time as a woman of intellect and enterprise: accordingly she possesses none of those qualities which are attractive to a young princess whose mind is directed to the luxury and splendour of life.

Prince Ivan Galitsin, the well-known and distinguished "master of the Court," who is imbued with the traditions of Kochubei, has troubled himself as little about the business and financial direction of the household as did the deceased *grande maîtresse de la maison*, who was even more "distinguished." This unthankful function has long devolved upon Oom, *secrétaire des commandements*, and a privy councillor. Oom has been in the service of the Court for a generation. He is the son of a highly respected mother (long since dead) who was directress of the large Foundling Hospital (*Vospitatelni Dom*), which belongs to the department of the reigning Empress. The directress was also brought up at the Court, and has left behind her a reputation for great energy. Among the ladies of honour (who, in contradistinction to the maids of honour, are married, and do not live in the palace), Princess Elise (Betty) Baryatinsky (widow of the field-marshal) is the best known, because she was in her day one of the queens and leaders of the fashionable world, and gave it its tone—qualities which have nothing in common with intellectual importance and actual influence. For this reason it is not worth while to enter into the connection of Baryatinsky with the Dolgorukies, and the part played by this family. They are of no account either politically or officially.

Only a few of the higher officials maintain regular relations with the Court and Court society: the majority of the Emperor's advisers and dignitaries belong to circles of an entirely different description. They are immersed so deeply in official cares that they have no time left for the excitement of the salon. In spite of all "Conservative" traditions, the days are past in which "elegant men" and high dignitaries were convertible terms, and this applies to St. Petersburg with as great, if not greater, force than to the rest of the European capitals. The doings of exclusive society have lost the last remnant of their significance and content, from the very time when Liberal ideas went out of fashion, and when political salons exercised no longer an influence on the State. Such circles as were to be found thirty years ago in the Michael Palace, and at times in the Marble Palace, exist no longer, and cannot exist, for the watchword has gone forth from the highest place, that affairs of State concern the Emperor alone and his officials, and that society must confine itself to pastimes and representations. The example set by the Empress in this domain *is* authoritative, and the society which she leads is not in a position to raise itself above the level marked out for them by her. It has always been considered *bon ton* to show readiness in yielding to the highest wishes, with the exception of the short period of the Liberal exuberance which lasted from 1860 to 1864. The present position is more absolute than ever: a generation has grown up which takes a delight in opposing, for the sake of opposition, the tendencies of the former reign, and which believes itself to be "national," when it stands aloof from West European and other ideas.

IV.

THE SMALL COURTS.

THE private lives and characteristic peculiarities of the brothers, uncles, and cousins of the Emperor Alexander III. are as well and perhaps better known both in and out of Russia than they deserve to be. The romantic relation (probably ending in a secret marriage) which subsisted for years between Alexis, the Emperor's second brother, and a lady who is at present living in Dresden and married to an officer, has long been a favourite subject with German novelists of the third class. The so-called Count Paul Vasily has thought it necessary to go into a multitude of details with regard to Alexis's more or less Platonic affection for the beautiful Countess Zeneida Beauharnais (*née* Skobelev). What goddess is at present being worshipped by the Grand Duke I do not know, and perhaps the inconstant Amadis does not know himself. Alexis is forty-one: he has remained a bachelor—a thing which has never happened before in the annals of the house of

Gottorp-Romanov. His position in the imperial family is an exceptional one. As is fitting for an admiral of the Russian fleet, he as a rule spends part of the year abroad, and when at all possible in a "port town of the future," namely, Paris. Admiral Shestakov (successor of Pechurov) superintended the marine department from 1882 : he has been succeeded by Admiral Chichagov, for many years the director of the Black Sea Company. It is as well known that Alexis has preferred dry land to the sea, and has worshipped other goddesses than Thetis, as that the influences (female as well as male) brought to bear upon him have usually been as violent as they are short-lived. His preference for cities, "dont le diable a fait son paradis," he shares with his youngest brother, the Grand Duke Paul, whose bachelor days, however, have been cut short through his marriage with the Greek Princess, Alexandra.

The position which the Grand Duke Vladimir, the eldest of the Emperor's brothers, occupies, or has been made to occupy, in the State and in society, is an incomparably more important one. On several occasions the "favourite brother of the Emperor" has stood in the foreground of public notice. The first time was when the Emperor, in the event of his early death, conferred the regency upon him while the successor to the throne was still an infant (1881), the second time (1887) when he was commissioned by the Emperor to visit the Baltic provinces, in order to put down the political discontent which was raging there. In the first case he had not the opportunity of proving his qualities as a statesman, in the second the desired opportunity remained unimproved, because it was in the main factitious, and because Vladimir had received instructions from Russia against which his counter proposals were in vain, and which excluded from the very first all possibility of success. The whole undertaking presented on a small scale a pendant to Von Kaulbar's Bulgarian mission; the only difference was that no imperial chamberlain of the quality of Sluchevsky had been attached to the latter to act as the chronicler of its failure. Since that time the favourite brother of the Emperor has been talked about so little except by scandal-mongers, that his ill-humour is easily explained. Agricultural and other exhibitions, in which the Mæcenas of "agriculture" had taken an interest, have not been held for a considerable time. The duties of the generalship of the first *garde du corps* and of the first military district might have been entrusted to Kostanda, the general of artillery and chief of the staff, without leaving unsatisfied Vladimir's very moderate desire for business.

Vladimir's wife, Maria Pavlovna, the Mecklenburg princess, is of an active disposition; she is undoubtedly the most intellectual woman in the imperial family, and next to the Empress is more talked about than any one else. Her position from the beginning has been a difficult one. She had the courage and the honour, on the occasion of her marriage, to make conditions guaranteeing that she should be allowed to retain her old religious belief. A similar case had not happened for a hundred and fifty years.[1] Her difficulties have increased since it has become known that she possesses a certain independence of judgment, and is not thereby prevented from enjoying the friendship of her imperial sister-in-law. Absurd stories, invented by French pamphleteers, and echoed by Russian dunces, have been circulated about her. She is represented as the champion and agent of Bismarckian ideas, as the fomenter of far-reaching German intrigues, and as the destroyer of everything essentially Russian. These charges are not worth a moment's notice. The princess is persecuted and slandered because she is Lutheran, and has remained so, and because she has independence enough not to deny her German origin and culture. Besides, with her experience of life she understands too well what she owes to the position which she occupies as a member of the imperial family, and the duties entailed by the dependence of her husband on the head of the State, to think of

[1] Peter the Great's daughter-in-law, Charlotte of Brunswick (the wife of Alexis, the Tsarevich), did not change her religion.

defying the Russian national sentiment, or of interfering in the smallest degree in questions of a political nature. In the present condition of things even the appearance of a certain independence or the tendency to appreciate nationalism at its true value is sufficient to rouse the slanderous disposition of the "loyal" autochthonous champions. In all cases where the claims of the national mania remain unsatisfied, its prophets immediately spread accusations and calumnies which would have been morally impossible under former Governments. It would be difficult to say positively whether Maria Pavlovna always takes the right course from a social point of view. It is a matter of fact that she shows tact in defending her married position without injuring herself, that her relations with the imperial family are entirely satisfactory, and that she has been able to make herself respected even in those quarters where nothing but malevolence was shown her. But with all these advantages she has to suffer. Persons of princely rank are more harshly judged than ordinary mortals if they are real personalities, and differentiate themselves as such from the non-entities, who enjoy the popular favour because they regard swimming with the stream as the essence of all wisdom.

Besides the Grand Duchess Maria Pavlovna the imperial family includes two other members who do not belong to the Greek Orthodox Church—a circumstance which may be connected with the new ukase with respect to the creed of the Empress and with the preference for Montenegrin marriages which has come into fashion. The amiable Princess Elizabeth of Hesse, niece of Queen Victoria, who was married five years ago to the Grand Duke Sergius, third brother of the Emperor, remained true to her creed until within a short time since, and the wife of the Emperor's cousin, the Grand Duke Constantine Constantinovich, *née* Princess of Sachsen-Altenberg, still retains her old faith. These ladies are too young and too diffident to make their influence felt in society or to cut out a path for themselves, but they enjoy a deserved popularity, especially the former, whose position in society is in this respect different from her husband's. The fact that the good examples of rulers are not so eagerly followed as their blunders and their outward demeanour, has been shown also in Russia, where the example of the Emperor's excellent domestic relations has unfortunately been imitated least of all where it was to be expected.

The social position of the two uncles of the Emperor deserves only a moment's notice. The Grand Duke Constantine Nikolaevich,[1] who was at one time general-admiral and vice-regent of Poland, passed out of notice, when he retired from the influential position which had been assigned to

[1] Died in 1892.—ED.

him during the lifetime of his brother the Emperor. In spite of the severe strictures which have been made against the character and conduct of this exceptionally capable prince, and in spite of the seclusion in which he and his benevolent and noble wife have lived for a number of years, it must be confessed that Constantine Nikolaevich's removal left a perceptible gap. The second son of the Emperor Nicholas dominated his immediate environment not only by reason of his natural endowments, but even more by the cultivation of his faculties. It was of special value that at least *one* Court could be named in St. Petersburg where learned men and artists could frequently meet together, and where other interests than those of society and external show were cultivated. Even after the Grand Duke had laid aside the violoncello in which he was fairly proficient, and after the death of his brother artists, Knecht and Davuidov, musical entertainments were not unusual in the Marble Palace, recalling the classical times long since passed away of the Grand Duchess Helena, of the two Counts Wielchorsky, and of General A. Livov. No trace will be left of this and of much else when the Grand Duke dies. His eldest son is a " lost man," who is not permitted to leave the place appointed for him years ago on the Asiatic frontier; the two younger Princes, Constantine and Dimitri, are imperial aides-de-camps, and enjoy a good reputation; the elder, as has been said, is the husband of Princess Elizabeth, the younger is unmarried.

The second uncle of the Emperor, Grand Duke Nicholas, who was commander-in-chief from 1877, general field-marshal, general inspector of cavalry, &c., has long since ceased to play a public part.[1] Of his private doings it will be better to say nothing. The Grand Duke Michael, besides holding other offices, is president of the chamber, the highest position of rank there is in the Russian Empire. The former governor of the Caucasus has, on account of his military vigour, his temperate zeal, and the integrity of his character, won the favour of his imperial nephew, and retained it in spite of differences of opinion. His wife, a Princess of Baden, who is reputed to be extremely clever and active, has made him the father of a numerous and good-looking family, consisting of six sons and one daughter (the wife of the Grand Duke of Mecklenburg-Schwerin). Although—or because—the Grand Duke is president of the Reichrath's plenum,[2] he has never taken a conspicuous part in politics, but has devoted himself entirely to his military duties. He is a member of the committee of the ministry, a general director of artillery, general of the ordnance, and general field-marshal.

[1] Died in 1891.—ED.   [2] See Appendix, Note 9.

V.

PERSONALITIES OF THE COURT AND THE STATE.

IN Russia there is no ministry and no ministerial council: there are only individual ministers, who as chiefs of departments are directly subordinate to the Emperor, and transact affairs directly with him (which is called in official language "making a *Doklad*"—a "report"): the so-called committee of ministers over which Bunge, the former minister of finance, presides, is an administrative court of appeal whose strictly limited power is of a formal nature, and excludes essentially political decisions.

Of the advisers of the Crown only one belongs to the small number of the Emperor's personal friends,—Count Vorontsov-Dashkov, minister of the household and the Court. His position differs from that of his colleagues in this also—that he belongs to the so-called "elegant world" and mixes in all its gaieties. Vorontsov-Dashkov is of the same age, and married at the same time as the Emperor. He has never manifested political ambition or shown any desire to take an active part in great political questions. He manages his considerable "unsquandered" (*nepromótannoye*) property with dignity, and has gained the reputation of being as honourable as he is unpretentious. As minister of the imperial Court, he has used his influence mostly in personal questions—outside this sphere he has never made himself felt; within it, very seldom. Count and Countess Vorontsov rarely allow themselves to espouse the cause of third parties, because they know they are surrounded by calumniators and slanderers of all kinds and by persons who are envious of them, and because they anxiously avoid the suspicion of misusing the confidential position, which they occupy, by forming a clique. Never to become tiresome by asking favours for one's self or others is the surest, the cheapest, and the only means of gaining a reputation for unselfishness in the eyes of royal personages. The observance of this duty is carried out without difficulty by people in the position of the Vorontsov-Dashkovs, as may be easily understood.

There are only two dignitaries among the Court officials who deserve to be mentioned—Prince Obolensky and General Von Richter. Obolensky, aide-de-camp and representative Marshal of the Court, married the clever and intriguing Countess Apraksin, formerly lady-in-waiting to the Empress, when she was still Grand Duchess. Because he is on terms of the greatest intimacy with the Emperor, he is the most respected and influential person at the Court. This respect he will undoubtedly maintain, as the possibility of entertaining an opinion different to the Emperor's has never occurred to him. Von Richter, the commander of the imperial head-quarters, director of the commission of petitions, imperial counsellor, and general adjutant, is marked out by the Slavophils and other national ultras as the head of the German party (as if there was one!), because he is a German and a Protestant, and does not deny the fact, and because he has no sympathy with the persecution of the Germans which has become fashionable. This has been sufficient to brand him as a partisan of Prussia and as a man of pronounced German sympathies, although he is extremely retiring in his disposition, prudent, and never occupied with questions of high politics. In truth the general, who has had close relations with the Emperor for years, and who is highly respected by him for his integrity and his loyalty, knows only too well the danger of the prevailing tendency, and the odium which rests upon his native province (Livonia) to allow of his entering upon a course which would neither benefit himself nor those concerned. Von Richter is a man of the *old* school, the chief articles in whose creed are: a belief in the traditional friendship subsisting between Russia and Prussia, and a certain faith in aristocratism: he is not a devotee of the new national political theory (Montenegro-ecstasy). The charges that have been levelled against him are the invention of a clique, to whom it is gall and bitterness that a German and a Protestant should hold a high position of trust at the Court of the national Tsar, and that this circumstance recalls the times when the names of Liewe, Benkendorff, Stuckelberg, Mayendorff, Pahlen, &c., were as popular on the banks of the Neva as those of certain Boyar races of old Muscovite origin. What is said of Von Richter holds good with respect to Von Giers, who has been excused his non-Russian origin, but at the expense of an attitude of caution and reserve from which his opponents and rivals believe themselves to be exempt.

Reference will be made later to the director of the synod, and to the ministers of foreign affairs, the interior, and justice. Next to these the name of General Vannovsky, the minister of war, is oftenest mentioned. He came into the Emperor's favour when he was acting in the capacity of chief of the staff of the army corps, commanded by the Tsarevich in 1878, and immediately after Milyutin's retirement from office (April, 1881) he was appointed as his successor. He is highly respected in the army for his soldierly qualities. With his predecessor he has hardly anything in common, except a pronounced dislike of the Prussian-German system, and a certain preference for France.[1] The present minister of war in questions of organisation and fortification has taken an entirely new departure. It is not Vannovsky, but General Obruchev, the chief of the general staff, who is regarded as the principal advocate of the Franco-Russo Alliance—an idea which has been spread throughout the Russian army. Obruchev's repeated visits to Paris during the last years of Alexander II., apparently for purposes of art, but really for the preparation of plans of alliance, have become impossible under the present *régime*. Neither the minister of war nor the chief of the staff ought to aspire to anticipating the decisions of the Emperor and the future, "which is known only to Providence;" but it is none the less certain that they have certain ideas of their own about the future, and that they hold fast to the opinions of Skobelev, the great national hero.[2]

The minister of education, Count Delyanov, has thrown in his lot with the men of the future and with nationalism: he is a man who really stands with both feet on the ground of the past. Behind this Russian sounding name there is hidden an aged Armenian, whose real name is Delajanz. As the *protégé* of M. A. Korff, Delajanz first rose to power, then he played the part of a Liberal for some time, and finally made his way as the obedient pupil of the great Katkov, who some ten years before dictated

[1] See Appendix, Note 10.   [2] See Appendix, Note 11.

to the then assistant of Count D. Tolstoi the programme for the organisation of the intermediate scholastic institutions, and for the reform of the universities—that is, a scheme for emasculating them and making them innocuous. In spite of his Armenian and plebeian origin the upstart Count Delyanov plumes himself in belonging to the highest society. His wife is regarded as fashionable, she holds receptions, and receives diplomatists. His colleague, Volkonsky, however, is really distinguished, and being the descendant of the late field-marshal and minister, Peter Volkonsky, is connected with half the nobility. Lastly, Privy-Councillor Polovtsov, who is imperial secretary and chief of the *chancellerie*, is intimately connected with the highest society. He is of a gay disposition, and married the adopted daughter and heiress of the richest banker of St. Petersburg, Baron Stieglitz. He entertains largely: high politics are sometimes discussed at his house, but it is questionable whether the discussions lead to anything.

Most of the statesmen of the former reign are dead (Count Valuev, Count Milyutin, Abaza, Reuter, &c.). The survivors have so completely vanished from the scene that an examination of their characteristic peculiarities would go beyond the scope of the present work.

VI.

VON GIERS.

IN 1864 Alexander II. said to a general governor of non-Russian extraction, on his dismissal from office, that it was only with the help of Russians born and bred that he (the Emperor) could keep national and orthodox fanatics in check : the *non-Russians and non-orthodox were suspected by the national masses from the very beginning*, and consequently were bound hand and foot.

These words of the Emperor (intended as a consolation) explain why Von Giers, the present minister of foreign affairs, occupies a more difficult position than any one of his colleagues: the remark also applies to the only *German* minister of the present Government, General Hübbenet (from Livonia), who was entrusted some months ago with the direction of public buildings and roads.[1] Both men left their homes years ago ; both were brought up in St. Petersburg educational establishments, and both were steeped in Russian modes of thought; but

[1] He has already received his dismissal.—ED.

because German blood flows in their veins they are looked at with envious eyes, and they must show themselves as doubly national if they do not wish to be branded as "traitors." Alexander III. intended to take the direction of foreign affairs into his own hands, and to emulate his grandfather in this department. Nothing could have been more favourable for the carrying out of this idea than the transference of the inheritance of Gorchakov to an official with a foreign name, a Finn, who was altogether dependent upon the person of the Emperor, and was surrounded by those who envied him and were his enemies. Von Giers has, however, not only become minister—he has remained one (which means much more). For this he has clearly to thank himself, and not the dependent position to which the un-Russian sound of his name seems to condemn him.

It is assumed that the reader knows that the present minister of foreign affairs had filled the higher offices of the State even in the time of Alexander II., that he began his career as consul-general in Moldavia-Wallachia, and there married a relation of Gorchakov's; that he subsequently filled several positions in various embassies (Teheran, Stockholm, &c.); that about the middle of the 'seventies he was appointed to the senate, and that he undertook from 1877 the double office of director of the Asiatic department and assistant-minister. It must, however, be called to mind that the nomination of 1877 (the eve of the Turkish war) caused extraordinary sensation at the time and gave rise to many comments. It was the general opinion that Privy-Councillor Stremukhov, the then director of the Asiatic department, had long been destined to be the successor of Westmann, who time out of mind had been the chancellor's associate, but who was then hopelessly ill. But to the astonishment of everybody, Stremukhov was passed over: he was so mortified that he sent in his resignation, and thus the two most important positions in the ministry of foreign affairs had to be filled up at the same time. Two different versions were current as to the cause of this notorious incident. According to one, private matters of a very dubious character had made Stremukhov impossible as an aspirant to the ministry; according to the other, considerations arising from the hostility which existed between Stremukhov and Ignatiev decided the question. It is a matter of fact that they had been deadly enemies for years, and that the ambassador at Constantinople was at the height of his power in 1877. Suffice it to say that Von Giers profited by this hostility, and that Ignatiev also gained an indirect advantage from the election which had turned out in favour of the Finnish baron. Had it not been for the intervention of Giers, the prophet of the "infallible bankruptcy of Turkey," who had been brought to book for the numerous lies he had circulated during the conduct of the war, would hardly have been permitted to take part in the proceedings of San Stefano—a circumstance which, be it noted, contradicts the opinion that Von Giers is a determined opponent of the traditions of the Russian Eastern policy.[1] Even during the last years of the chancellor's life he was virtual director of the foreign policy of the Government, and after Gorchakov's death he was appointed minister.

That the best-abused Russian statesman of the present day has been successful in maintaining his position is due to several circumstances, and especially to the preference which the Emperor has shown for men of an orderly, reliable, and respectable character. The "renowned" Prince Gorchakov could hardly be said to belong to men of this category. Personally avaricious, he was entirely indifferent to the expenditure which had to be borne by an already overburdened State. As long as Westmann remained in good health and capable of performing his duties, he had looked after the bureaucratic and financial administration in the department of foreign affairs; but after the death of this hard-working and capable official an economic system prevailed, which, taking even the traditional standard, seemed unauthorised. Von Giers had already, as colleague of the minister, brought about

[1] See Appendix, Note 12.

some change in this respect, and because his quiet, serious, and modest disposition was personally agreeable to the Emperor, he was entrusted, first provisionally, afterwards definitively, with the chancellorship. Silent, cautious, with no inclination for the frivolities, intrigues, and vanities of high society, he possessed two special qualities which endeared him to the Emperor—minute acquaintance with actual political relations and the method of transacting business, and the power of making his authority felt at the right time and the right place. He goes from point to point, and knows and says exactly what has to be done under the given circumstances; on the other hand, he is a thorough disbeliever in stereotyped systems and principles, and sets himself resolutely against explanations of a general nature. By never anticipating the wishes of the Tsar, and by always confining himself to the practical questions of the moment and their solution, Giers makes it possible for the Emperor to feel that he himself is the real head of Russian policy. Von Giers, who is of a retiring and taciturn nature, has never yet disclosed his views to anybody on the Slav or the Eastern question; nor has it ever leaked out whether he has embraced the cause of France, or of the powers of Central Europe; whether he strives after a permanent or a provisional condition of peace, or what he thinks of the future of Russia and Europe. He seems to have been so moulded by nature as to feel little desire to form definite opinions of his own; hence it may be easier for him simply to act as the docile executor of his monarch's orders, in which capacity he is ably assisted by the highly-gifted Sinovjev, a colleague of Ignatiev.[1]

Von Giers deals only with the immediate present, and then only when the necessity for action has arisen. There are good grounds for the opinion that he is always to be found on the side of discretion, of peace, and of reason, and that he is an opponent of the Panslavist fanatics and the French-disposed enemies of Germany; but pronouncements and avowals to that effect cannot be produced. If Von Giers ever expresses himself on these questions it is done in the form of dry interrogatories. With the greatest possible quietness and attentiveness he interrogates the sages of the bold and "truly national" policy as to the chances which the *moment* offers for the attainment of their national *aims*, as to the resources at their command for undertaking their great enterprises, as to the prospective operation of a disturbance of the peace, on economic relations and the budget of the current year, as to the names of those Parisian statesmen with whom alliances can be concluded against both the central European monarchies, and with whom arrangements of a more certain nature could be made than with the leaders of the policy of the above-mentioned powers. "Poli-

[1] See Appendix, Note 13.

ticians of genius," to whom a handful of bank-notes are of no consequence, regard such considerations as paltry and narrow, and complain with a shrug of their shoulders that the cold Finn fails to comprehend the "expansive Russian nature." Their dry interlocutor's questions, however, remain unanswered.

The Emperor has the feeling that Von Giers is a faithful, clear-headed, and serviceable statesman who never encroaches upon the rights of others. This quality has had more weight than all the charges and calumnies that have been levelled against the so-called "un-Slav" policy of the minister for foreign affairs. Well acquainted with the difficulties that surround him, this minister observes a prudence which makes the work of his calumniators a thousandfold more arduous.

Von Giers, who is neither Russian nor a Boyar, wisely avoids the kind of trump-cards affected by the deceased Count P. A. Shuvalov, and is careful not to fly directly in the face of public opinion. He has never fallen short in questions of patriotism or passing phases of public feeling, nor has he ever gone too far. He acts as a diplomatic man of business who transacts current affairs in accordance with the lofty intentions of the Emperor. Von Giers never says *that he is in truth more*, nor does he allow himself to appear more; it may be that he has no strong self-consciousness to suppress. He apparently values public distinctions, honours, and tokens of good-will as much as others; but he is resigned if they are not bestowed upon him. He knows the considerations which weigh with the Emperor, and which often coincide with his (the minister's) interests, and he never makes himself inconvenient to his master by putting forward claims or expressing desires. If measures which he has opposed are put down to his charge, or if successes which he has brought about are attributed to another, he is equally indifferent, for the actual possession of influence is of more value in his eyes than its mere appearance. He stands out among modern Russian statesmen in this respect as an *avis rarissima*.

Since the death of Jomini, the last of the diplomatists of the old school, the director of the ministerial *chancellerie*, Prince Valerian Obolensky (to be distinguished from Prince Peter Obolensky, adjutant to the Grand Duke Vladimir) has been looked upon as the most competent man at the foreign office. In contradistinction to his *chef* the prince is a lion of the salons, and a man of great conversational powers; his praises are especially sung by female lips. The future will show whether that will avail him much. Cleverness, *as a profession*, has lately gone out of fashion in Russia, as it has in the West. Privy-Councillor Vlangali, who is descended from a Wallachian Boyar family, occupies the position of adjutant minister. Baron Osten-Sacken is at the head of the Home Department. The Asiatic

Department is administered by Sinoviev. Sinoviev is considered by many as much more important and influential than the real assistant of the minister. It would be impossible to name the presumptive successor of the present minister. In former times it used to be taken for granted that ministers' assistants never became ministers. That the rule, "Tel brille au premier rang qui s'eclipse au second," has not applied for a long time, is shown in the case of Makov, A. Lieven, Giers, and recently Durnovo. The present assistant of Von Giers, who has reputation for extraordinary shrewdness, has not, however, hitherto been looked upon as his presumptive successor.

VII.

POBYEDONOSTSEV AS MINISTER.[1]

THERE are two classes of fanatics, the cold and the hot—that is, fanatics from reflection and fanatics by temperament. It is easy to know to which class Pobyedonostsev belongs. His looks betray him. He is old and of a spare build, his nose is pointed, his eyes are keen and penetrating, he wears spectacles, his forehead is fringed with a few grey hairs, his face is clean-shaven, and his expression is keen. There is no need of a physiognomist to tell us that he is one of those cool, calculating natures whose temperament enables them to steer clear of difficulties, because they are guided by the head and not by the heart. At first sight the *oberprocouror* of the Synod might be taken for a Prussian privy councillor or a Dresden Court councillor. Serious and thoughtful in his manner, he is more like a *savant* than a statesman.

He lives exclusively for the office, which was

[1] This designation corresponds to the position better than the official title.

transferred to him in 1880 on the retirement of Count D. Tolstoi, and for the ideas according to which he administers it. This office, which Tolstoi (the Minister of the Interior from 1882 to 1887), had filled for fifteen years from 1865 to 1880 in conjunction with the Ministry of Public Instruction, is a ministry by itself, and might be defined in Western European terminology as being nearly equivalent to the "Ministry of Public Worship." The *oberprocouror* of the Synod, as a representative of the Emperor, is invested with full powers, and is the only secular member of the highest ecclesiastical administrative body of the Empire. This institution comprises the metropolitans of Novgorod-St. Petersburg, of Moscow-Kolomna, and of Kiev, and nine bishops and higher clergy who are called upon from time to time. No decree of this institution is valid without the previous approval of the *oberprocouror* of the Synod; in important cases he appeals to the decision of the Emperor, and sends in his reports directly to him; the ecclesiastic educational establishments (academies and seminaries) of the orthodox faith are under his superintendence and direction, and the parochial Consistories depend immediately upon him. He is a member of the ministerial committee and of the imperial council, he stands on an equal footing with the other ministers, and has to be heard on all subjects either directly or indirectly affecting the State Church.

The importance of this office, which was instituted by Peter the Great, has always been very great (Galitsin's short period under Alexander I. excepted), but never greater than in the present reign, and in the hands of its present occupant. Pobyedonostsev having gained repute as a jurist and as an authority on Russian legislation, was, on the death of the Tsarevich Nikolai in 1865, entrusted with the instruction of the present Emperor, who was then twenty, in the principles of Russian public law and administration. Unlike the majority of his colleagues at that time, Pobyedonostsev knew how to impress his august pupil first by the earnestness and zeal with which he devoted himself to his duties as an instructor, and secondly by the rigid dogmatism of his political and scientific views. Instead of making things easy and pleasant to himself and his listener, Pobyedonostsev went to work seriously and energetically, and fearlessly emphasised the importance and difficulty of the task which he had undertaken. The important point, however, was that Pobyedonostsev had pressed his pretty extensive historical and juridical knowledge into the service of an idea, the idea, namely, that absolutism and orthodoxy, as being divine and founded on history, formed the only sound basis for a Russo-Slav state system, and that they were mutually supplementary. Pobyedonostsev has adopted the same methods and made use of the same abstractions as enabled Joseph de Maitre in his day to reconcile the ideas of popery and legitimacy, and to form them into a modern articulated system apparently satisfying the demands of science; he understood how to deck out the famous doctrine of the providential destiny of the Eastern Church to regenerate the heathen West in such a way that it was perfectly manifest to his pupil. The self-confidence and *self-abandonment* [1] of the preacher of this new wisdom were in such marked contrast with the instability of the other doctrines, which oscillated between Liberalism and Loyalism, that it could not fail to make a permanent impression on a nature which always felt the need of leaning upon authority.

The inexorable logician, whose eye was always directed to the attainable, *who never thought of self*, never obtruded his own personality, and whose system recommended itself by its "grand" simplicity—this logician appeared to stand in character as well as in intellect far above those opportunists who were constantly changing their point of view, whose conclusions lay open to the most contradictory explanations, and who above all tried to ingratiate themselves. When it is added that the national garment in which the orthodoxy of Pobyedonostsev stalked about, corresponded to the inclinations of his august pupil, it will be easily understood why this man immediately obtained an authoritative position

[1] Pobyedonostsev's opponents have tried to cast doubts on his integrity, but unjustly.

which was denied to others. Long recognised as an energetic worker, and recommended to the highest position on account of his educational success, Pobyedonostsev was installed in 1880 in one of the two offices which until then had been vested in Tolstoi. Privy-Councillor Saburov, a Liberal imbued with European ideas, was entrusted with the other office: his appointment was strictly in keeping with the contradictory character of the former reign, and was regarded by its adherents as a " particularly happy solution."

In spite of the regard in which he was held by the late Emperor, the new *oberprocouror* of the Synod had to be satisfied during Alexander II.'s lifetime with a subordinate position. Even after Alexander Nikolaevich's liberal enthusiasm had cooled down, he remained " European " in his ideas, and, as such, looked askance at all kinds of fanaticism, and especially all religious eccentricities. It had also to be taken into account that the ministry of the Interior, which has numerous relations with the Synod from having to transact the affairs of the "foreign religions," as well as those of the ancient superstitious beliefs, was at that time in the hands of Loris Melikov, a man who was thoroughly acquainted with the views of his imperial master, and who was neither fitted nor inclined to play the part of the old Russian-Byzantine zealot.

All this was changed when the pupil of Pobyedonostsev ascended the throne. A complete revolution took place when Count Tolstoi, Pobyedonostsev's predecessor, was entrusted with the direction of the ministry of the Interior (May, 1882). Tolstoi had won his first spurs as the author of a violent polemical treatise against Catholicism: he never deviated from the course which he had once taken, and his overmastering idea was that the restoration of strict "orthodoxy" (*pravoslavïe*) formed the essential basis for the renovation and establishment of national absolutism. Pobyedonostsev went hand in hand with him: he began his work of Church reform, and favoured by Katkov and his successors, he carried it out with extraordinary apparent success. He is the originator of those persecutions of the Catholics and other bodies in Poland, Little Russia, and Lithuania, which even Anatole Leroy-Beaulieu, the most zealous partisan of Russian ideas in France, has declared to be unwise and barbarous, and which he has been obliged unconditionally to condemn. The orders of 1864, by which Alexander II. had allowed religious freedom to children born from mixed marriages in the Baltic provinces, were re-instituted at his instigation. It is due to him that new Catholic and Protestant churches, even in the Polish and Baltic provinces, can only be built after the previous consent of the Greek-Orthodox bishops of the district; that all missionary activity on the part of Catholics and Protestants, whether at home or abroad, is interdicted under penalty ; that dozens of Polish and Livonian priests have been proceeded against or removed on the faintest suspicion, and that processes of this kind are no longer conducted before Catholic and Protestant consistories, but before secular judges, who are influenced by the State. And all this is done with a quiet, pedantically cold rigour, and with the help of a juridical sophistry, which avoids the appearance of violence as far as possible, but at the same time leaves room for tricks of interpretation, which impose upon the ignorant and "captivated" Russian masses and the unprincipled press. The doctrine that the end justifies the means has been taken for granted everywhere at all times, and long before the publication of the "Medulla" of Busenbaum by men of Pobyedonostsev's stamp ; but the author of the circular to the "Evangelical Alliance" has spoken out with regard to his aims and his blind hostility to the churches of Western Europe with a frankness which has been received with indignation by the whole civilised world.

In private life Pobyedonostsev is quiet, cool, serious, and sensible. He takes a certain pride in displaying his knowledge of the most recent legal and theological literature, and in showing his acquaintance with modern thought. He occasionally appeals to the solidarity of interests of all who believe in positive Christianity, and (as he said to Pastor

Dalton) he looks upon disputations with believers of other confessions as an important means to mutual advancement. That does not prevent him, however, from using the most violent means, where mere arguments produce no impression, or from pursuing a policy in ecclesiastical matters which differs in no particular from that of the coarse and brutal fanatics of former times.

The *oberprocouror* of the Synod shows the uprightness of his character not only by his perfect indifference to external honours and distinctions, and by his integrity and devotion to the service of the State, but by the frankness with which he recognises in his yearly reports certain failings and faults of the clergy who are placed under him, and notes the alarming increase of superstitious heresies and of heathen, almost Thibetan, idolatries. He holds fast to the conclusion that drastic and fearless measures are more necessary now than ever, and that the propaganda which is the privilege of the State Church should be used to the uttermost to extirpate all superstitions and heresies. "Standing on the heights of culture," he acts as his reactionary predecessors did before him, with this difference— that these spared themselves the trouble of theological or other reasonings. The means of modern culture, which Pobyedonostsev has at command, serve him simply to furbish up the brutal and monstrous practices which have been handed down to him by his predecessors of the old schoolmen whose severities against sectarians, Catholics, and others twenty years ago excited the horror of civilised Russia. The apostles and prophets of "orthodoxy" in the time of Nicholas were men of the world without strong convictions, pleasure-seekers without claims to culture and without religious feeling, officials whose religiosity and morality differed in no respect from those of other people, and laid claim to no pretensions. But Pobyedonostsev is honourable and pious, so honourable and pious that he makes no secret of his bigotry, but retires periodically for a certain time to some cloister or other which is encircled with the odour of special sanctity, in order to be able to devote himself undisturbed to religious exercises and profound meditations.

In the good times of the Emperor Nicholas it often used to be said by a certain class of quasi-Liberal officials (and at times by even non-Liberal officials) that in Russia the zealous, honourable, and convinced dependants and tools of the prevailing system (and these especially included the German Russians) were the worst and the most dangerous. Even the worst coercive measures remained tolerable as long as they were administered by Russian nationalists, and were suited to "circumstances." But alas! it was a bitter day when pedantic Germans and other *honourable* persons took the matter in hand, formulated the Government ideas into a system, and drove things to extremes! " Les zélés, les fidèles—les croyants sont les pires." The contemporaries of Pobyedonostsev's *régime* have been the first to understand in all its fulness this expression which was so often in the mouth of Alexander Herzen. Honour, zeal, and fearless and sincere devotion to an object which is base, false, and hollow at the core—power over the modern means of culture in the service of a worthless retrograde end! Is there a worse or more dangerous combination possible?

VIII.

SECRET POLICE.

I.—*The Minister of the Interior.*

PRIVY COUNCILLOR IVAN NIKOLAEVICH DURNOVO, as has been mentioned, was appointed successor to Tolstoi in the ministry of the Interior.[1] He is a precise, cool-headed official, without any great antecedents or high connections. He is a minister who observes a certain routine, who has no initiative, and who acts on the instructions of others. Durnovo has set himself to carry out the work of Tolstoi—that is to say, to deprive the provincial assemblies of the last vestige of their former significance, to re-establish the corporative and social position of the nobility, and to uproot the weeds of nihilistic and revolutionary ideas. This last point is the most important, as it most nearly concerns the Emperor. Since the abolition of the "Third Division of his Majesty's Chancery" (which was the department of so-called State police), in the time of

[1] See Appendix, Note 14.

Loris Melikov, both classes of police, the ordinary police and the political police (*gendarmerie*), have been placed under the ministry of the Interior, and the chief of this department is thus responsible in a double sense for the security of the Emperor and the imperial family. The momentous importance of the duties of this office is seen in the organisation of the ministry. Of the *three*[1] ministerial subordinates who assist the Minister of the Interior (all the other ministers have only one assistant), one is almost exclusively occupied with the direction of the political police and its ramifications. General Orchevsky, a "fashionable" officer conspicuous for his ambition, unscrupulousness, and love of intrigue, filled this office some years ago. But the reign of this so-called Richelieu was of short duration. There is nothing to be said of his successor, Shebeko.

It is generally known that nihilism is less talked about than formerly, that its resources are exhausted, and that the attractive power of its secrets has lost its former charm. But no one could say with certainty that its danger had decreased. It is the opinion of those who have a minute acquaintance with the inner working of Russian revolutionary, secret societies that *acute* nihilism has decreased, while *chronic* nihilism has increased. The number of fire-brands who are ready to sacrifice themselves in perpetrating criminal acts has become smaller,

[1] Now two.—ED.

but the mass of the discontented, who at the present moment expect salvation from disastrous events, unsuccessful foreign wars, and the like,—this mass has, on the other hand, constantly increased. Not to speak of the distrust with which our modern nationalists meet every stranger, the spread and ramification of secret political agents and informers inside as well as outside St. Petersburg has increased so enormously that political discussions are avoided with an anxiety which is foreign to the habits of Russian life and Russian character. Even the inclination to play the part of the opposition, and to gird at existing institutions and persons in authority —a tendency which is deeply rooted in the national character, and which is really harmless—is almost entirely crushed: people are more cautious than they were in the time of the Emperor Nicholas, to say nothing of the days of Alexander II. The discussion of public affairs has almost entirely ceased in those circles of society in which bold radical expressions formerly passed from mouth to mouth like everyday words. The educated classes who take a serious interest in politics confine their exchange of views to intimate circles. The former freedom of discussion only prevails where it is a question of abusing or criticising foreign countries. The public emulates in this respect the attitude of the periodical press, which displays its courage and its firmness so abundantly in its criticisms on Prince Bismarck,

Count Kalnoky, Lord Salisbury, and M. Stambulov, that the guarded silence which is observed with regard to internal questions appears in this way to be almost compensated for.

II.—*Voluntary Secret Police.*

"Misunderstanding and distrust have spread like a blight over Russia; they have marred the proportion, form, and colour of all the manifestations of our life. Between the nobility and the people, the Government and society, the educated and the ignorant, nay, even between members of the same classes of society, there exist distrust and harassing misunderstanding. Everything is out of joint, everything has lost its foundation, discontent is everywhere:

> "'Wir reden klug, doch sind es leere Worte,
> Vom Leben reden wir, doch ohne das wir leben.'"

With these words, which were printed in the last days of the year 1881, Ivan Aksakov concluded his characterisation of the first ten months of the reign of Alexander III. That this severe judgment was literally true must be recognised even by those who wished to know nothing of the celebrated Ivan Sergyevich and his periodical "Rous."[1] Such a year

[1] *Rous* as well as *Rossia* means "Russia," but the first is an ancient and popular term, while the second is of later and official origin.

as this had never been experienced in Russia since the days of the great interregnum. Nicholas had ascended the throne after quelling a conspiracy, and had roused the dread fear of reaction throughout his wide empire—the heir of the murdered Alexander II. awakened apprehensions threefold greater in their intensity. Along with the dread of new revolutionary crimes arose the fear of blind reaction and the fear of fear.

The last was the most grievous, for the most painful surprises might be expected from a terrified Government. The Liberals were prepared for the worst, after the new ruler had dismissed three "free-thinking" ministers of his father on one day. The honourable Conservatives complained that an adventurer (Count Ignatiev) had been chosen as the most confidential adviser of the Tsar: the masses stood under the weight of two new criminal attempts, the fact that a revolutionist—Soukhanov—together with six companions, was detected among the officers of the imperial fleet, the revolutionary fermentation discovered in the military school of St. Michael, and the gross carelessness which had been brought home to several police officials. As the secret printing presses of the nihilists could not be discovered, it was believed that fresh outrages might be perpetrated at any moment. It was an open secret in the highest society that the Emperor was not sure of his life for a moment, that the apprehensions of the omnipresence and omniscience of the nihilist conspiracy had accompanied him to Gatchina, and that these phantoms continued to haunt him night and day in this asylum. The slightest rumours were believed, the most trustworthy servants suspected, the most ordinary occurrences magnified to tales of horror. Undermined bridges and streets, bombs of dynamite hidden in the park of the castle, threatening letters found on the Emperor's table, assassins masked in Court livery—these and similar horrors were such a constant source of terror to high and low that at last it was impossible to say where the real danger ended and the imaginary began.

Under the influence of this unrest and excitement an extraordinary scheme was originated in the circles of the younger Court officials and officers, which had for its object the formation of a secret society similar in every respect to the nihilist conspiracy. The aim of this society was to entrust the safety of the imperial family to the best blood of the land, and at the same time to meet the conspirators with their own weapons—that is to say, to find out the nihilist plans both at home and abroad by means of a conservative secret organisation. The existence of a State institution devoted to this purpose, viz., the political police, was just as little thought of as the wonderful impression it would make if the flower of the Russian nobility formed themselves into a corps of political secret police, and raised espionage to the rank of an elegant pastime. The word of command was given, the high-sounding name of the "holy band" (*swäshchénnaya drouzhina*) was adopted by the new organisation, and the enterprise was so far advanced that some young men of the noblest families put themselves at the head of the movement. The necessary resources were to be raised by subscriptions from the highest society, but as a matter of fact the millionaire, Prince Demidov San Donato (nephew and heir of the husband of the Princess Mathilde Buonaparte), paid the greater part of the expenses out of his own pocket. The Grand Duke Vladimir and Count Vorontsov-Dashkov obtained the Emperor's approval of the statute of the new secret society, and its operations began in the summer of 1881. First of all a number of paid agents[1] were obtained to do the "dirty work," and then the attempt was made to come to terms with the police of those foreign states which called for special consideration as neighbours of Russia or on account of their harbouring political refugees.

The Berlin officials had hitherto had too many unpleasant experiences of the unreliable character of Russian secret agents to receive the new species with open arms. In London and Geneva, on the other hand, things went better, and a certain *rapprochement* was brought about with influential police officials. In Paris, however, two "famous" veterans of the

[1] See Appendix, Note 15.

former Napoleonic secret police were actually enlisted in the good cause—in consideration of handsome rewards! Immediately afterwards branches were formed in the interior of the Empire, and young nobles were invited to join the league. The fashionable and aristocratic appearance of the scheme, the travelling and other expenses that could be made out of it, and the prospect of alliance with the highest society, exercised so irresistible an attraction, that men of the most different ranks and ages enlisted in immense numbers in the new service, and even "sons of good houses" declared themselves ready to accept subordinate but well-paid positions. To be able to go on a secret mission and at another's expense to Odessa and Kiev, or even to Paris or Geneva, appeared as interesting as it was amusing, and all the more amusing as these patriotic services voluntarily rendered to the fatherland were paid for. The times in which the cultivation of Liberal ideas and expressions had been considered as *comme il faut* were gone for ever, and nothing more was to be heard of the Russification of Poland and Lithuania.[1] Was it more derogatory to spend one's leisure hours in acting in the capacity of a secret policeman than as was formerly the case in fulfilling the duties of a tribune of the people or a political missionary?

[1] A field for the exploits of adventurers who wished to get a good salary for "patriotic work" in the second part of Alexander II.'s reign.—ED.

The *official* State police naturally looked upon the new system with anything but friendly eyes. Since the abolition of the celebrated "third division" (August, 1880), the high police functionaries were placed under the Ministry of the Interior, and entrusted to the guardianship of the chief of a division. The occupant of this office was at that time a man of great ambition, General Cherevin. For the sake of the Grand Duke Vladimir he acted not only as the champion of the "holy band," but expressed his readiness to undertake the superintendence of the hopeful new society. Plehve, the technical leader of the police department, an earnest official with a full sense of the responsibility of his position, thought otherwise. At the first glance he recognised that he had to do with a set of pretentious idlers, who were dangerous to the unity and organisation of his administration. But on account of the reputation which they enjoyed, nothing was left for him but to bide his time.

The beginning seemed to be promising. The "holy band" boasted that they had made important discoveries, which "somehow or other always escaped the official spies." Much was made of the great services of one of the Parisian ex-policemen who was sent to Baden-Baden, a gentleman who had been trained under M. Pietri, and pretended he had found out half a dozen nests of dangerous nihilists. The impression which the news of these successes produced in the salons of St. Petersburg was so great that the "holy band" began to be looked upon as the salvation of Russia, and its members as having given the death-blow to the revolutionary dragon. General Cherevin thought the time had come to carry out his ambitious plans. In a memorial addressed to the Grand Duke Vladimir he explained that recent experience showed that it was absolutely necessary to form a special ministry of police, and that the new department should be brought into "organic connection" with the "holy band." A series of most disagreeable revelations followed close upon the great success of the aristocratic voluntary police. As persons accused of criminal offences could neither be imprisoned nor surrendered without the previous approval of Plehve or his subordinates, Plehve took good care that a searching examination should be made into all cases that were brought before him. As a result of this examination it was found that there had been mystifications of the grossest kind in numerous cases, and that the suspects were for the most part harmless travellers against whom nothing could be urged. In other cases the collection of incriminating documents was so completely neglected that well-founded charges could not be made; and lastly, the arrest of two innocent men caused very painful complications, and compromised the officials who were concerned in it.

On account of these occurrences Plehve presented a complaint to the Emperor, and warned him of the dangerous consequences that resulted from the well-meant but injurious action of the Holy Band. He also pointed to the confusion which threatened to dislocate the newly organised dual administration. About the same time two old respected functionaries condemned the proceedings of the Holy Band as being contrary to the honourable traditions of the past: the members of this informers' league, they said, looked upon their vocation either as a by-play or as a means of enriching themselves, or as an opportunity for indulging in adventures which brought neither advantage nor honour to the country. If Paul Demidov wanted to spend his money for patriotic ends he might find a more suitable channel, &c.

These reasons had the more weight with the Emperor, inasmuch as violent collisions had frequently taken place between Vladimir, the patron of the Holy Band, and the Minister of the Interior. It frequently happened that the agents of the Holy Band and their myrmidons arrested whole sections of the State secret police: at other times the reverse happened. These grotesque scenes were the talk of the town. The number of the opponents of the new system increased in proportion as the enthusiasm for it decreased. Alexander III. came to the conclusion that it was politic quietly to dispense with the services of the Holy Band, and to content himself with the protection which Plehve afforded him. Plehve was subsequently appointed Secretary of State, but Cherevin was removed from his position. Cherevin's proposal to create a special ministry of police, which had been unfavourably received by the public as well as the bureaucracy, but which was publicly announced in December, 1881, was abandoned at the eleventh hour. Count Ignatiev, the Minister of the Interior, had once more beaten the Grand Duke Vladimir, the patron of Cherevin, and the Holy Band.

IX.

THE NECESSITY OF KNOWING RUSSIA.

THE following words are taken from a journal which professes to speak with authority: "We should be most pleased with 'Holy Russia' if we could keep ourselves from knowing anything about her." Life, it is true, would be more pleasant on our planet if we "had not to know" of all the troubles that disturb our repose, if we "had not to know" of cholera and foot-and-mouth disease, of phylloxera, social democracy, and anarchism, if we were not obliged to think of ways and means to check the ravages of epidemics, if we had not to study their nature, and if such study did not make it apparent that disaster in the main proceeds from ignorance of its causes, and is the consequence of a careless indifference which neglected to make the necessary sacrifice at the proper moment. Truly it would be an inestimable boon if we "could keep ourselves from knowing" all this.

The above sentence would be a mere commonplace if it did not mean that all disturbing reports about

Russia could be ignored with advantage. It is taken for granted that the nearness or remoteness of the storm which is apparently brewing in the East is a fit subject for discussion, and that it is necessary to take a cursory glance at the signs of the weather; but when it is proposed to establish a scientific meteorology of the East in order to indicate the precise nature and extent of the dangers that threaten from that quarter, and thus to take measures to ward them off, the objection is raised that this is not a subject of vital importance or of public interest; Europe is indifferent or apathetic—in fact " the most convenient thing is to 'keep oneself from knowing' about it."

It is apparent that we have to deal here with misunderstandings which arise from a too great eagerness to do good, from a " blind officious zeal " which does harm where it would confer a benefit; in a word, we have to deal with a false conception of the principle which underlies the European policy of peace.

Every year of peace establishes the solidarity of Europe and strengthens its power of defence; every year of peace completes Russia's isolation and accelerates her internal dissolution; every year of peace makes Russia less dangerous. The longer the outbreak of a war can be put off, the more confidently can Europe accept it. The longer peace continues, the longer its continuance seems assured. The maintenance of peace, although it has to be paid for at a high price, ought therefore to be the end and aim of all public action.

The wisdom of this principle which lies at the root of the European policy of peace will be of little avail if blind zeal, acting ostensibly in the interests of peace, diverts public attention from the condition of Russia, under the impression that the public "want to know nothing about it;" it is even seriously maintained that a knowledge of Russia might lead to a depreciation of its strength, and to a readiness to accept the challenge thrown down by it; or, on the other hand, that Russia might look upon the exposure of her faults as a provocation that would rouse a warlike spirit within her. All these apprehensions are both erroneous and injurious.

It is not necessary to show that those in authority have a knowledge of Russian affairs. This knowledge forms the hypothesis, the point of departure, and the firm foundation of the European policy of peace. But this policy can never be firmly maintained and supported by public opinion so long as the knowledge of the state of Russia is wanting. Without this knowledge the desire for peace on the part of the public has no sure foundation, and the various governments are deprived of a reliable support. At the critical moment questions of minor consideration might press for a solution, as the experience of the past and of the present clearly shows.

Are we satisfied that the Imperial Sanitary Authority should find out the nature of epidemics and study the means to prevent them? Do we not rather feel it incumbent upon us to teach the masses on these points, so that in case of necessity the instructions of the sanitary authorities may be the more easily carried out, and that the burdensome restrictions imposed upon them may not encounter opposition? Similarly the direction of the European policy of peace ought to act in concert with the knowledge of the people; it ought to be sure not only of their confidence, but also of their full knowledge of the nature and of the greatness of the danger that has to be guarded against. For if it is not so it always remains doubtful whether the necessary sacrifice will be forthcoming, and whether it will be sufficiently lasting; whether at the critical moment other less weighty considerations may not preponderate, and interfere with the unity of action. It will be remembered how political passion was led astray with regard to the dangers of war which later (*e.g.*, the Boulanger revelations) had to be avowed even by those who had formerly denied them. Think of the Italian parties who attempt to weaken the triple alliance. Think of the national efforts of the Austrian Slavs, who in their foolish blindness gravitate towards Russia; recall the time when France was deaf to the remonstrances of Barthélemy St. Hilaire that it would be a disgrace to aid Russia in her retrograde policy, and behold her even now coquetting with Russia! When all this is considered the conclusion must be drawn that the knowledge of Russia and of the dangers which are advancing from the East has not for a long time been sufficiently general, and that the nations are not even yet disposed to lay sufficient stress on matters of momentous importance..

And it would be a foolish mistake to suppose that clear insight into the decay of Russia and its dismal condition could lead to a dangerous depreciation of the enemy or even to a thoughtless acceptance of its challenge. On the contrary, it is the sight of Russian misery that first reveals in all their significance the dangers of a Russian war and the necessity for its prevention.

A knowledge of the state of Russia shows how much more difficult it would be to carry on a war against that country than against a European Power, and how much more difficult it would be to carry it through to a satisfactory issue; how much greater and longer continued sacrifices it would involve even in the case of success, and with how comparatively small means Russia's countless inhabitants could begin a war and continue it in their boundless solitudes. Without a knowledge of its condition no conception could be formed of the technical difficulties of war waged against Russia or of the greatness of the sacrifice which would have to be made. A depreciation of the dangers of war would in no case be caused by a knowledge of Russia and its people: quite the contrary.

In comparing the condition and efforts of Russia with those of the West of Europe the mind naturally reverts to the attacks and incursions which Western civilisation, both in antiquity and the Middle Ages, had, in spite of all its resources, to suffer from the rude and needy but hardy barbarians of the East and North. And the recollection of the past brings with it the apprehension that once again the countless barbarians of the East may possibly triumph precisely by virtue of their uncivilised condition and the smallness of their needs. If the knowledge of the state of Russia calls up such a gruesome picture of a possible future, there will be no tendency to depreciate the enemy, but rather a desire due to this spread of information to form a coalition of all the countries of the West for the purposes of resisting the advance of a barbarous Power.

No apprehension need be felt that the war-spirit of the Russians would be awakened and aroused by an exposure of their faults and misdeeds. For it is only gross ignorance that can suppose that the irritability of the Russian war-spirit is capable of being intensified, and that it can be repressed or silenced except by overmastering force. Who are they whose susceptibilities an excessive diffidence is so anxious to spare? Is it the ranks of the people? Is it the Russian press? Is it even the Tsar? On none of these factors of Russian public life can the European publicist exercise the slightest determinative influence.

The masses in Russia are in themselves eminently peaceable; they will never take the initiative in any foreign war. The criticisms passed by the European press on Russia can never irritate them, for they are mostly unable to read. It is only among the higher classes that war is advocated, war is their constant cry. Some of them are possessed with a fanatical passion for aggrandisement; they believe they are called to be the masters of the world by means of the Slavs. This war-spirit, like blind fury, is neither capable of being intensified, nor is it allayed by tender considerations; only overpowering force can keep it down. Others hope that a war will shatter to pieces the present arbitrary form of government and establish a better in its stead—a federal union or a communistic republic. Even those parties, who would go to war under any circumstances, and who long for nothing more than a defeat of Russian arms, are entirely indifferent as to whether Russia's faults are exposed or not. In the case of parties so decidedly and deliberately warlike in their tendencies it is useless to talk of provocation or the reverse. Only very few educated Russians recognise clearly that it is not war, but internal and especially ecclesiastical reforms that will bring about the regeneration of Russia. These few enlightened men have been the first to expose and condemn the internal state of the country; they would be the last to resent descriptions of Russia. On the contrary, they rejoice that the public opinion of Europe has been united, strengthened, and reinforced through becoming acquainted with the danger of Russia, and that it has felt itself called upon to resist the Russian desire for war.

It would therefore rest on a misunderstanding of the nature of the case if European publicists allowed themselves to be led astray by an over-scrupulousness with regard to the susceptibilities of the Russian people in the fulfilment of their duty. An attitude of apprehension would be still more futile, as the opinions of the foreign press very rarely reach Russia in an unmutilated condition; only a few editors and a few special individuals enjoy the advantage of reading foreign papers in their original form. The Tsar, whose reading is submitted to a rigid scrutiny, does not belong to this special class. For the Russian public the Russian press is alone available. It would be a mistake to suppose that this press erred on the side of excessive sensitiveness.

The Russian press is quite unlike the press of the West. It does not reflect the tendencies of other countries or the state of their affairs; it even ignores the drift of opinion at home. It cannot influence the people and the people's representatives,[1] and thus make its weight felt in the course of events, as is the case in Western Europe. The Russian press is only the mouthpiece of the ruling coterie, which has suppressed all other organs advocating different views. It does not allow freedom of discussion, and alone enjoys the cheap and cowardly satisfaction of displaying itself publicly, but without exercising any special influence in important decisions. This imperial press serves up to its readers nothing but what is whispered to it daily by the powers that be, and by them in turn to the Emperor. Russia is calumniated by Europe and threatened with attacks; facts are found and false documents produced by way of proof. Under such circumstances it is clearly quite irrelevant and without influence on Russia's peaceful or warlike position if information with respect to the condition of Russia is spread in Europe for its protection, and especially irrelevant if the evidence of Russians themselves is used. In its reproduction there is nothing else to be found than what conspicuous and patriotic Russians have themselves said of their country's condition.

Lastly, it would be a mistake, and a depreciation of Alexander III.'s disposition and character, to suppose that the European press has anxiously to

[1] As there are none.—ED.

consider the moods of a Tsar whose nod would be sufficient to kindle the torch of war. If Alexander III. were not naturally one of the most peaceable and sober-minded men in his Empire, national Chauvinism and desperate nationalism would have had many opportunities of rousing in him an irresponsible desire for war. It is not to be attributed to the character of Alexander III., but to the horrible circumstances of his accession, that the pernicious elements maintained an overmastering influence over him, that they were prejudicial to the weal of his Empire, endangered the peace of Europe, and could not fail to compromise the respect due to the ruler who was held fast in the meshes of their deceptions. As a matter of fact there has never been a ruler naturally less prone to approve of wrong, or to promote persons of doubtful character to an influential position, or even to tolerate them in his presence. Nevertheless it has been understood as lending authority to the opinion that the Tsar does not want to know the truth, as if it might be said of him, *vult decipi*. What a desirable end would be attained if he could once know to what extent his people deceive him! How they deceive him as regards the state of his Empire and the tendencies of other countries; how they impose upon him, for example, in making him believe that absolute religious freedom exists in Russia, and that every adult subject of the Empire is at full liberty to profess and act up to his religious convictions. And an inestimable service would be performed to the Tsar, his kingdom, and even all Europe, if his eyes could be opened to the actual condition of the country and to the accursed action of the orthodox national camarilla.[1] If this were attainable a new era in Russia's internal and external policy would commence. This policy would be absolutely peaceable externally and internally, it would prepare the way for a blessed transformation of the national life by introducing genuine religious liberty and ecclesiastical reforms. Consequently accurate information about the condition of Russia would be in no way hazardous as far as the Tsar is concerned; it could produce no effect if it were withheld from him, and its influence would be beneficial if it were brought to his knowledge.

Although information with regard to the condition of Russia is, as we have shown, to be regarded as permissible, imperative, and useful, yet the subject is attended with peculiar difficulties, and it appears hardly practicable to do more than spread the information which we get from Russians themselves as to the state of their country, because the reports of foreigners run the danger of being considered as either exaggerated or untrustworthy.

The Western European who was formerly accustomed to look upon Europe as being influenced and

[1] See Appendix, Note 16.

almost dominated by the mighty prestige of Russia felt himself compelled to institute a parallel between the civilisation of the East and the West, and expected that the reforms of Alexander II. would succeed in bringing to a glorious development the powers of a nation which had apparently all the freshness and vigour of youth.——The Western European even now finds it difficult to believe his own eyes when he is brought face to face with Russian civilisation, which compels him to see that this vaunted prestige was by no means a proof of power and inner worth, but rather of Europe's weakness, abasement, and want of cohesion, and that the reforms of Alexander II. have only had the effect of giving freer play to the despotically-bridled and only half-tamed savagery of the Russian nation. It is difficult to convince a Western European that Russia is in reality an entirely different and hardly intelligible world to the West. It is a country which has already become effete, and is either on the point of retiring from the scene of history, if at the eleventh hour a salutary reversal of the march of development does not set in, or taking advantage of the factions and want of unity and cohesion among its natural enemies, it will devote itself to its historical mission of destroying the culture of the West and of bringing about the doom of the history of the world.

X.

MISDOINGS OF THE CLERGY.

The following extract, which is derived from a Russian source and is of recent date, will be sufficient to show the radical difference between Russian and Western civilisation, and to rouse feelings of horror and a sense of common danger in the minds of those who usually take no interest in Russian affairs. The woman who fell a victim to an act of orthodox fanaticism was not an obscure individual, but occupied a high position, and had relations who were highly respected at Court — Princess Anna Livov. The extract, which is translated from the French, is entirely trustworthy, as it comes from a friend of the princess. It is as follows:—

"Anna Livov had paid a visit to one of her uncles in the province of Kalaga, and had spent several days at his house very pleasantly and in the best of spirits; thence she went to a well-known cloister in the same province to perform her devotions and to ask advice with respect to the founding of a hospital which she wished to build on the estate where she had spent her life in works of charity. The prior of this cloister advised her to go to the nunnery of Tikhopovsk, telling her that there she would be likely to get more accurate information, and could at the same time visit the holy well. Indefatigable in her zeal, Anna betook herself to the nunnery, but the tedious journey had exhausted her strength. When she arrived in the neighbourhood of the well she saw that the pilgrims, men and women alike, were being forcibly pushed into it by the nuns (every immersion was doubtless a source of income). Anna hesitated to approach the well, especially as the water was very cold. The nuns set upon her and upbraided her as an atheist. Anna defended herself and told them her name. They cried out that she lied, that she was mad, &c. They then threw her into the water time after time, with the result that she was seized with cramp, and concussion of the brain set in. The nuns now became alarmed lest charges should be brought against them; they therefore locked her up in a room, where she was thrown half-naked upon a bed without a covering, and her arms so tightly tied that the blood began to spurt. One window of the room was left wide open by the nuns, and the crowd of people were urged by them to look in upon one who was possessed of a devil. Anna was left in this state for several days—without food, without water, without attention. It happened by chance that a woman who had arrived as a pilgrim, and had desired to see the one 'possessed,' was none other than a former servant in the family of the Livovs. This woman recognised Anna, and Anna recognised her in a lucid moment, and begged her to inform her brother-in-law, Olénin, of her condition. The woman went away, but—whether from stupidity or nervousness—she could not make up her mind to speak of the matter for several days. At last she summoned up courage and told Olénin everything. He set out at once, taking a doctor and Anna's lady's-maid with him. When they arrived they were not allowed to see Anna: it was only after using threats that Olénin gained admittance. Anna was not recognisable, so great was the change that had taken place in her appearance. In a lucid interval she called out, 'Alexander, save me!' and then the delirium again set in. She was brought to Moscow and nursed with the greatest care: a slight improvement took place, and there was again room for hope, but the power of resistance was gone, and Anna Livov succumbed on September 19, 1888."

The following may be added by way of supplement. The Princess Anna was unmarried, and was a distinguished and highly respected woman. Although by position belonging to the highest society, its frivolities and superficialities had no attractions for her. The sad occurrence caused great sensation in Moscow and St. Petersburg;

but it has not transpired whether any decisive action was taken to bring the criminals to justice. On the contrary, all the legal proceedings which the relatives of this unfortunate victim of brutal fanaticism and low greed sought to take were without success. And it is added in the extract that violent immersion is as prevalent as ever.[1]

Why, it may be asked, were the distinguished relatives of the unfortunate Princess Livov unable to obtain satisfaction for the crime which was perpetrated on her? Why were the authors of it left unpunished? Any one who puts such a question has neither any conception of the system which prevails in Russia, nor of the arbitrary power of its present representative, Pobyedonostsev, the *oberprocouror* of the Holy Synod. Everything must be put down by force which might by any possibility shake the Caesaropopism which has been called to universal dominion, and which "stands on guard at two divisions of the world." There is no single act of the Holy Synod which it is permissible to condemn; it matters not whether it concerns the violent measures taken to spread the doctrines of the Greek Church, or the brutal suppression of heretics. No one dares at the risk of his life to oppose this arbitrary power,[2] and the barbarity of this aggressive system imagines that it can silence an officious zeal by attempting to prevent the European press from taking no notice of it.

[1] See Appendix, Note 17.   [2] See Appendix, Note 18.

The "Russian atrocities" were brought to light by the publication of diplomatic reports in the English Blue Book (Russia, No. 1, at the British Embassy, March 5, 1877), but at that time they did not receive the attention which they deserved, on account of the uncertainty which prevailed as to whether a war would break out, and whether it would be possible to localise it. As serious efforts are being made to divert public attention from Russian affairs, it appears advisable to recall those terrible events, so that every one may know the consequences that would follow to Europe, especially in the religious domain, if Russian arms were successful. The following particulars, which are entirely trustworthy, are taken from these documents.

First of all attempts were made to awaken Russian orthodox belief in Poland and Lithuania by distributing sums of money among the people, and promising them exemption from taxes and military duties.[1] As these inducements were unsuccessful, more drastic measures were taken. In the district of Myncievicz those who remained true to the faith of their fathers were flogged by the Cossacks: "fifty blows with the 'nagaika' (Cossack whip) were given to every adult man, twenty-five to every woman, and ten to every child, irrespective

[1] No. 12, Lieut.-Col. Mansfield to Earl Derby Warsaw, Jan. 29, 1875; and No. 13, Mansfield to Earl Granville, Warsaw, Feb. 10, 1875.

of age or sex; one woman who was more vehement than the others receiving as much as a hundred." On account of the crowded state of the prisons and dwelling-houses the religious prisoners were crammed into yards and sheds in the severe weather.

"Scenes similar to that which took place at Myncievicz, of January, 1874, &c.,[1] have been repeated in many localities, varying only in the amount of casualties, killed and wounded."[2]

In certain places the mission work was carried on with even greater severity. "The peasants were assembled and beaten by the Cossacks until the military surgeon stated that more would endanger life; they were then driven through a half-frozen river, up to their waists, into the parish church, through files of soldiers, where their names were entered in the petition, and passed out at an opposite door, the peasants all the time crying out, 'You may call us orthodox, but we remain in the faith of our fathers.'"[3] In order to escape from their persecutors the "peasants bivouacked in the forest, where the mortality among them was frightful; and orders were given to the Cossacks to hunt them down back to villages."[4] Furthermore, "cruelties of the most revolting nature were committed by the military

---

[1] Mansfield to Granville, Warsaw, January 29, 1874, No. 3.
[2] Ibid., February 18, 1874, No. 4.
[3] Mansfield to Derby, Warsaw, January 29, 1875, No. 12.
[4] Ibid., January 1, 1875, No. 9.

authorities—cruelties which can only be compared with those resorted to in the darkest ages of the Inquisition."[1] As these violent measures were of no avail, the signatures of so-called converted peasants were forged, and "the peasants declared that in signing the addresses they did not know what they were doing; in others, that they had given no authority to the delegates; in others, the older peasants said that they had only given a personal adhesion, and under compulsion."[2] "In one village a peasant suffocated himself and his family with charcoal rather than have his child baptized by the Government pope," *i.e.*, the parish priest.[3] Not a few being driven to misery and despair have taken refuge in suicide.[4] In spite of all this it was impossible to make the peasants give up their religion. "The Uniats[5] who were 'converted' in the previous year are far from subscribing to their conversion: they neither attend the churches nor take the sacrament; the 'popes' are neither allowed to baptize their children nor to bury their dead; and they never

---

[1] Lord Augustus Loftus to Earl Derby, St. Petersburg, February 16, 1875, No. 4.
[2] Lieutenant-Colonel Mansfield to Earl Granville, Warsaw, February 10, 1875, No. 13.
[3] Lieutenant-Colonel Mansfield to Earl Derby, Warsaw, January 1, 1875, No 9.
[4] Lord Augustus Loftus to Earl Derby, St. Petersburg, January, 28, 1875.
[5] See Appendix, Note 19.

submit to the 'popes' marrying them."[1] Measures of a different kind were taken against the most obstinately recalcitrant : "In some parishes the most obstinate have been sent to the interior of the Empire or Siberia."[2] Of these latter, three hundred small landowners were compelled to give up their parcels of land, they were torn ruthlessly from their wives and children, and sent as exiles to the province of Kherson. Three hundred others were exiled to the province of Ekaterinoslav. One man was apportioned to each village, the elder of the village being responsible for the Uniat, who was forbidden to have any communications with his family or friends, or to receive his letters or money. They received eight copecks, or twopence halfpenny, per day ; but, in consequence of their stubbornness, this allowance was cut off. They looked upon themselves as martyrs, and would rather die than give up their belief. About 20,000 Uniats were deported to Saratov and other provinces, and Russian priests ("popes") were sent by the Russian Government to proselytise them, but the Uniats drove them away. The Uniats who were left behind were imprisoned and tortured, and Cossacks were billeted upon them whose excesses knew no bounds.[3]

[1] Lieutenant-Colonel Mansfield to Earl Derby, Warsaw, February 14, 1876.
[2] Ibid., January 29, 1875.
[3] Consul-General Stanley to Earl Derby, Odessa, June 29, 1876, No. 21.

And after all this the procuror of the Holy Synod can hold up his head and boast before the whole of Europe that Russia is the land of religious toleration! And in the summer of 1888 he celebrated the twenty-fifth year of jubilee of the conversion of the Uniats with all the pomp of Church and State! Russia, he announced, was marked out by Providence as the "guardian of two divisions of the world," and from this dominating position was entrusted with the mission of regenerating the world with its "pure Christianity."

XI.

FINLAND.

The area of the grand duchy of Finland is equal to seven-tenths of the surface of the German Empire: the country is therefore about one-tenth larger than Prussia, and two and a half times as large as the kingdoms of Bavaria, Würtemberg, Saxony, the grand duchies of Baden and Hesse, and the Imperial State of Alsace-Lorraine put together. On the other hand, Finland contains little more than one-seventh of the total population of these countries, and numbers as compared with their average of 92 only six inhabitants to the square kilometre (16 in the south and most populated, Nyland-län, and only one in the most northern, Uleåborg-län). The rapidly increasing population amounted at the end of 1886 to 2,232,378 inhabitants, 92 per cent. of whom were peasants, engaged in agriculture and the rearing of cattle, and not quite 8 per cent. were living in towns; 98 per cent. are Lutherans; 85 per cent. speak Finnish, and not quite 14.5 per cent. Swedish. The latter constitute the country population only in the southwestern coast and island districts; the remainder belong to the nobility, clergy, and civil service, as well as to the commercial and industrial classes.

With regard to the configuration of the country, Finland was covered during the glacial period, as Greenland is still, by a huge unbroken mass of ice, so that the land appears as a system of glacier beds, running from north to south, and resting on a foundation of granite. At one extremity of these glaciers are found thousands of lakes, often very extensive, and containing numerous bays; at the other, interminable moors, in addition to small tracts of carefully cultivated land, which are separated from one another by chains of low hills, covered for the most part with pine forests, but amongst which are found numerous bare and totally unproductive granite ridges. The extent of the whole forest area was some time ago estimated at 63 per cent. of the total surface of the country, whereas the returns of the districts then surveyed (about 70 per cent. in the south) showed 8·65 per cent. of cultivated land, *i.e.*, tilled fields and meadows, 26 per cent. of moorland, and 11·6 per cent. of water surface.

The general impression produced on a visitor when he first sees the country is a very peculiar one; nowhere else does he find such subdued melancholy loveliness. The view of the innumerable lakes in the distance is interrupted by the prettily undulating lines of wooded heights; the rural scenery is rendered striking by the delightful and delicately graduated variations of the atmosphere; but it is, so to speak, a picture of still life. This is not due to the scarcity of human dwellings. However scattered the farms of the Schwarzwald (in Germany) are, the sounds of merry laughter, expressive of comfort and contentment, penetrate from its valleys to the loneliness of the forest above; whereas in Finland the general poverty of nature lends the picture its fundamental tone. An air of silence and melancholy in the scenery harmonises with the gray walls and brown shingle-roofs of the unpretentious wooden structures which isolated farms and scattered groups of houses present to the eye.

Totally different, however, from this general impression is that produced by every scene of human activity. The smallest parcel of ground as well as the more extensive cultivated field is tended with all a horticulturist's care. The houses in both town and country are extremely well built. The peasant's home is kept spotlessly clean; the high windows with their neat curtains and bright flowers give it an air of cheerfulness. Well cared-for cattle of pure breed testify to the solicitude of the farmer. Everywhere, both in town and country, the people are well dressed and evidently well fed. The roads from one end of the country to the other are well kept, and the rapidity with which travellers are conveyed, and the excellent and cheap accommodation to be obtained at the numerous clean posting-stages, or at the rustic inns, are in themselves sufficient evidence of the perfect arrangement of things in Finland.

As to the capital of the country, the poverty of which was at one time almost proverbial, and which in its own national song calls itself poor,[1] a traveller wrote twenty years ago: "On entering the Finnish capital one can form at once an idea of the 'poverty' of the country. If the statistics of European capitals were to be compiled from the architectural value of their public buildings, and if, in so doing, the extent of the period during which they were erected were taken into consideration, and if the wealth of the city were estimated by the sums expended yearly on its structures (so much for each inhabitant), then Helsingfors would undoubtedly appear as one of the wealthiest cities of Europe. The greatness of Riga, for instance, dates many centuries back; the prosperity of Helsingfors only began a few decades ago. Riga has been for centuries the emporium of an extensive inland country; the value of the Helsingfors trade scarcely amounts (1870) to a seventh of that of Riga. The larger buildings of Riga are almost exclusively the property of individual corporations, whereas those of Helsingfors are national institutions. Apart from its splendidly picturesque situa-

[1] See Appendix, Note 20.

tion, Helsingfors must strike every stranger as being the capital of a promising country."

* * * * *

The conversion to Christianity of the lands to the east and south-east of the Baltic, and their subjection to German culture, has been accomplished everywhere within almost exactly the same historical period, but under circumstances which differed according as the colonisation emanated from Germany or from Sweden. These differences should be glanced at, because one of the principal Finnish characteristics cannot otherwise be properly understood.

The work of conversion, which was set on foot at the end of the tenth century, was unsuccessfully begun among the Slavonic Prussians by Bohemian and Silesian missionaries, and was continued by the Poles, but with only temporary success. It was not till after the settlement of German Cistercians in the latter part of the twelfth century, and the support granted by the Teutonic Order, that German culture began to develop in Prussia, and not even then, as is well known, without uninterrupted, bitter, and often unsuccessful struggles with the natives, and strong opposition from the Poles. German culture, unless it had been assisted by the mother-country, would have been doomed to destruction if, after the secularisation of the Teutonic Order at the Reformation, a series of powerful princes had not succeeded in recovering and maintaining the ascendancy of the German element in Prussia.

In Livonia likewise until the twelfth century Slavonic (or more correctly Russian) influence tried to make itself felt, but without any lasting success, and without leaving behind the slightest traces of civilisation. It is well known that about the middle of the twelfth century some Bremen merchants first landed on the coast of Livonia, that the country immediately became the permanent home of a German mission, and that in a very short time, after some comparatively brief but energetically conducted struggles with the Finnish tribes of the Livonians and Esthonians, a well-ordered federal state in connection with the German Empire was established in the territory of the present Livonia, Esthonia, and Courland by the spiritual princes of the country, the military order, and the autonomous towns. This state enjoyed brilliant prosperity for several centuries; but after the repeated attacks of its powerful Eastern neighbour, and after enduring terrible sufferings in war and frightful devastations—the German Empire not lending the least assistance—it lost its unity and independence (1561), though not without stipulating for the preservation of German customs.

Unlike Prussia and Livonia, Finland was first visited by the Swedes, not for missionary purposes, but in the course of a war undertaken in order to put an end to the plundering of the Swedish coasts by Finnish pirates. Among the expeditions which gradually extended the Swedish borders, and finally led to the permanent acquisition of Finland by Sweden, the most noteworthy are those undertaken in the years 1157, 1249, and 1293. It is to be noticed that the annexation was accomplished under obviously favourable conditions, and particularly that "little resistance was offered to the spread of the Swedish administration; at least no complaint against the violent imposition of foreign laws has been handed down to posterity, as has been the case in so many other countries."[1]

To these striking circumstances must be added another of paramount significance. In both Prussia and Livonia the right of feudal investiture was not only asserted to the fullest degree, but in many cases led to excesses notorious under the name of feudal rights, and especially to the diminution of the rights of the free peasantry, and finally to its reduction to the level of serfdom. Sweden, however, and more especially Finland, in spite of its national difference, totally escaped this degradation. This circumstance, which distinguishes the Scandinavian world from almost the whole of Europe, is not only accounted for by the necessity too often imposed on the Swedish kings of relying on the help of the peasantry in order to resist the encroachments of an arrogant aristocracy, but also by a peculiarity of the Scandinavian character which pervades all classes of society. As early as the second half of

[1] See Appendix, Note 21.

the thirteenth century, under King Magnus, the commoners were protected by law against the arbitrary power of the nobles. About two generations after the final conquest of Finland it was set down in the Finnish Charter obtained by the layman, Niels Thuresson Bjelke, and Bishop Hemming (1362), that in addition to the Finnish laymen and clergy, twelve Finnish peasants should take part in the election of the king. Since then, for nearly five and a half centuries, the Finnish peasantry have uninterruptedly enjoyed political and social equality, and have had a voice in all decisions respecting questions of legislation and taxation.

If we compare the mutual relations existing at the present day among the peoples of the countries just contrasted, we shall necessarily, to a great extent, have to trace the differences resulting from this comparison to the historical events that have meanwhile occurred in them. Nevertheless it cannot be denied that the beginnings of civilisation in these countries have exercised a lasting influence on their future development. The colonisation of Prussia was attended with extreme harshness. There was a time when the thought was seriously entertained of rooting out the recalcitrant natives, and replacing them by German immigrants, and even at the present time there is no district on the Baltic which has remained so far behind in intellectual culture as East Prussia. There the peasant is far below the level of the Esthonian or Lett, and his relations with the German are by no means of the most friendly.

Although in Livonia the lot of the subject population has been from the very first somewhat less hard (under Swedish rule much was done to lighten it), although the emancipation of the serfs and the suppression of forced labour among the Esthonians and Letts took place much earlier than in many parts of Germany, and although the country population—thanks to the initiative of German fellow-citizens—enjoys a free and independent communal administration of justice and autonomy probably unparalleled, yet the effects of past memories are plainly recognisable. But for these the Muscovite would never have been able to bring about a revulsion—transitory, it is true, but at times very serious—against German institutions.

Certainly the acts of violence indiscriminately perpetrated against the country during the last few years have had the effect of drawing Letts, Esthonians, and Germans more closely together than they have been for the last seven hundred years. Had the beginning of Livonian civilisation been milder, perhaps its present existence would be less threatened. In the whole history of Finland, but especially in the dangers of the present time, it is obvious of what auspicious importance it has been for the country never to have known real feudal servitude, and only to have been inhabited by free men, politically equal. The promise that the good deeds of the fathers should bring a blessing upon thousands has proved itself true here if anywhere. For in spite of ethnological differences in the population, the people of Finland has, from the commencement, possessed the consciousness of its continuity without interruption through whatever disturbances.

In vain has the Muscovite policy expanded all its skill to exasperate Swedes and Finns against one another, and to blow into the flame of a political and hostile opposition the harmless and purely *literary* movement of the Finnish patriots.

Upon the first appearance of a menace to the laws of the country Swedes and Finns stood shoulder to shoulder for the purpose of defence, with the same resolution, the same patriotism, and without allowing any separation to come between them.

There is not the least doubt that all that unanimity in passive opposition can do has been done with the greatest stedfastness and in inviolable co-operation by the brave little nation against the gigantic oppressor. The last centuries during which Finland was under the rule of Sweden—that is, since the time when Sweden became an important factor in the politics of the North—were for the already scantily-provided country nothing but an unbroken series of sufferings of all kinds. And yet throughout this period the history of Finland is as rich in memories, which the patriot may recall with pride, as any other country. This, owing to the limited space at our command, cannot be even cursorily dealt with. Only one very special and characteristic moment in the peculiar history of Finland must be noticed, as it probably nowhere else stands out so prominently. It reflects the highest honour on the people of Finland, and is well calculated to secure for them the sympathetic recognition of the whole civilised world.

From the earliest times Finland's position in her union with Sweden was that of equal rights. Scarcely had one generation passed, after the final annexation of the country by the peace of Nöteborg (1323), and Finland had already a voice in the election of the king like the other provinces of Sweden. It appears, from many decisions of the General Legislation of 1442, that Finland was then enjoying the same rights as the other provinces, but at the same time that it was something more than a mere territory administered by Sweden—that is, it possessed an individuality of its own. This is clearly shown in the legislation which repeatedly names Finland side by side with Sweden. Certain rights were acknowledged in the case of the nobility "of Finland and of Sweden"; the regiment kept up under the standards of the nobles was not to be employed outside "Finland and Sweden"; the "Swedish as well as the Finnish" peasantry were guaranteed certain privileges.[1] This distinction is all the more striking when contrasted with the transmarine possessions acquired at a later period—*i.e.*, the Baltic provinces and the German territories, where Swedish rule never fully asserted itself. Finland appears equal to Sweden proper, both as regards its representation in the diet of the realm, and in all other judicial and political respects. The Swedish law was not foreign to Finland, but was based on the native customs, coupled with rights developed by the representatives of the country, and rooted in the purely Finnish population.

The distinction from the beginning of the period mentioned acquires a most regrettable significance, if not in political yet in, so to speak, practical respects, because Finland is gradually relegated to the undeserved position of a neglected and injured step-brother — undeserved in two respects: first, because of its importance as a frontier land, and second, on account of the exceptionally loyal conduct of the people.

It was by no means ignored by Sweden that, from a military point of view, it was of the utmost importance to maintain the Finnish frontier in the best possible defensive condition against its aggressive Eastern neighbour. Resolutions and measures were repeatedly taken to ensure this object, but

[1] Mechelin, pp. 245, 246, and *passim*.

each time ostensibly more important tasks diverted attention from Finland and its effective defence. At the eleventh hour, when the power of Sweden was broken and the loss of Finland was only a question of time, an attempt was made to fortify the southern coast, which was more immediately threatened by Russia; but, as on former occasions, the land was almost entirely denuded of defensive troops, and had to rely on the improvised armies of the local population.

But, apart from its importance as an advanced frontier post, the value of Finland was by no means overlooked, but was repeatedly acknowledged and emphatically insisted on. The great Swedish kings, Charles IX. and Gustavus Adolphus, proved their superior capacity for ruling by the care which they devoted, during prolonged visits to the country, to the restoration of order in its shamefully neglected affairs. Axel Oxenstjerna, who distinguished himself in the same manner, remarked emphatically that a well-administered Finland might almost equal Sweden, only, as a matter of fact, it was the weaker portion. And Peter Brahe the younger, after travelling as governor-general through all parts of Finland and studying them thoroughly (1638), acknowledges, in his first report, that Finland was by no means an insignificant kingdom. As early as 1581 John III. recognised the brilliant achievements of the Finns in repelling Ivan the

Cruel, by raising Finland to the rank of a grand duchy. At the coronation of Charles IX. (1607) the heir to the crown, Gustavus Adolphus, bore the standard of Finland as "Grand Duke of Finland," &c.

In estimating the value of Finland, the most important factor surely was not what is noticed in the second place by Peter Brahe—the great abundance, considering the number of inhabitants, of fish, furred animals, forests, and minerals, and its extent—for imperishable treasures of another kind have at all times formed the inexhaustible and greatest wealth of the country. Inexhaustible indeed, for, with but a few rare exceptions, the government of the Swedish kings and nobility has almost systematically, one might say, endeavoured to repel Finland, and estrange it from Sweden. Nevertheless, Finland at all times, and uninterruptedly, distinguished itself more than any other province of Sweden, by its steadfast loyalty and cheerful willingness to make sacrifices, as long as it was not actually given up and definitely handed over.

That Finland was left without aid and protection from Sweden in the direst necessities of war has already been adverted to. A few striking examples will supply the proofs.

In spite of constant menaces of war, the troops of Ivan IV., who invaded the country in 1573, did not meet with any serious resistance in either

Finland or Esthonia. In the year 1577, after repeated devastations by the Russians, only the town and castle of Reval remained of the two coast territories in the possession of Sweden. But, under the leadership of the Finns, Tott and Fleming (later also Delagardie and Tawwast), *with only the troops stationed in Finland*, aided by bands of Finnish peasant volunteers, the Russians were not only totally driven out from the two coast territories and Ingria, but even Carelia (which afterwards remained with Finland), together with its capital, Kexholm, which had the reputation of being impregnable, was taken (1580 and 1581). It is true that for these achievements Finland received the honourable title of a "grand duchy," but otherwise it was very badly rewarded. Not only had the country, during a war which lasted nearly nine years, been harassed by levies, bad harvests, devastations, and plagues, but after the conclusion of the truce it actually became the booty of undisciplined unpaid soldiers, and what was most vexatious, as being a constant and permanent oppression, it fell a prey to unprincipled Swedish officials — the "law-readers" — who delighted in extortion, &c. Repeated Finnish deputations entreating the king to do away with these abuses remained unnoticed by him.

Under circumstances essentially similar though of shorter duration, the sufferings were revived eight years after, when Finland, left undefended, was inundated by the devastating bands of Boris Godunov. The honourable peace of Teusina (1585) did not end the misery, as a deplorable civil confusion broke out in Sweden—namely, the struggle between the lawful king, Sigismund, then absent in Poland, and Duke Charles, who abrogated to himself all the royal power as regent of the realm. It is worthy of notice that Finland then, in spite of all the vexations it had been subjected to, placed itself on the side of legality and of the rightful sovereign, whose representative in Finland (Fleming, the viceroy) had, by exercising an arbitrary and illegal pressure, driven the people in self-defence to civil war (the "War of Clubs," 1592-1600), which was only ended after the deposition of Sigismund had been legally accomplished. In the Swedish religious differences which were then raging, Finland, threatened on two sides, preserved a doubly honourable position, making a stand against Swedish puritanism and Lutheran intolerance, as well as against the Jesuitic counter-reformation, and holding aloft the banner of religious liberty.

The successes connected with the powerful position of Sweden under Charles IX., extending to the peace of Stolbowa (1617), viz., the "rescue" of Moscow in 1610, the second capture of Kexholm, the storming and occupation of Great Novgorod, the call of Gustavus Adolphus, *i.e.*, of his brother Charles Philip to the throne of the Tsars, &c., were due to

Finnish men—Klaus Boije, Arevid Wildeman, Ewert Horn, Jacob Delagardie (the last named, though born at Reval, was brought up in Finland)—all of them leaders of Finnish troops. Thus was Sweden actually in a very special way advanced by Finland.

Finland, however, proved of the greatest value to Sweden in the great "German War" (Thirty Years' War). While only expected to supply one-fourth of the total military armament of Sweden, the Finnish contingent in this war amounted to fully two-fifths (*i.e.*, of thirty regiments twelve were Finnish), amongst which the Finnish cavalry formed the best part of the Swedish picked troops. Their war-cry, "Hakka pääle,"[1] produced a regular panic.

These great services and sacrifices were accomplished by Finland, although it had been nearly annihilated by the almost incessant frontier wars, for which it had had to depend entirely on its own resources, as well as by the extortions of Swedish officials (its population scarcely numbered more than 250,000 to 300,000 people, and, according to the testimony of Oxenstjerna, whole districts were totally uncultivated and only contained wild animals), and although the benevolent rule of Charles IX. and Gustavus Adolphus had scarcely had time to produce favourable results. But if Finland was indebted to the intelligent administration of Oxen-

[1] This cry cannot unfortunately be accurately translated. It combines the meaning of "At them" and "seize them!"

stjerna and Peter Brahe the younger for many benefits that could never be forgotten, such as the reform of sundry abuses, the foundation of the Abo University, improved means of communication, &c., yet it was only then that the real period of suffering commenced for the not only neglected, but actually misused and maltreated, step-brother.

During the minority of Christina the wasteful throwing away of the land, which yielded the chief revenue of the realm, began; under her frivolous government disorder reached its highest point. Christina alone created eighteen counts, forty-two marquises, and four hundred nobles, and endowed them all with hereditary landed possessions. Finland was the specially favoured country for such investitures; in Finland alone (where hitherto there had only existed one county and two baronetcies) no fewer than eight counties and twenty-one baronetcies were instituted by Christina. On her abdication Finland was a bundle of little principalities: two-thirds of the country and one-third of the revenue had been given away to noblemen living in Sweden, who were for the most part foreigners. Finland had become the plunder-ground of the Swedish aristocracy, who were, moreover, granted oppressive privileges—church patronage, judicial and political powers, &c. The abuses and sufferings which resulted to Finland need not be pointed out in detail.

Matters were destined to become still worse in consequence of the ambitious plans of Charles X.; his defeats as well as his successes proved alike injurious to Finland. To provide for the expedition undertaken against Poland, Finland was entirely denuded of all its military strength (1656), so that, while 20,000 Finns were quartered in Poland, Finland was quite defenceless, when it was invaded by the Russians, who took the part of the dethroned king of Poland, John Casimir. A hastily summoned Finnish reserve sprang as it were from the ground; instead of every tenth man, the peasants gave every eighth; and local diets voted war contributions to an extent never heard of before. In 1657 Kexholm was relieved and all danger from the Russians removed; Finland gave up half of its newly-raised military power for continuing the war in Livonia, and received from Poland in return—the plague. This war, conducted at the cost of so many sacrifices, but otherwise abortive, was ended in 1658 by a truce, and was followed in 1661 by the peace of Kardis. Time gradually heals the wounds of war, but the successes of Charles X., as has been remarked, were far more fatal to Finland than his defeats, *e.g.*, the acquisition of the Southern provinces by the peace concluded with Denmark in 1658 at Roeskilde. Hitherto, in consequence of the achievements of the Finns, the brotherly relations between Finland and Sweden had at least theoretically and academically become increasingly sympathetic; the loyalty of the Finns had become proverbial ; it was acknowledged that the Finns were justified when they boasted of being bound to Sweden not as slaves, but as partners; in Sweden the Finns were recognised as "brothers and comrades," and the relations existing between Sweden and Finland was termed an "alliance." From the time, however, that Sweden extended its frontiers to the south, its interest in Finland began to cool. It became more and more evident that the fidelity of Finland to the State was one-sided and not reciprocated.

Under the last governments, whose efforts were principally directed abroad, a serious neglect, nay, even an oppression, of Finland had set in. The improvements effected by Gustavus Adolphus, Oxenstjerna, and Brahe, had disappeared ; Finland was again exploited by greedy and corruptible Swedish judges and officials; trade and industry were paralysed by the monopolies granted to certain privileged companies and to Swedish markets. Money and talent no longer found an opening, and therefore migrated to Sweden. Finland began to lose its culture. All these evils were intensified under the aristocratic regency which followed, for, instead of improving the finances by effecting the "reduction" which had been decided on, *i.e.*, recovering lands and endowments which had been thrown away or obtained by cunning devices, new grants were made, and, although the treasury was almost empty, the persons in power allowed themselves to be persuaded by France to join her in frivolous military adventures, &c. This mismanagement weighed more heavily on Finland than on the provinces, yet Finland, nevertheless, repeatedly distinguished itself by its loyalty to the Crown, and voted at the diet of Abo abundant supplies for conducting the "useless" war, with the proviso, it is true, that these supplies should be chiefly spent in placing the country in a proper state of defence against Russia, which was then arming in order to make up for the peace of Stolbowa.

Under the ensuing absolute rule of Charles XI. Sweden enjoyed twenty years' peace; order was restored to its finances, its resources were re-established through strictly carried out "reduction," and an orderly administration, together with civic freedom and security, was obtained. Although the king never visited Finland, and bestowed no special care upon it, even in many respects treating it like a step-father (in 1689, for instance, the Finns were excluded from the rank of officers), it nevertheless derived some indirect benefit from the general improvement, and all its subsequent administrative institutions may be said to date from this epoch.

It is noteworthy that a distinction, though merely theoretical, between Finnish and Swedish, is then met with for the first time. While, on the one hand, a total suppression of the Finnish language was aimed at, on the other the first beginnings of Finnish ethnography and philology were made—a fact which at any rate points to an invigoration of the native intellectual vitality. In economical respects, however, this period was one of the most lamentable ever experienced by Finland. Besides a persistent artificial paralysing of trade and industry, Finland was visited by a long series of bad crops, famines, and terrible conflagrations. At the beginning of the reign of Charles XII. it would have required years to heal the wounds from which the country was suffering; instead of this necessary period of peace, there were constant miseries of war, such as had never before been experienced, which were obviously intensified by the total neglect and abandonment of Finland by Sweden.

It is too well known to need amplification that, during the twenty years' Northern war, the Baltic provinces bordering on Russia and Poland were entirely abandoned by Charles XII. for the sake of his plans, which were directed towards the South. We need only mention Finland's share in the sufferings thereby incurred. After the great victory of Narva, which was more than half due to the Finns, Finland was entirely denuded of troops, and was called upon to supply a second army. During the first year of the war (1700), scantily populated as it was, it had supplied no less than 20,000 soldiers, not even a third of whom were allowed to be used in defence of their own country. The want of men was at that time so great that even fathers of families and holders of farms had often to be called out, and even this was not the last demand for men! Nevertheless, the unflinching fidelity of the Finns to the State and the king constantly rendered it possible to send out peasant volunteers to serve in other than the, so to speak, official war operations! Nothing was done by Sweden for the defence of Finland; authorities and archives were shipped off, and the country was entirely abandoned to itself. Although in 1707 a new army had to be got together, it was able in 1710 to arm another 8,000 men, who, however, were powerless to save their country. Half the troops, whom Charles XII. in 1713 led from Bender to the fertile districts of Rügen, would have sufficed to deliver Finland. Instead of this help being given, the very last soldier was withdrawn from Finland to protect the Swedish coast, and the land, thoroughly exhausted by the distress produced by a fourteen years' war, became for the third time the prey of the Russians, who for seven years (1714-1721) committed unbounded excesses.

Under such provocation it would not have been surprising if the loyalty of Finland had relaxed, and if the diplomatic schemes to marry Charles Frederick of Holstein, the nephew of Charles XII., with the daughter of the Tsar, and to make him the ruler of an autonomous Finland, had been gladly welcomed. Instead of this, Finland's fidelity remained unshaken, and, even under Russian sway, the Finnish partisan war was carried on obstinately and without interruption!

After the peace of Nystadt in 1721—by which, in order to retain Livonia, Esthonia, and Ingria, the greater part of Finland (except Viborg, &c.) was given back to Sweden—the government of the Swedish nobles, which had just begun, was at first very attentive to the restoration of the country's welfare. But Finland was soon again neglected. Only one of its harbours obtained the right of trading with foreign countries. This was Abo, which, not having any important inland country at its back, could in no way compete with Stockholm, Gefle, &c. Even the representatives of Finland at the diet were reduced in number. Stockholm alone had as many representatives as all the Finnish towns put together, &c. But the exceedingly thoughtless and wild rule of the nobility, disgraced by the constant party hatred of the "Hats" and "Caps," contributed more than any oppressions, slights, or neglect, towards estranging the hearts of the Finns from the State and detaching Finland from it. Finland was treated, over the heads of the Finns themselves, as goods for barter by the leaders of the Swedish policy. On the one hand, the "Caps" in 1741 carried on negotiations, with a view to constitute Finland an autonomous neutral state " under Russian protection." On the other hand, the " Hats " expressly declared, among their reasons for declaring war against Russia (1741), that the war was not dangerous, because it would at most bring about the devastation and loss of Finland. Indeed, the whole of Finland was occupied for the fourth time by the Russians, and administered by them for two years (1742-1743)—this time, however, in rather an indulgent manner. The Empress Elizabeth, who by a manifesto of 1742 had raised hopes as to the autonomy of Finland, afterwards preferred its incorporation with the Russian Empire, and compelled the Finns to do homage. In the treaty of peace of Abo (1742) the cession of Finland was offered by Sweden as the price of Elizabeth's consent to the choice of an heir to the throne agreeable to the " Hats "; in short, Finland was heartlessly treated as something to be bought and sold. The treaty, it is true, allowed the greater part of Finland to remain under Sweden, but the Finns were wounded in their tenderest feelings, not only in that their national territory was rent asunder, but also because the new frontier regulations deprived the southern harbours of their inland connections, and the inland country of its harbours!

During the ten years of the wildest party struggles between the " Hats " and the " Caps " that followed,

Finland had to pay the greater part of the reckoning. It was brought to light by the deputations to the diet how much Finland was injured, and neglected in favour of Sweden; how all payments out of the "manufacturing fund" were withdrawn; how only three Finnish seaports, as against twenty-one Swedish, obtained the right of trading abroad, &c. Instead of allaying the increased discontent in Finland by refraining from acts of injustice, the Swedish nobility preferred to introduce a regular reign of terror, by making use of a severe press-gang system, and by keeping a strict watch over all malcontents, who were speedily brought to trial and executed. Native Finnish officials were dismissed and replaced by Swedes. It was even proposed to replace all the Finnish military by Swedish forces, after the plan of placing Finland in a general state of defence had been given up, because of the fear that the Finnish country population might prove unreliable! Such was the gratitude for the sacrifices cheerfully made for centuries by the loyal Finns.

What truth there was in the pretended unreliability of the Finns was first shown at the diet of 1765, when, chiefly by the aid of the numerous Finnish representatives, the restoration of the royal authority, which had been degraded by the excesses of the nobility in power, was effected; the freedom of trade, which had been lost for 150 years, was regained; the liberty of speech and of the press was inscribed in the fundamental law of the land, &c. And soon after Gustavus III.'s coronation, it was in Finland that the decisive steps were taken to restore the royal power, and to place it on a satisfactory basis.[1] All the attempts of the Swedish nobles, who for the sake of their own plans had always been ready to give up Finland, failed on account of the fidelity of the Finns to their king!

With the accession of Gustavus III., the golden age of Finland appeared to dawn. He had already issued a special manifesto from Versailles (1784), the "Letter to the Finnish nation," and his endeavours to raise the state of defence of Finland to the same level as that of Sweden, and to support the Finnish nobility, which had been neglected by the Swedish Estates, soon became evident. He visited Poland, accompanied by the Crown Prince Gustavus Adolphus. The gratitude of the "Finnish nation" for all the benefits he had conferred was expressed to him in a solemn form. It appeared for a moment as if the intimate understanding between Finland and its king was to be disturbed, when a personal quarrel occurred between the king and the younger gifted Sprengporten, whose discontent was made use of on two sides—by the Freemasons, who aimed at the autonomy of Finland,

[1] See Appendix, Note 22.

and also by the Queen-mother, whose dearest wish it was some day to see her favourite son, Duke Charles, raised to the position of an independent Grand Duke of Finland. To realise these plans, Sprengporten entered the service of Russia, against whom Gustavus III. had illegally, without consulting the Estates, declared war, whilst Russia was occupied in Turkey, hoping thus to take advantage of the opportunity offered to recover Viborg, &c., and, in addition, he sought to foment a conspiracy in Finland, with the object of severing the country from Sweden. Although the latter plan ended in complete failure, yet the so-called Aujala league, formed by the malcontent Finnish military officers, which, though faithful to the State, called on the people to resist the king—*i.e.*, to arrest the war, consolidate the national rights, and at the same time also defend the country to the last—affords the only example in history of an attempt made in Finland to rebel against the king. The Aujala league, however, met with no support from public opinion in Finland, which declared itself decidedly in favour of the king, and thus once again gave a striking proof of its fidelity.

Gustavus IV. likewise left behind him a grateful remembrance of his regency in Finland, because of many beneficial economic arrangements — the foundation and endowment of the Economical Society ("Finska Hällningssällskapet"), &c. He liked and favoured Finland because it showed itself decidedly averse to the prevailing revolutionary ideas. The final fate of Finland, however, its severance from Sweden, was brought about by the king's mortal antipathy to Napoleon, "the scarlet beast of the Book of Revelation," whom he, a second Charles XII., intended to overthrow by a bold onslaught. Of course it did not come to this, but, repeating the grievous wrong inflicted by Charles XII. on Finland, he almost entirely denuded the country of troops, at a time when it was threatened with war by the East. Far from complying with the categorical demand of Russia, Napoleon's ally, to exclude the English from the Baltic, he even undertook, with the assistance of England, to conquer Norway, and abandoned Finland to its fate.

In an obstinate and desperate struggle Finland gave the last proofs of its fidelity to king and realm, but unfortunately in vain, since, in spite of brilliant military achievements and martial ardour, the Finnish troops, under the bad leadership of Klirgspor, had to relinquish one favourable position after another, and lastly they were obliged to retreat into Swedish territory. While the whole country was occupied by the Russian troops the peasants took up arms wherever an opportunity presented itself. Before the eyes of the Russian garrison, Mathias Colonius, then an old man of seventy, interpreted the feelings of every Finn when he said in his rectorial address, "Although the fortune of war has placed our bodies in the power of our enemies, and compelled us to resign ourselves to the fortune of arms, yet our souls cling with incorruptible loyalty and unutterable obedience to our native king; for as long as the issue of war is still uncertain, and until a peace shall have been concluded by which our ruler himself resigns his rights, it is not permissible for a subject to abandon his duties, if he does not wish to be branded as a traitor." And when Von Dobeln announced to the Finnish soldiers the purport of the treaty of peace, he pronounced words which conclude the Swedish period of the history of Finland in a dignified and truthful manner:— "Through the loss of the noble Finnish people Sweden has forfeited its most reliable support, and the Swedish army its most solid and most efficient element."

* * * * *

Alexander I., who by the favour of Napoleon made himself master of Finland, recognised the value of the acquisition. The intellectual and moral gain were appreciated more by him than the territory which had been annexed. Finland was to serve as a lasting model of culture to the old undeveloped Russian Empire. Just as a century before Peter I. had not wished to possess Livonia and Esthonia by virtue of the brutal right of war, but by the bonds of mutual confidence, so Alexander I., after Finland was given up by its former ruler, united it to his Empire by the solemn pledge of the letter of security of the 15th (27th) of March, 1809, "to preserve entire and unchanged the religion and fundamental laws of the country, as well as the privileges and rights which every estate, and all the inhabitants in general, have enjoyed in virtue of their constitution."

When the diet assembled on the 17th (29th) of March, 1809, at Borgâ, to do homage to the new ruler, he and the constitutionally elected representatives of the national estates took a solemn oath to be faithful to one another and to the law of the land. This sacred vow has since been solemnly renewed on every change of government, and also by Alexander III., on his accession to the throne.

Soon after the erection of the grand duchy of Finland into an autonomous state, personally united with Russia, its national territory was again restored through the incorporation of the "government of Viborg" with Finland. This province under Russian rule had remained behind in its delevopment, and had become in a relatively short time so degraded in respect of culture that the traces of this degradation even now, eighty years after, have not totally vanished.

The oath of fidelity mutually taken at Borgâ has always been observed by Finland to the letter. The same cannot unfortunately be said with regard to the other contracting party. For half a century the assembly of the diet of the Estates, prescribed by the constitution for the levying of taxes and making of laws, has not taken place. The realisation of true constitutional administration was not agreeable to the reactionary and gloomy policy of the last period of Alexander I., to say nothing of the autocratic spirit of Nicholas I. At that time, at any rate, the country, through the intermediary of its senate, was ruled in accordance with its old institutions, and in complete harmony with the Russian Empire, so beneficially that at no period of its existence did Finland enjoy such undisturbed and thorough development.[1]

No doubt in many departments of civic life the antiquated legislation, the want of development of the financial system, &c., were keenly felt, but as the country from the earliest times had been used to a capable self-government, it was possible to take circumstances into account, and to find contentment and satisfaction even within the narrow limits assigned.

All possible steps were taken during the liberal period of the beginning of Alexander II.'s reign to renovate and vivify the political condition of Finland. Under the auspices of the enlightened Governor-General Berg, who was well acquainted with the circumstances and requirements of the country, an

[1] See Appendix, Note 23.

assembly of Finnish notables and persons acquainted with its affairs prepared a programme for a second diet, which was opened by Alexander II. in person on the 15th of September, 1863, and to the general satisfaction of all, sat during his presence at Helsingfors until the 15th of April, 1864. The limited space at our command does not permit us to give even a brief account of the legislative measures which were voted by the Estates then as well as at the third diet (26th of January to May 31, 1867) for the real regeneration, completion, and consolidation of the Finnish administration, and were afterwards sanctioned by the Grand Duke. All these agreements between the Finnish people and their ruler may be briefly described as a late but all the more felicitous realisation of what Alexander I. had promised the Finnish people on the day when the diet did homage to him, viz., that he would raise them to the rank of a nation (that it would be *placé désormais au rang des nations*). Indeed the Finnish people has attained a highly honourable position in the European family of nations, and it is easy to understand why it faithfully clings with an inborn and long-tried tenacity to the advantages obtained after long sufferings.

The sincere fidelity of the Finnish people is shown by observing the feelings with which the Finn at no distant date looked back from an untroubled and prosperous present to the painful recollections of the Swedish past. In his "History of Finland"[1] the national Finn, Koskinen, writes as follows:— "The people of Finland, although they were subjugated, obtained the same political rights as their masters the Swedes enjoyed. Both peoples afterwards marched side by side through good and ill fortune, and although the lion's share of honour always fell to the Swedes, and the burden of suffering to the Finns, yet the people of Finland gained advantages from the political union which, left to themselves, they would never have been able to obtain in the same degree and in the same time. . . . The old bond of union, though snapped as if by a decree of fate, left behind recollections which will always remain dear and sacred to the Finnish people" (pp. 562 and 563).

Even those who did not come to the same conclusion by themselves, may gather from the above that the quite recent truly happy relations between the Finns and their Grand Duke produced on their part exceptionally faithful and warm feelings of gratitude and esteem towards that potentate. And these they were quite prepared to pay to him. Yet what fate arranged so happily and pleasantly is now to be destroyed by one blow of a rough hand.

The Grand Duke in his most recent manifesto may tell the Finns that they need have no apprehen-

[1] From the earliest times to the present day. (German edition, Leipsig, 1874.)

sions, that it is not proposed to interfere with the rights of the faithful Finnish people, and that the only desire of the Russians is to form a closer union with the grand duchy; but it is a contradiction in terms. For Finland has no other union with Russia than that which is conditioned by the personal union of the crowns and by the community of the leadership of the army and the diplomatic representation. All other "union," if it is not voted by the states of the grand duchy, is a manifest act of violence and an undeniable wrong.

The people of Finland remember only too well the barbarity which was practised in the "province of Viborg" shortly after its "union" with Russia. And have they not before their eyes the example of the German colonies on the Volga, in Southern Russia, and Bessarabia, colonies which enjoyed an enviable prosperity, until a pretext was found to deprive them of their efficient self-government, and, by inoculating them with Russian bureaucracy, "to make them members of the great Russian family"? And as a result the colonists were driven to such despair that they preferred to leave the country and wander into foreign lands.

The Finns are not ignorant of the fact that in Livonia, Esthonia, and Courland the people were deprived of their rights, and that Russification of the worst kind was introduced by a similar manifesto. The Grand Duke Vladimir, while on his tour through the Baltic provinces, had no sooner declared in the name of the Emperor how much he loved and cherished his dear Baltic subjects, how he would in no wise interfere with their position, but would rather "make them members of the great Russian family," than all at once a blight fell on all departments of public life: order, security of rights, and means of education were destroyed, and the country was overrun with Muscovite officials.

Alexander III. may have acted in all good faith in signing the manifesto to the Finns which deals only with the future. But had not the immediate past and the present already given sufficient grounds for uneasiness? Were not the pernicious beginnings of violence and of the destruction of all security of rights already visible?

Was it a trifle that the well-ordered financial relations of Finland and its stable monetary system were destroyed with a single stroke of the pen, while the Russian paper rouble was forced into circulation at a value to be determined by the Russian Minister of Finance? Add to this the ruination of trade and manufactures in Finland through the introduction of arbitrary Russian custom-house measures!

And was it nothing to hand over the well-organised postal system of Finland to the disorderly management of Russian officials? What a terrible misuse has been made of the power of intercepting letters! At the present day confidential communications can only safely be sent in Finland, as in "Holy Russia," through the intermediary of personal friends. And the Russification of the railways is only a question of time. And an army of Chinovniks thrown upon the land! No European can have any notion of the resemblance between all this and an infectious epidemic.

Was it not a gross infraction of the rights of the land when the members of the Finnish senate were compelled to resign in consequence of an official note from the governor-general, in which, by a flagrant violation of the constitution of the grand duchy, the Emperor's will was declared to be supreme, and the senate was requested to subordinate itself to the orders of the Russian Government? It amounts to this: the substitution of Russian caprice for orderly Finnish administration, and the destruction of all rights of person and property. That is what is meant by "unification" and "admission as members of the great Russian family." It is nothing but the fanatical degradation of culture to the lowest depths of barbarism.

Truly it is not without cause and for no slight object that the minds of the Finns are agitated. Their whole culture, which has been painfully acquired after hundreds of years, is at stake. An impressive spectacle is presented to the eyes of Europe— the spectacle of a small courageous people united as one man to resist the encroachments of their giant oppressor by means of passive resistance. What may be the result no one can tell. But this sorely tried people have one consolation. Some unforeseen calamity may overtake their giant oppressor at any moment, for his body is corrupt and covered with sores; while the healthy and vigorous may hope, Antæus-like, to derive fresh powers from their past culture, and with resigned and steadfast love of their "poor" home, they may say in the words of the national song:—

> "Men detta laudet älska vi ;
> För oss, med moar, fjäll och skär,
> Ett gultland dock det är.
>
> Din blomning, sluten än i knopp,
> Skall mogna ur sitt tvång :
> Se, ur vår Kärlek skall gå upp
> Ditt ljus, din glans, din fröjd, ditt hopp :
> Och högra klinga skall en gång
> Vår fosterländska sång." [1]

---

[1] See Appendix, Note 24.

XII.

THE AKSAKOV FAMILY.

I.

At the end of 1888 a book was published at Moscow under the title of "Ivan Sergyevich Aksakov in his Letters" (two vols., 1839 to 1848, and 1848 to 1851), which is one of the most remarkable in recent Russian literature. It is, in a double sense, of more importance to literary history than any work published in the Russian language during the last twenty years.

The recent political history of Russia is so intimately connected with the literary movement in that country, that the one cannot be understood apart from the other. The dominant idea in Russia under Alexander III. is that of a national separateness and exclusiveness, an idea adopted by the Government of St. Petersburg from a literary party, that of the so-called Slavophils. The history of the Slavophil party, again, is indissolubly connected with the fortunes of the Aksakov family. Not that either Aksakov the father, or one of his sons, was the founder of the school; that position is recognised as belonging to the poet Khomyakov, whom the Aksakovs always regarded as their master. But the scholars far outstripped their master, who died young, in influence and in active propagandism. They completed the details of his system, and deduced from it political consequences foreign to the purpose of the originator; they introduced Khomyakov's ideas to wider circles, and prepared the way for their realisation, and for their distortion and exaggeration, perhaps even more effectively than they themselves knew or desired. For more than a generation the house of Aksakov formed the centre, the Vatican, so to speak, of the doctrine of the only saving power of the Russo-Slavonic nationality. The father, who died in 1859, and his eldest son, Constantine, who died a year later, did not live to see the abolition of serfdom, and the new era opened in the history of the Russian people and State by that event; but the surviving younger son, Ivan (born 1823), followed the traditions of his ancestors with a talent and energy which have secured him an important place, unique of its kind, in the annals of his country. He certainly produced no tangible political results comparable to those produced by Katkov; but his moral and literary influence was far greater than that of the famous editor of the *Moscow Gazette*.

But there is another sense in which the history of the Aksakov family was important to Russia. Its earlier chapters have been narrated in a book which is unequalled in Russian literature. The history of his ancestors, his parents, and his own early years, written by Sergy (Sergius) Aksakov, the father of Constantine and Ivan, under the title of "Family Chronicles," is one of the most delightful, instructive, and artistic memoirs ever written, a masterpiece both in form and contents. The author sketches, in short, nervous strokes, a picture of Russian country life, and of the patriarchal housekeeping of the eighteenth century, which, although or because it is limited to the chronicles of one family, gives at the same time a lively history of Russian manners and culture in the days of Elizabeth and Catherine II. The narrative is fascinating in its poetic warmth and feeling. The author's grandfather appears as the representative of the old Russian patriarchal life, and as a pioneer of the colonising activity by which the half Tartar countries of the Lower Volga have been subjected to Russian and Christian civilisation.[1] He seems, in spite of his rough ways and autocratic temper, to have been an estimable old man. His son, the father of the author, is half modernised, weak, and insignificant; yet he is capable of a deep and ideal attachment to a young girl, intellectually

[1] A German translation of the "Family Chronicles," by Racynski, has been published by W. Engelmann, of Leipsic.

greatly his superior, the clever and beautiful Sophie of the novel, whose real name was Marie. She became the mother of the narrator. She was born in Kasan, and was the daughter of an official in a high position, who had given her an unusually complete education, procuring for her German and French teachers. Yet the admired beauty decided to give her hand to the timid and insignificant squire, whose passion for her knew no bounds, and to follow him to the modest house of his uncultivated and still half-barbarian father. The "Family Chronicles" describe with the utmost tenderness the relations that grew up between these two apparently widely separated and yet allied natures. The young wife learns to understand the strength and nobility of the despotic old man, and he the aptitude and moral superiority of his daughter-in-law.[1] Accustomed all his life to abuse, and occasionally to kick, the women of the neighbourhood, he becomes the friend and protector of the representative of a higher civilisation and humanity.

The grandson, born in 1791, received his first impressions of life among the romantic wilds of his grandfather's estate of New Aksakovo (called in the story New Bagrovo). Here he learnt to know and love his mother-earth, its products, and its inhabitants, to recognise trees by their shadow and birds by the sound of their flight, and to observe each

[1] See Appendix, Note 25.

detail of the life of the trout in the brook and the animals he hunted in the forest. Here he acquired a feeling for nature, which an innate disposition to poetry and a refining education developed into artistic perfection. He who reads only the last chapter of "Bagrov's Childhood," which is the continuation of the "Family Chronicles," will gain an idea of its nobility. The old man describes the mysterious fascination of the spring night which he, then seven years old, spent in prayer before the coffin of his grandfather. The next volume gives an account of the early years of study which the author passed in Kasan, and affords remarkable glimpses of so-called education in Eastern Russia eighty years ago. It stops at the young man's entry upon the customary official career.

The son's account begins where the father's breaks off. The first volume of "Ivan Aksakov in his Letters" is preceded by a clearly-written sketch of the later history of the family, begun by the writer of the letters, and completed by the anonymous editor. From this sketch we take what follows.

His official position in St. Petersburg was so little to the taste of Sergy Aksakov, the chronicler and the father of Ivan, that he gave it up as early as 1812, married four years later, and returned to the house of his parents, where he lived for a long time as a landlord and an enthusiastic huntsman. The romance of the home of his youth had meanwhile given place to an uninspiring prose. The accomplished and amiable mother had become an ailing and imperious old woman, who felt herself burdened by her ascendency over her nonentity of a husband, but who none the less treated her children with a want of consideration which led them to remove to a neighbouring estate of the family, and later (1826) to settle in Moscow. There Sergy Timofeevich lived, at first as an official of the censorship, afterwards in private life, until his death in 1859.

The son gives a detailed sketch of both his parents, and dwells on the influence they exerted upon the development of their children. It is in every particular the opposite of the well-known—

> "Vom Vater hab' ich die Statur,
> Des Lebens ernstes Führen;
> Vom Mütterchen die Froh natur."[1]

Sergy Aksakov enjoyed life and its pleasures. He was essentially an artist. A passionate friend of the theatre, a passionate hunter, a passionate gambler, he was an artist in the chase and at the card-table; he could forget everything in the occupation of the moment. The tender husband and father "could spend the entire day in hunting, entire nights in card-playing; yet he recognised his weakness, and

---

[1] "My height is like my father's height,
Like his, my life is earnest;
My mother's is my nature bright." (*Goethe.*)

was therefore free from self-conceit, and was a lenient judge of others. . . . When age and sickness had curbed his activity and dulled his passions, his mind rose to that peaceful, objective observation of life which arouses such pleasant emotions in the reader of his works. . . . He was a complete stranger to the interests of the politician and the citizen. His delight in nature and his part in literature occupied his thoughts so completely, that, though he was enlisted in the militia, even the year 1812 passed over him without leaving a permanent impression. Although Russian in the full meaning of the word, he was never a 'patriot' in the current acceptation of the word in his time. Political schemes were so far from him that he laid claim to no kind of heroism, and used in jest to call himself a coward, in spite of his decided personal courage. . . . Although his education was limited, he was recognised as an authority in the circle of his friends, for the most part scholars and highly-educated men. He had a thorough knowledge of life, and of all the emotions and weaknesses of the human heart."

The above criticism corroborates in a striking manner the incidentally stated opinion of Ivan Turgenev, that Aksakov the father belonged in no sense to the Slavophil party, and that it could consequently be truly said that not one important poetic talent, and not a single work of art, had been produced by that school. The author of the " Family Chronicles " did indeed, for the love he bore his son, wear the Russian national costume, and take part in other national extravagances, when already an old man; but he did so because he was politically indifferent and had no definite connection with the public affairs of his country. The disposition and development of the brothers Constantine and Ivan, sons of the narrator, were principally determined, both in politics and in other matters, by their mother, Olga Semenovna, *née* Saplatin. This remarkable woman was the daughter of a general who had become prominent in the Turkish campaigns, and of a Turkish woman, made prisoner at the siege of Bender. Until her marriage she was the companion of her father, who had early been left a widower. For years she supplied the place of secretary and reader to the veteran, who devoted the evening of an eventful life to the diligent study of the historians and poets of his time and country. She possessed, according to her son, a high spirit, inclined to stoicism and to an idealistic view of life, and she considered the mother of the Gracchi as the highest pattern of womanhood. She was severe in her judgment of herself and others, and averse to all luxury and artificiality. She was frank and truthful to a degree, considering it a sin to deny herself to unwelcome guests. In questions of conscience she was inaccessible to the influence even of the husband whom she loved and honoured. Like all strong characters, she had little inclination or capacity for entering into the nature of people of a different mould. Her influence upon her sons was far-reaching. Daughter of a general of the time of Catherine and Suvarov, she was an ardent patriot, and much more Russian than her husband, who in earlier years had devoted much of his time to the literature and the drama of France. "She lived entirely in the Russian manner, held fast by Russian customs, Russian ritual, and Russian cookery; she took a full and warm delight in the scenery of her country; she exercised the Russian hospitality and sociability, and far from seeking to limit these qualities in her husband, she lent a special charm to the gatherings at his house."

For our purpose we must look more particularly at the nursery, in which the two leaders of the Slavophil party received their first impressions of life. Constantine Aksakov was six years older than Ivan, who was born in 1823, and, in spite of the profound difference in their characters, he was the favourite, and afterwards the most confidential friend, of the father he adoringly loved. While the other sons were sent in their childhood to schools in St. Petersburg, Sergy Timofeevich could never part from his eldest-born. For forty-two years, until the death of his father, Constantine lived under his roof, and left it only once for the short period of four months; and it is not surprising that, though in the prime of his life and of herculean proportions, he utterly broke down at his father's death, and followed him to the grave nineteen months afterwards. He succumbed in 1860 to a lung-disease, of which until 1859 no trace had ever existed.

With so close a tie binding him to his poetic father and his father's interests, growing up at the knees of the literary celebrities of Moscow, who taught him in his father's house, and systematically trained to patriotism as he was by his mother, Constantine Sergyevich showed, even as a boy, the fantastic sympathies by which he became remarkable as a man. At an age when others are learning to read he knew by heart a large portion of the older Russian poets. His pride in his nationality, awakened by his mother, and further developed in his father's ardent manner, became so soon a mania with the boy, that he rejected the usual Russian word for father (*pápenka*, or *papásha*) as half foreign, and substituted one of his own invention, a diminutive from *otets*, father. The plays and puppet-shows arranged by him, and acted in the nursery, always dealt with events of national history or legend, and treated by preference of Russian deeds of heroism against Germans and other "heathens." At the age of twelve he worked the tragic end of a Slav prince, Vachko, who fell in a battle against the Germans, by whom he was besieged in

Cuxhaven (sic),[1] into an epic, which he rehearsed with his brothers, dressed up in fantastic costumes. He declared that he had ascertained that the birthday of the Slav hero, who had been so meanly forgotten, fell upon the third of November (the Russian St. Andrew's Day); and he chose that day for a solemn performance for the benefit of the family. A certain dangerous impatience and arrogance appear soon to have followed on these manifestations of childish patriotism. When letters in the French language to his mother from her friends fell into the hands of the young purist he used to summon his brothers to form a tribunal, which commenced proceedings by solemnly piercing the criminal foreign document, and ended them in an *auto-da-fé*, accompanied by poetic execrations. These scenes were finally forbidden by the good sense of the father, but they prepared the way for the time when the son of the cosmopolitan friend of literature and the translator of Molière forbade the employment of French, not only to himself, but to the entire household, and succeeded in enforcing his commands. The child was father to the man who built up an entire history of Russia to correspond to his theoretical suppositions, on which ground he rejected everything but the Muscovite old-Russian Slav nationality, and was finally led to declare a war against Little

[1] In reality that Prince is supposed to have been besieged in Uriev (now Dorpat).—ED.

Russia and White Russia, similar to that with which he sought to threaten the "heathens" of the West.

II.

In spite of the influence exerted upon his development by his elder brother, Ivan, the junior by six years, showed at an early date that he was of a completely different disposition. While the principles inherited from his mother worked chiefly upon the fancy of Constantine, who in this resembled his father, the sober, practical, and yet fanatical nature of Olga Semenovna appeared in the younger brother. He, too, in boyhood, in youth, and in adult life, made many attempts in the sonorous exercise of rhyme and musical rhythm. But he was always essentially a politician, far more disposed to a practical carrying out of his convictions and principles than to their artistic representation. His brother was unwilling to look beyond the walls of Old Moscow, and had to force himself to do so. Ivan Sergyevich, on the contrary, was a diligent reader of the newspapers, followed the fortunes of non-Russian Europe as attentively as those of his own country, and betrayed a desire to be instructed about the world as it was, and about its component parts. It was not without a considerable influence on his character that he quitted Moscow and his father's house at the age of fifteen, and went to St. Petersburg, where for four years (1838–1842) he studied at the school of law, and prepared himself for the higher branches of the Government service in that institution of aristocratic repute. In spite of his aversion to bureaucracy and imperialism, Sergy Timofeevich was sufficiently in harmony with his time and his position to lay more weight upon the "career" of his children than he cared to acknowledge. Two of his sons had to study law, and the third to enter the corps of pages, a preparatory school for officers of the guard, which enjoyed an unenviable reputation as a nursery of aristocratic libertinism. Ivan was an industrious student, who employed all the means of education at his disposal in St. Petersburg, and kept aloof from the follies of his frivolous environment. Yet he made himself so thoroughly respected by his comrades that they allowed him to continue in the way he had chosen. The student of law in the hated town of Peter the Great was for some time considered half a renegade by his more fanciful brother and his brother's friends. He acknowledged the value, from many points of view, of a foreign education; he observed the precepts of the "Orthodox" Church only under certain limitations; he went by preference to the French theatre, and declared openly that it was more entertaining than the Russian, with its indifferent actors and its repertoire of translations. But at bottom the young man had already become the exclusive Russian, hostile to all foreign elements, that his whole life proved him to be. The difference was only that he took things more soberly, and examined them more thoroughly, than the hastier Moscow Slavophils, who were prone to judge by exteriors. He wished to study Europe, in order reasonably to judge and condemn it. He wished to obtain a clear idea of the Russian State mechanism, that he might be able to mark out in detail the boundaries drawn by his friends between the State and the people. He considered it necessary to observe the "people" (from whom the deliverance was to come) in their various employments and daily intercourse with one another, and to separate the national wheat from the chaff. His pride and his common sense forbade him to adopt, like Constantine, the Russian peasant's dress, to discard foreign languages and foreign educational systems, and to make a profession of lauding the national mode of life. Occasional jests on the subject of the French tailors, who supplied the Aksakov family with sleeveless jackets and particoloured trunk-hose, occur pretty frequently in Ivan's confidential letters. But it is evident, from the decisive severity with which he met the sarcasms on the subject in others, that they were not meant in earnest, and that he accorded his relations the same liberty which he claimed for himself. Though he had a considerable share of the extravagance characteristic of the Aksakovs, he was of a different type from his brother and his brother's more intimate friends. He was as fanatical as they, but he was a fanatic by reflection, and was therefore able to distinguish between what was attainable and what was desirable, and was ready, if need were, to compromise with the existing, and for the time being unalterable, disposition of Russian affairs. He possessed, besides, a decided talent for dealing with practical and administrative problems, and the ability, inseparable from it, to get on with men of a different stamp.

The two volumes of letters which we are now considering belong exclusively to the bureaucratic period of Ivan Sergyevich's eventful life. They give an equally clear idea of the then condition of the Russian official world, and of the character of the young man who, at the age of twenty, had to deal with problems such as in civilised countries fall to the lot only of mature and experienced men, exceptionally qualified for the task. He was employed chiefly upon ministerial commissions of revision and examination, *i.e.*, exceptional institutions, which embody the governmental mistrust of its officials, and attest to Old and New Russia the questionable integrity of the administrative mechanism. He was occupied for eighteen months as secretary to the second division of the sixth department of the Senate, which was domiciled in Moscow. He was then, at the age of twenty, and with the style of "Titular Counsellor," attached to Senator Prince P. P. Cagarin, afterwards president of the imperial council, who was charged with the "revision" of the province of Astrakhan. His eleven months' residence in the half-Asiatic town on the Volga gave the young official the opportunity of becoming acquainted with the most different branches of the administration, opened out to him a sphere of activity much above his age and his position, and formed an important period of his life. From that time he cherished the wish of being henceforth employed exclusively in similar duties, *i.e.*, in exceptional missions; but his wishes were at first not fulfilled. On his return from Astrakhan (November, 1844), Aksakov had for some time to retire into his position of senatorial secretaryship. In the autumn of the following year he was appointed assistant to the president of the Kaluga criminal court, and remained for two and a half years in that office.

The letters he wrote from Kaluga are extremely valuable contributions to the history of the rule of Nicholas and the state of the provinces of Russia at that time. They form in substance the sharpest possible condemnation of the "old system." An enthusiastic champion of his nationality, an enemy of everything foreign, and especially of everything German, as he was, the patriot looks in vain for evidence of a healthy development of Russian life in state and society. The higher classes fill him with contempt, because of their profound neglect of morality and their pitiful semi-culture. The people, on the other hand, he maintains, vegetate in a dull sloth and hopeless subjection. The corruption of the nobility begins to affect the middle classes of the city population, for whom the imitation of misunderstood German and French manners and fashions forms the climax of modern civilisation. He tells his brother again and again that the original nature and strength of the true Russian, of which he had dreamed, are nowhere to be found, and that the traditions of the "good old times," which yet remain among the rural population, threaten to be strangled by the pressure of servitude and the corrupting influence of officialism. And yet, in spite of his keen observation and sober judgment of details, he clings to his theme, representing the rejuvenating power of the "pure" nationality, the poisonous influence of Western culture, and the universal damage done by the reforms of Peter the Great.

A short residence in St. Petersburg, in the autumn of 1848, followed the time spent in Kaluga. It gave rise to a most unfavourable judgment of the town, which had become unendurable to his Muscovite sympathies, but which yet helped him, when wearied of the judicial service, to a mission to Bessarabia. There he devoted himself, for fourteen months, to improving the condition of the followers of the old faith, and never wearied, in spite of the persecutions heaped upon them, in his praise of the glory and the blessings of the Orthodox Church, undeserving as its servants for the most part were. He spent the winter of 1848-1849 once more in St. Petersburg. There the wild reaction caused by the fear of revolution in governmental circles had in the meantime reached its highest point, and a system of espionage, extended to all classes of society, suppressed every trace of independent action. Even Aksakov, the son of a patriotic house, which detested foreign customs as it did revolution, was finally entangled in the meshes of this system. Accustomed to inform his father of every detail of his outer and inner life, he had not concealed the painful impression made upon him by St. Petersburg. In spite of the advice of his experienced father, he had imprudently committed his Moscow letters to the post, which was at that time one of the most active branches of the famous "third section of the imperial *chancellerie*," *i.e.*, the secret police.

We shall leave Aksakov's book to speak for itself upon what followed, with the remark that we have been able to give only selections from the curious document we extract from it, on account of its great length.

Ivan Aksakov was arrested on the evening of the 18th of March, 1849, and consigned by Lieutenant-Colonel Löwenthal to the staff of the corps of gendarmes. He was lodged in a room belonging to the residence of Count Orlov, chief of the third section. The reasons given for his imprisonment were his near relations to Juri Samárin (an agitator arrested shortly before for having written his "Letters from Riga"), and the boldness of certain expressions in family letters which had fallen into the hands of the secret police.

A number of written questions was put before him, which he answered with characteristic frankness and outspokenness. These answers form, from many points of view, the Slavophil confession of faith. In what follows we give word for word the most important questions and answers, with the notes made upon them by the hand of the Emperor Nicholas. Aksakov was liberated on the 22nd of March, after a detention of scarcely four days.

QUESTION SHEET OF THE THIRD SECTION OF THE IMPERIAL *CHANCELLERIE*.

Question III.—Is there not among your papers a letter from your father, in which he calls your attention to the biting and rather obscure style of a letter of the 24th of February, and hints that you might be taken for a Liberal? Give a full account of the entire contents of your above-mentioned letter, and, if your memory permits, verbatim where possible, especially in the expressions referred to by your father.

Answer III.—Although it may injure me, I am prepared to answer this question openly. My father's reference is to a letter of mine, the gist of which is the following. I had written to him: "The restoration of the former state of things in Europe calls a triumphant smile to the faces of our St. Petersburg aristocrats. They feel themselves suddenly revitalised. Every time I walk over the Nevski Prospect I become very despondent. You cannot dream how my soul revolts at the sight of these 'half-Frenchmen' and 'half-Germans'—these people who are everything but Russians, who distort their mother-tongue, who wish to lord it with the luxuries of Western industry and live in the most un-Russian way! 'Thank God!' is written on their faces, 'we can now fearlessly go on, as we have done before—that is, we can guzzle and carouse, and suck our peasants dry!' Last year these gentlemen were alarmed by the disturbances in Europe, and they sang exulting hymns in praise of Russia and the Russian people. For my part I could find in their hymns only this meaning: 'What a good, long-suffering, excellent people is ours! We despise it, we drain it of its last penny, and it endures it all patiently, and bears us no malice.'" These are the expressions, with the obscurity of which my father reproached me, when he said that it might be inferred from them that I was a Liberal, while (he added) you are, on the contrary, an opponent of the Liberalism of Western Europe. He is perfectly right. I take this opportunity to express my unspoken ideas and to represent them clearly.

In my opinion the former disposition of European

politics was as false as the present. (Marginal note by the Emperor Nicholas: "Perfectly true!") And precisely because it was bound logically to lead to the present revolutionary condition. The inner falsehood of the principles of historical life in Western Europe must be crowned by unbelief, anarchy, proletairism, egotistic concentration of every idea upon the material possessions of life—by a proud and insane trust in human power, and in the possibility of replacing God's watchful care by human legislation. (Marginal note by the Emperor: "This is the gospel truth!") Western Europe was brought to this pass by the authority of Catholicism, by Protestant rationalism, and by the one-sided vindication of personality, so opposed to the humble spirit of Christianity. (Marginal note by the Emperor: "Thank Heaven!") It was not so in Russia. The orthodox faith saved our country, and brought into its life quite other essential conditions, which the people regarded as holy. The people look to the Tsar as the autocratic head of the entire orthodox community of Russia, who for the public weal takes upon himself the whole burden of care and labour. The people have complete confidence in him, and are firmly convinced that to require guarantees would but disturb the intimacy of the mutual relationship, and lay useless restrictions upon freedom of action. And finally, they are convinced that only that restriction (*sc.*, of the governing power) is justified which the spirit of the Christian doctrine enjoins on every one in connection with his fellow-men. This relation of the Russian people to its ruling house has found expression in the official commentary on the well-known manifesto of February or March of last year, in the words: "Every form of government, however perfect, has its faults," &c. (Note by the Emperor: "All this is true!") Yet let no one think that I desire to flatter; Heaven forbid! This is my conviction:—Under Peter the Great the upper circles of society became alienated from the people. They surrendered themselves to the seductions of the West, they were corrupted by the brilliancy of its civilisation, and they despised the original and essential principles of the Russian nationality. It was not only that works of art and of industry were imported into Russia from without. No! Russian tailors were actually banished for making Russian costumes (cf. the complete collection of the Russian laws), and the Russian language was disfigured by foreign words; the administration, with its German arrangements and nomenclature, strangled all life by its formality; the officials, with their German divisions of rank, occupied a dishonest and false position in relation to the peasantry, who not only understood them with difficulty, but could scarcely pronounce their names. The nobility separated itself completely from the people. It deduced from its pitiful civilisation the right to disbelieve what they believed; to neglect the ordinances of the Church, with which they lived in accordance; to be ignorant of its mother-tongue; to forget its history and traditions, and to regard the people only as material from which to extract revenues. (Note by the Emperor: "Much of this is true, but thank Heaven not universally so!") The following generations allowed themselves to be driven forward along the same lines, without looking round them, and without taking thought. This society has to answer for it to the Government, that it turned the sympathies of the population away from it,—society has prevented the government from seeing Russia in the true light. . . .

While "educated" society lived this semblance of a life, and aped the West, the people fortunately remained unchanged or nearly so. I say nearly so, for the example of corrupted manners, which we give, begins already to work evil in the country. The lower classes were at first repelled from the great towns, when they saw, as, for example, at Lent in Moscow, that, while they rigidly observed the fast, as they went to early mass or returned from confession, "good" society delighted itself with nocturnal drives over the ice-fields, accompanied by torches, singers, fortune-tellers, and gipsies. Afterwards the people became accustomed to such sights, and adopted similar bad habits. (Note by the Emperor: "Naturally—if this be true, it is scandalous, and should not be permitted by the authorities in the towns in question.") I admit that under the present Government the consciences of many have been awakened. Are we not answerable, they ask, for the Russian people? and is it not our duty to help Russia to a new life?

This regeneration of the Russian nationality was effected in science and in literature. The pioneers of the movement are men who serve Russia with all their strength and with all their hearts, who have patiently sought the treasures of the intellectual riches of the people, who have regarded as holy the national origin of their being, and have steadfastly adhered to orthodoxy. These men,—why Heaven only knows!—are called Slavophils, although their relations to the Western Slavs are limited to a cordial sympathy with the position of their kinsmen by blood and by faith. I count myself among these people, and I believe that it is consequently our duty—that is, the duty of educated society—to do penance, to cleanse our ways, and to become genuine Russians. (Note by the Emperor: "Because behind the sympathy with the alleged oppression of the Slav peoples the criminal idea is hidden of a rising against the legal governments of neighbouring and in part of allied kingdoms,—the idea of a general union of the Slavs, which they anticipate, not from God's decree, but from a revolution which would bring ruin upon Russia. . . . This I regret, because it means a confusion of criminal and sacred things.")

The events which took place at the beginning of last year[1] led us to hope that educated society had found its senses and was about to reform. But it was quite otherwise. Society, especially that of St. Petersburg, was at first alarmed—a new proof that it does not know the Russian people, for every revolt, every path that leads to violence and revolution is odious to them, and is opposed to the principles of a populace saturated with the spirit of the faith. (Note by the Emperor: "Charming! now we shall see what the Russian according to Aksakov really is!") But society was soon tranquillised, because it did not see that it bore in its own heart the germs of the mischief which had broken out in the West. It continued in its false direction, and believed, as has been well said, that it could create in Russia its own West, and intoxicate itself with impunity upon the sweetness of all those sins which prepared the downfall of Western Europe. (Note by the Emperor: "Natural enough!") Therefore, I say it openly, it has always been repulsive to me to see before me an empty-headed libertine, the lord of thousands of peasants, who work patiently and zealously to defray by the sweat of their brow the senseless extravagance of their masters. (Note by the Emperor: "Such people exist, but they expose themselves to the contempt and condemnation of all better thinking men, who are still numerous enough, and, thank God,

[1] 1848.—ED.

daily increase in number.") Such a man stupidly despises the "clownish ignorance of the peasantry," when he himself cannot even write his name correctly, and believes himself delivered from the duty of even an external respect for the Church and her commands. Instead of learning wisdom and patience from the people, their master, when he has perhaps entered the service of the State, is prepared at once to instruct them in his own way, and to load them with all possible theories but those which are Russian. There are many such. One meets them in St. Petersburg at every step. My father expressed the fear that my indignation upon this point might be taken for Western Liberalism. (Note by the Emperor: "But one should not give occasion to such a misunderstanding by one's manner of speaking, exaggeration, and dogmatism. These things are due to arrogance and inexperience, and distort the true intention.") If that should be so, all who believe it are in error. I have already pointed out that all violence is abhorrent to the Russian people, and in consequence to those who, like me, claim to be Russian in thought and feeling. I am convinced that violence only begets violence, destroys the moral purity of every cause, and never leads to good; and I can never believe that the end justifies the means. Rather I believe what our Lord said to the disciple who would have defended Him by force, "All they that take the sword shall perish with the sword." And for this reason I desired that we ourselves should notify each other of our errors, and so strive to find the right way. We must use all our powers to establish the existence of our nationality, to the salvation of Russia and her people. And we must do it with the co-operation of the Government, which has the best intentions, but cannot always accomplish them, although they are a hundred times better than those of our own society. It is only from the Government that the regeneration of the Russian nationality and the independent development of a Russian life can come.

My answer to this question has been somewhat long. I considered it necessary to expound my views at length, in order to avoid the possibility of a misunderstanding. I have written everything unreservedly. (Note by the Emperor: "I believe it, but people can make mistakes with the best intentions. *C'est le ton qui fait la musique.*")

Question VII.—Your brother Gregory, in a letter from Simbirsk, in which he mentions Jellaczicz, the Ban (of Croatia), with special praise, and calls the assembly of Frankfort stupid, expresses the hope that Austria may be converted from a German into a Slavonic monarchy. Do you and your relations profess Slavophil ideas, and in what do they consist?

Answer VII.—My brother Gregory, in one of his letters, calls the parliamentary assembly of Frankfort stupid. . . . I fancy that not even those who question me can have any doubt of that. He is loud in his praise of Jellaczicz. . . . Was he then unworthy of the praise? His imperial master had the same opinion of him, for he rewarded him with an order. With regard to my brother's opinion that Austria will be converted from a German into a Slavonic monarchy, it is mine also; the German element of that state has become corrupt, and Austria would have long since fallen to pieces, had the Slavs not supported it. One may therefore conclude that Austria will execute a *volte-face*, and become converted into a Slavonic kingdom. I should much regret the change, for a strong Slavonic monarchy, springing up beside independent Russia, would draw to itself the Southern Slav races which we are alienating, and Russia would thereby be defeated in its mission as the chosen defender upon earth of orthodoxy and Slavonic principles. But perhaps Austria may continue her existence with her present constitution. As to my Slavophil ideas, I and my relatives are by no means Slavophils in the sense implied in the question. We do not believe in Panslavism—nay, we consider it impossible: firstly, because it would require the adoption of a single faith by all the Slav races, and the Catholicism of Bohemia and Poland would bring a hostile foreign element into our community, which could not be amalgamated with the orthodox faith of the other Slavs; secondly, because the individual elements of the Slavonic nations must previously be dissolved and fused into a differently characterised, more powerful, more united, and mighty nationality—namely, the Russians ; thirdly, because a large part of the Slavonic races is already infected by the influence of barren Western Liberalism, which conflicts with the spirit of Russian orthodoxy. Russia is far more to me than all the Slavs, and my brother Constantine is reproached with absolute indifference to all Slavs outside the Russian kingdom, nay, outside Greater Russia. (Note by the Emperor : " And he is right, for everything else is madness. God alone can determine what is to happen in the far future. Even if every circumstance should combine to lead up to this union, its accomplishment would be the ruin of Russia.")

III.

The Aksakovs had lived for a long time in Moscow, as a letter of the now dead author, Panaev, informs us, and occupied a large and roomy house in the Smolenski market-place, which had the appearance of a country seat transplanted into the town. The exterior corresponded to the internal arrangements, the prodigal hospitality of which was characteristic of Moscow, and was of a quite patriarchal nature. The large wooden building, in which the family lived, was surrounded by stables, outhouses for the servants, a wide court, and a tastefully laid-out garden, in which not even the old-fashioned bathing-house was wanting. Guests came and went at every hour of the day. They were always certain of a cordial welcome, usually felt themselves at home after a short time, and seemed as if they belonged to the family. Even on days when there was no reception there was generally a crowd of men and women, who amused themselves with play, dancing, and innocent conversation, and often remained until daybreak.

The head of the family, Sergy Timofeevich Aksakov, at that time about fifty years of age, was the type of the easy, pleasant country nobleman of the old school. Of herculean build, powerful appearance, and harmonious voice, the amiable father concealed behind the unpretentious heartiness of his manner a wide range of culture and a delicate feeling for art. No one divined in him the man who was in the evening of his life to take the first rank in literature, and by his "Family Chronicles" far to outstrip the poetic talent of his famous sons. It was known that Sergy Timofeevich had read more than others, had translated a few of Molière's comedies, and had written here and there a theatrical criticism in his enthusiasm for the stage, that he was fond of declamation, in which he was a proficient, and that he took an eager part in the philosophical studies of his sons and their friends. But these appeared to be the only differences between him and other people of a similar disposition.

The Slavophil party, the history of which was to be indissolubly connected with the name of Aksakov, was at that time still in its infancy. The eldest son of the house, then two-and-twenty, belonged to a circle of philosophising students, who had grouped themselves round the young Stankevich, a landed proprietor, who was an ardent disciple of the newly imported systems of Schelling and Hegel. His companions were Bakunin, Alexander Herzen, and Byelinsky (the subsequent founders of the young Russian Radical school), from whom he differed chiefly in his enthusiasm for Moscow. The whole family was devoted to the worship of the old-Russian capital. The father, an unwearying pedestrian, was for ever discovering fresh points of view from which to admire the beauties of the "white-stoned" town he loved; the son was firmly convinced that Moscow was not only the heart of Russia, the centre where were gathered together all the advantages of Russian life, but at the same time the first town of the world. He never spoke of St. Petersburg without a certain dislike. He was never weary of showing and extolling to strangers the magnificence of his adopted town, and he considered that the title of "a genuine Muscovite" was the highest conceivable praise.

Constantine was naturally not behind his father

in his love for Moscow. He once took young Panaev, the afterwards well-known Radical writer, then a guest at the house, for a walk, with the intention of showing him the most picturesque views of Moscow. The two friends, favoured by delightful summer weather, lay down on the grass at a high part of the bank of the Moskva, opposite the Dramilov bridge. There they rested after their walk, and admired the picturesque town spread out before them in the splendour of the setting sun. They had taken off their coats and given themselves up to the enjoyment of the moment, which the enthusiastic young Aksakov appreciated from the bottom of his heart.

"Is there anywhere in the world," he said to his companion, "another town where one could be so free and unconstrained as here? We are but a little way from its centre, and yet we could imagine ourselves in the country. Look how effectively the small houses on the hill stand out from the green of the grass! There are many such spots in Moscow, all equally picturesque, and many of them only a few steps from the centre of the town. How delightful this life is—and how can you endure existence in the cold, wire-drawn, granite St. Petersburg? Stay with us! Your heart is Russian; but only here, in the midst of historical remains which call up pleasant emotions at every step, can a Russian heart beat happily. It is impossible not to love Moscow, for she has made so many sacrifices for Russia."

Aksakov spoke for a long time, and more and more passionately. With gleaming eyes, clenched fist, and a voice choking with excitement, he exclaimed at last, "It is high time that we should think of our nationality, but here only is it possible. The time draws near when we must become one with our people, and discard these unbecoming German swallow-tails that make a distinction between us." With these words he contemptuously flung away the fashionable overcoat lying beside him; then he continued more excitedly, "Peter the Great made us cut off our beards, to alienate us from the people; we must grow them again too. But you, dear Ivan Ivanovich," he went on, laying his powerful hand on Panaev's shoulder, "you must cast off St. Petersburg and come over to us. . . . Think it over thoroughly."

"Five years later," thus ends Panaev's account of this characteristic scene, "Constantine Aksakov amazed the whole of Moscow by appearing in public in high boots, a red shirt, and the national sleveless coat (the so-called *mourmólka*). At the same time (about 1840) he had a scene with Mademoiselle K., the most fashionable beauty of Moscow, which gave rise to much talk. "Mademoiselle," he said to her at an aristocratic ball, "give up that foreign dress, and set a good example to our ladies by wearing the national sarafan. It would admirably become your charming face!" As the fiery apostle of the people urged her with increasing vehemence, the aged Prince Shcherbatov, at that time military governor of Moscow, who had grown up in the traditions of the eighteenth century, came up to them. The lady repeated Aksakov's words, and the prince ironically observed: "Then *we* shall all have to wear a caftan like M. Aksakov's." "True," said his interlocutor, highly excited, "the time will soon come when we shall all wear the caftan." The horrified prince hastily beat a retreat; and Chadaev,[1] who had been an onlooker, jestingly related how Constantine Sergyevich had tried to induce the military governor to wear the sarafan.

IV.

The Aksakovs and their friends were suspiciously watched in certain quarters, and the all-powerful Count Zakrevsky (formerly Minister of the Interior, appointed Governor-General of Moscow in 1848) regarded them as members of the "red" party. Alexander Koshelev, who at that time held daily intercourse with the Aksakovs and Khomyakov, and often saw them at his house, tells in his memoirs of the close watch kept by the police on all the doors through which real or suspected

[1] See Appendix, Note 26.

Slavophils went out and in. Lists of suspected persons had to be periodically handed to the Count, who was highly astonished that the old Prince Sergy Ivanovich Sagarin (a highly respected "member of the imperial council," who could not well be accused of revolutionary ideas) should associate with Koshelev and Aksakov. "This circumstance," says Koshelev, "may have kept Zakrevsky from employing the arbitrary measures which he had planned against me. . . . In St. Petersburg they dreaded us like fire. . . . When Constantine Aksakov paid a visit to A. S. Norov, the Minister of Education, at the time of his residence in Moscow, that benevolent and harmless man exclaimed in astonishment, 'I made the acquaintance of Constantine Aksakov; I expected to find in him a tiger or a bear, and I found a polite and, as it seems, a very good-natured young man.'"

V.

Only for a short time did Sergy Timofeevich enjoy the fame to which he attained in his latter years. He died in May, 1859, six days after the death, at the age of ninety, of Alexander von Humboldt. The news of both deaths was announced in St. Petersburg at about the same time, and it was debated for several days which was the greater loss. This circumstance is characteristic of the rapidity with which purely national views had taken root in St. Petersburg, formerly so cosmopolitan. Admiration of Aksakov had, by the middle of the 'fifties, become so extravagant in Moscow, that moderate men like Granovsky, the historian, entered a protest against it, and held themselves obliged to remind people that the fashionable comparison of the "Family Chronicles" with the Odyssey was entirely attributable to the imperfection of Russian education, and to the Slavonic tendency to senseless exaggerations. It was only a few years since Constantine Aksakov had called Gogol the Russian Homer, and declared his "Dead Souls" to be an unique work in the literature of the world. The audacity of this opinion had been combated in an exhaustive criticism by Byelinsky, an old friend of its eccentric advocate, in which he reminded Aksakov of the proverb, "Sunt certi denique fines." The same Byelinsky was one of Gogol's earliest and most enthusiastic admirers, and had done justice to the deeper meaning latent in the works of that genius of humour, at a time when none had suspected its existence.

Constantine Aksakov survived his beloved father by only a few months; he died in December, 1860, at Zante, whither he had retired on account of a lung disease. At his death he was barely thirty-seven years old. Panaev, who had an honest personal affection for him, judges him as follows:—"To the end of his days Constantine Aksakov remained a child in his relations to real life. He grew up to manhood under his father's roof, to which he clung like a snail to its shell, and he was unable to exist without the support of family life. The death of his father, and the change it produced in the household, was the last blow to his already broken health. He could not survive the loss, and died soon afterwards, a virgin bachelor."

Panaev adds some account of the almost comic part which the naturally talented young man played whenever he had to move outside the circle in which he had grown up, and which had become the indispensable foundation for his romantic opinions of the world and of life. During the only journey he made in his father's lifetime (to Germany, *viâ* St. Petersburg, in 1840) he was practically lost. "The day after his arrival in St. Petersburg," writes Panaev, "he paid me a visit. After we had warmly embraced each other I ventured to hope that he would stay some time with us. " Oh no," he answered; "what should I do in this odious town? I am going to foreign countries. This town oppresses me. Your Petersburg seems to me like a huge endless barrack; your masses of granite, your chain bridges, your eternal drum-beatings irritate me. I cannot see a genuine Russian face in the whole town; the environs are nothing but marsh and fen. God forbid that I should have to stay long here!"

We went out, and Aksakov looked upon men and houses with equal disfavour. The noise of the carts and the hurry of the streets seemed to distract him. As if he wished to escape from his disagreeable surroundings, he looked up at the sky, which was bright and clear but for the passage of a fleecy cloud. He caught my hand, stopped, and began enthusiastically to declaim:

> "The clouds sweep by! Once more the sun is beaming,
> And down to earth the blue of heaven is streaming."

He recited the long poem so loudly and excitedly, that people began to stare and to crowd round us. I pointed this out to Aksakov, and he shook his head sadly: "I see I have forgotten myself; I thought I was in Moscow, where nobody is surprised if a poem is recited in the street. It is probably not the custom here, so these people crowd about us. In Moscow they know what freedom means, and there is room for a free soul to beat its wings. . . . But here! forgive me if I have compromised you."

It was Aksakov's intention to spend a year in foreign countries; but after four months in Germany he could no longer master his passionate longing for Moscow, and returned to the family hearth, away from which he could not live. Europe did not impress him favourably; after his return he was a more one-sided Muscovite than before, and he became a declared hater of the West, and a fanatical Slavophil.

Dislike to St. Petersburg and inability to find one's bearings in the world of Western culture were certainly not specific peculiarities of the Slavophils. They were tolerably well marked in the majority of the thoroughgoing Muscovites of the time. Turgenev says of Byelinsky, the valiant champion of Western culture and civilisation, that during his residence in Germany and France he felt like a fish out of water, and showed neither desire nor capability of entering into the real spirit of the Western world. Another advocate of Western culture and vituperator of the limitations of Moscow, Ketcher, the translator of Shakespeare, and the close friend of Herzen and Ogarev, was almost beside himself after exchanging the old-Russian capital for the imperial residence on the Neva. He bewailed again and again the narrowness of the arrangements of St. Petersburg, which did not suit the "broad nature" of the genuine Russian, and allowed no freedom of movement. "Here," he said, "there are no comfortable little houses in which a man can live independently, no little gardens where he can plant his own cabbages and occupy his leisure in gardening. Crammed into the same house with hundreds of strangers, chiefly poor, forced to be content with a small parlour and with dirty stairs, cut off from courtyard and garden, from free air and exercise—such an existence is physically and morally impossible for the Muscovite, who is accustomed to better things."

The above-mentioned memoirs furnish many statements concerning the moral condition of the then society of Moscow, so renowned for its "genuineness" and its unadulterated nationalism, and of its intellectual leaders, which really means the shallowness of the materialistic and pleasure-seeking life in which that society wasted its time. The high-minded men who thought themselves called to renovate the state and the society of their country, and differed one from the other solely as to the means of doing so, floundered, in their relations to everyday life and practical morality, in the same morass which their much-despised neighbours were accustomed, "with little wit and much comfort," to wade through. The one and the other class could live only in an artificial world; they therefore never attained to an unobstructed view of life, or to an energetic concentration of the strength and capacity they possessed in so large a measure. In truth, it hardly mattered whether the flight from this little encouraging reality was cloaked by old-Muscovite or by European-Radical illusions; pretended activity, self-deception, and back-stair gossiping were the result in both cases. Freedom and unconventionality were certainly more frequent in Moscow than in St. Petersburg; but they were not put to a profitable use, and were in many aspects dangerous to the community. "This lazy, apathetic Moscow," said Professor Korsh of that town to Panaev, "seems to me like an old woman who boasts of her aristocratic family and the conquests of her youth, lives upon her former reputation for intellect, and brags of an independence which in reality is most doubtful. Like other provincial towns, Moscow depends upon the favour and the whims of its high officials. . . . To be a dependant is always disagreeable, but I had rather be a dependant of the master himself than of the servants who lick the dust before him. Moscow is a capital place for people who live from one day to another, and for those who are stationary or have become tired out; but there is no field there for vigorous men, desirous of action and enterprise."

VI.

At the time we speak of, besides the house of Sergy Timofeevich, the salons of a certain Mme. Elagin formed a social centre for intellectual and philosophical circles. This lady had first married a M. Kiryeevsky, and by him became the mother of Ivan and Peter Kiryeevsky, both of them close friends of Khomyakov. Her reception rooms were open both to the friends of her sons and to Herzen, Ogarev, Granovsky, and the other leaders of the "Western" party. Herzen and Khomyakov were usually the foremost champions in the tournaments fought in the salons of Mme. Elagin. They excelled all their companions in their brilliant oratory, their surprising readiness, and their unwearying eagerness for disputation, and they conducted their arguments with the courtesy of knights at the joust, which gave them in the salon an inestimable advantage over the others. According to the thoroughly reliable evidence of a contemporary adherent of the Western party, P. V. Annenkov (a literary man, and an intimate friend of Herzen and Turgenev), Khomyakov was so deeply read and so skilled a tactician in debate, that he was able successfully to support the boldest opinions, and caused his talented and witty opponent many a bad quarter of an hour. To be a match for his rival, and to be able to control his citations of the fathers and of the decisions of councils, Herzen had to study the voluminous ecclesiastical histories of August Neander and of Gfrörer, and even the acts of œcumenical councils. Khomyakov, again, made himself acquainted with the more recent achievements of Western art, science, and technics, while his scholars, distorting the teaching of their master, declared such knowledge unnecessary. Whether it was the new and much-talked-of novels of George Sand, or the writings of social reformers such as Comte and Proudhon, the authorities cited by the Western party were counted by Khomyakov's scholars (not by the master himself) worthy of no consideration. They said that Europe could achieve something in the spheres of natural science, finance, technology, means of intercourse, and so on, and that she could bring forth comfort, riches, and luxury. But they denied her the capacity to create healthy works of art to satisfy the religious and metaphysical wants of humanity, and they declared that she possessed no means to realise the ideas of right, justice, and fraternity. Those who listened to these remarkable discussions are unanimously of opinion that Khomyakov's criticism of the intellectual and social condition of Europe was moderate and elegant in form, yet of quite overpowering acuteness and discrimination. It undoubtedly had a certain influence even upon his opponent Herzen. The detailed essays which he published many years later upon the failure and the untenable position of Western Europe show traces of Khomyakov's influence, of which it is possible that Herzen himself was never aware.[1]

An end was put to the good-fellowship between the friendly rivals in an unexpected and peculiar manner. It was due to Byelinsky, who in 1839 had been one of Aksakov's warmest friends, like him an ardent admirer of Hegel, and had remorselessly condemned Herzen's political radicalism as a departure from

[1] Cf. the essay addressed to Georg Herwegh, and published in Herzen's "From the Other Shore."

true Hegelian principles. It was he who gave the first signal for an open rupture between the Slavophils and the Western party, and after 1840 ceaselessly attacked the doctrines of his former friend as obstacles to the civilisation of Russia, and to its conversion to European principles.

The period of the literary and social life of Moscow from 1830 to 1850, which we are now considering, was affected by Byelinsky's literary activity only in so far as it influenced the relations between the two sections of Stankevich's circle. At the time of the first publications of Byelinsky's later period, a peculiar combination of circumstances excluded those elements which had formerly been means of accommodation. Soon after his return from foreign travel Stankevich died of consumption, to which he had long been predisposed. Bakunin, whose pre-eminence in debate was universally recognised, had left Moscow for Berlin. The mantle of these men seemed to have fallen upon Granovsky, the historian, a high-minded, moderate young scholar anxious to act as mediator, and connected with both Herzen and Aksakov.

But it was only a seeming inheritance. In the much-admired lectures on mediæval history which Granovsky delivered at the Moscow University he did not once mention the Orthodox Greek Church and its pretended vocation in the history of the world, and he professed conceptions which shut out the theory of the renovation of Europe by the orthodox Slavonic races. His mediation between Slavophils and Westerns was consequently at an end. But it was the first article written by Byelinsky after his change of opinion which did away with all hope of accommodation. The champion of Western ideas made a most violent onslaught upon the *Moskvitänin*, a journal published by the old-Russian reactionaries, Pogodin and Shefirev. Khomyakov, in spite of the numerous differences between his views and theirs, was connected with this journal.

Constantine Aksakov's gentle disposition caused him to make a long struggle against a rupture with his friendly opponents, for whom, as men and as his comrades of many years' standing, he had a high regard. The close of Granovsky's course of lectures, which had met with an unexampled success, was celebrated by a banquet given by his colleagues and auditors. Aksakov persuaded the more important members of his party to take part in this banquet, hoping that the opportunity might bring about a reconciliation. Khomyakov and Petr Kiryeevsky were willing to agree to the proposal, and Shefirev, in spite of his dislike to Granovsky, had, as his colleague, to take part in the celebration. Thus the co-operation of the Slavophils was actually brought about. Panaev, who was by chance in Moscow, gives the following account of the celebration:—

"After the conclusion of Granovsky's last lecture, amid applause and cheers, the majority of the audience accompanied him to the house where the banquet awaited the guests. Herzen and Constantine Aksakov were masters of the ceremonies, the former as representative of the Westerns, the latter of the Slavophils. Granovsky took the place of honour, with Shefirev beside him. We were no less than three hours at table.

"The first toast, that of Granovsky's health, was received with unanimous applause. He answered by drinking to the health of Shefirev, and then the prosperity of the University was pledged.

"At last Constantine Aksakov rose. His eyes gleamed, and he struck his fist upon the table, crying out in a voice of thunder, 'Gentlemen, I propose the toast of Moscow!'

"The cheers for the old-Russian capital had not yet died away, when suddenly the vesper-bells began to peal from all the numerous towers of the town. 'The bells of Moscow reply to the toast!' cried Shefirev, raising his voice.

"The transparent intention of these words caused some to smile, and delighted others to the highest degree. Much moved, Constantine Aksakov walked up to and embraced the speaker. He then, with evident emotion, recited his well-known poem,

"'Old capital, so oft belauded.'

"Shefirev then walked up to Aksakov and sank into his arms. After the enthusiasm of the Slavophils who were present had found fitting expression, one of the Westerns began to speak. 'I propose,' said he, 'a toast in honour of all Russia, not excluding St. Petersburg.'

"Shefirev changed colour, rose from his seat, and asked leave to speak. 'Allow me to remark,' he began, 'that the toast which has just been proposed is unnecessary, for the whole of Russia was comprehended in the toast of Moscow, which we all drank with enthusiasm. Moscow is the heart and the representative of Russia, and comprises in her muster-roll, as M. Constantine Aksakov has aptly said in an admirable essay in the *Moscow Gazette*, all other Russian towns.'

"Panaev then rose and said, 'Petersburg is not included in the muster-roll of Moscow, because it did not exist when that roll was drawn up. Why will you exclude Petersburg from the general toast?'

"Shefirev answered, evasively, 'I am very willing to drink your health, dear Panaev.' And while a number of Granovsky's younger adherents noisily drank to the prosperity of St. Petersburg, Panaev and Shefirev clinked glasses together."

The end of this historical banquet was the usual one in such cases. Those who at the beginning of it had refrained from an open quarrel only out of regard for their honoured guest, fell into each other's arms when the wine began to take effect. But next day all was forgotten. The differences which had once existed reasserted themselves, and very little was sufficient to convert the former allies into open and decided enemies.

It must be admitted that the banquet itself gave rise to a touching scene. Byelinsky had aroused Aksakov's displeasure by an attack upon the *Moskvitänin*. Khomyakov's brother-in-law, the dissolute poet Yazuikov, had, in his poem, " Our Non-Allies," called the catholicising Chadaev an apostate, Granovsky a corrupter of the young, and Herzen " a lackey in a Western livery," and he had insinuated that these men were traitors to their country. After these occurrences Constantine Aksakov appeared, at a late hour of the night, by Granovsky's bedside, wakened his unwitting friend, wept upon his neck, and told him in a broken voice that they were for ever separated from each other by the events that had taken place. The tender-hearted man took an equally emphatic leave of Alexander Herzen, the real originator and spokesman of the new young-Russian school. But the personal sympathies which formerly existed between the more important members of the circle of Stankevich were never entirely extinguished. Although there was no longer any personal intercourse between them, Byelinsky and Granovsky preserved a cordial feeling for the high-minded Constantine Aksakov; and Herzen spoke of him in his memoirs of "*Nos amis, les ennemis*" (an expression first used in a song of Beranger's), which appeared many years later, with unmistakable regard. Neither he nor his friends were ever willing to count Pogodin, Shefirev, and the other panegyrists of vulgar realities and old-Russian despotism among the true Slavophils. Byelinsky once wrote as follows, in grateful recollection of the years of his development: "Outside our circle I have known excellent men, men of greater merit than we were; but I have never anywhere met men with so insatiable a thirst of life, so great demands from life, and so far-reaching capabilities of sacrifice in the cause of an idea."

XIII.

M. N. KATKOV.

The name of the most influential Russian publicist of his time is only occasionally encountered in the fairly comprehensive body of memoirs which appeared between 1830 and 1850. The remarkable memoirs of Koshelev, the Polish Director of Finance, make but an incidental mention of the famous publisher of the *Moscow Gazette*. Turgenev's "Reminiscences of Life and Literature" pass over in complete silence the contemporary and fellow-student of their author. Panaev's memoirs, and the letters of Granovsky the historian, restrict their information on the subject to relatively modest proportions. The reasons for this are not difficult to divine: in spite of his indubitable and recognised importance in the intellectual world the comrades of his youth considered Katkov intolerable; and the witnesses of his great successes held him to be a self-seeking and dangerous man, whom it was better to avoid. Turgenev's posthumous letters attest that the all-powerful publicist was absolutely hated by all who knew him intimately, and was considered so utterly regardless of others, that people entered even into business relations with him only when they were unavoidable. The Liberals of the old school, whom he had actively and continuously persecuted, considered him a renegade, whose desertion to the reactionary camp was caused principally by motives of vanity and ambition. Leontiev, on the other hand, the closest friend of Katkov and the companion of his labours, was always regarded, even by his enemies, as an honest man, and from a moral point of view far superior to his comrade in arms.

Born at Moscow in 1820, Mikhail Nikoforovich Katkov was the son of a noble family possessed of no property. He lost his father early. He studied at the University of Moscow at the time when a large number of its young alumini were becoming prominent. We find him about 1840 in the circle of assiduous votaries of German philosophy, which had formed round Stankevich the Hegelian, and which was composed of Alexander Herzen, N. Ogarev, Bakunin, Granovsky, and the critic Byelinsky. It is well known that these founders of the young-Russian democratic party belonged for the most part to honourable and noble families. It is equally well known that they were intimate with their future opponents, the Slavophils (Khomyakov, the two Kiryeevskys, and Constantine and Ivan Aksakov), and that their discussions with them were solely on the practical deductions to be drawn from the systems of Hegel and Schelling. Katkov, industrious philologist as he was, played but a secondary part beside Herzen, the advocate of French socialistic ideas, and the then conservative Bakunin. He was considered capricious, unreliable, and vain. He associated, Panaev tells us, principally with Bakunin and Ketcher, the translator of Shakespeare, because he sympathised much more with their advocacy of European culture than with the opinions of the Slavophils, whose national exclusiveness appeared to him narrow-minded. He was besides a devoted admirer of the German romanticists, especially of Th. A. Hoffmann, and in imitation of his favourite Heine he posed as a sacrifice to the fashionable "*Weltschmerz.*" While his companions chattered merrily over their champagne, in nightly exchange of jest and argument, he used to put on a sombre air, now folding his arms across his chest like a second Napoleon, now lifting his small and insignificant eyes rapturously to Heaven, *à la* Lord Byron. These airs and graces afforded his friend Ketcher, who was fond of a joke, an opportunity for endless sarcasms. At other times Katkov was in a frolicsome humour, which his friends laughed at as childishness. His whole manner was that of a poet in process of development, who cared nothing about the actualities of life. Among his favourite occupations was the translation of Heine's poems, which he afterwards listlessly read to his friends; but for his living he wrote criticisms, and worked at a translation of "Romeo and Juliet," the money got for which was to be spent on a journey to Berlin.

In April, 1840, Katkov paid a visit to St. Petersburg to prepare himself for the journey to Berlin. There he was for many weeks the guest of Panaev, who gives the following account of his visit: "When I think of Katkov I can scarcely imagine him but with his eyes fixed on the sky and his arms crossed on his breast. In that position he would declaim unceasingly the poems of Freiligrath; I can still hear his languid voice reciting 'Capitano, capitano.' He was very young, and had the most extraordinary crotchets. One day, for example, it suddenly struck him that Theodore A. Hoffmann, to whose works we were both devoted, used to spend his evenings in a Berlin wine-cellar. He at once proposed to me to go to such a cellar, and when I answered that there were no cellars of the kind in St. Petersburg, but that I would willingly send for wine, Mikhail Nikoforovich flew into a regular fury, and told me I wanted to play the aristocrat and toady to aristocratic prejudices. He would sweep away these prejudices, he would go to a cellar, and would bring in the custom of going to them; and so on. I had a great deal of trouble in calming him." Another ludicrous whim seized him while he was at an oyster breakfast with Panaev, Bakunin, and the poet

Yazuikov. He suddenly became melancholy, and then rushed into the street, and stood with folded arms in the middle of the Semenov bridge, where his extraordinary behaviour caused a small tumult among the people. A few days later he became so childishly enraged over a philosophical discussion with Bakunin that he challenged him to a duel, and was with difficulty persuaded not to fight it out in St. Petersburg, but to settle the dispute by a meeting in Berlin a few weeks afterwards.

Bakunin went forthwith to Berlin, but Katkov was detained for several weeks, as he could not obtain the money necessary to realise the darling wish of his youth. The money was to come from the fees for his translations of Cooper's novel, "Lake Ontario," and of "Romeo and Juliet." The fee for the first consisted in two hundred copies of the book, which a bookseller bought from him for 350 paper roubles (about £14). But the publisher of the translation of Shakespeare delayed so long to pay his debt, that the impatient traveller went off without the money, and had it sent after him.

When Katkov went on board the steamer that was to take him to Lübeck he had 100 paper roubles (scarcely £4) in his pocket. "And yet," says Panaev, "he was in good spirits, and buoyed up by the thought that he would in a few days be in Western Europe, to which he was so strongly drawn. The goal of his wishes was the University of Berlin, 'the sanctuary of science,' of which he had dreamed for years."

We may here remark that Katkov was by no means the only Russian nationalist who at that time, when the principle of nationality had not yet been discovered, carried his respect for German literature and science to the point of worship. One of his older contemporaries, the already-mentioned Slavophil, Koshelev, thus describes his emotions when he first trod upon German soil: "When I stepped ashore at Travemünde, the thought that I was in the fatherland of Kant, Schelling, Goethe, and Schiller called up in me a dream of delight. The modest dinner I ate in Travemünde seemed especially well-flavoured, the little inn I lived in a miracle of cleanliness and good order. Amid the antiquities of Lübeck I imagined myself in mediæval Germany, and Hamburg, with its '*Jungfernstieg*' and the promenade by the Alster, produced so powerful an impression upon me, that I wandered through the entire town, large as it is, in the course of a single day."

The same patriotic traveller has only this to say of Berlin, that the town reminded him at times of St. Petersburg.

We know nothing more of Katkov's Berlin student days except that he came in daily contact with Turgenev, Granovsky, and Bakunin, that he excelled his countrymen in industry and perseverance, that he studied philology and philosophy with success, and that he was personally acquainted with two famous teachers of the high school, Schelling and the æsthetic Werder (who had a great reputation with the philosophers of Moscow). The industrious student was respected but not loved by his fellow-students. Katkov was never a bosom friend of any of the young men mentioned. The highly-sensitive Turgenev appears even then to have been repelled by Katkov's overweening selfishness; Granovsky, the best-liked and most sociable Russian of his time, formed substantially the same opinion. These disciples of German philosophy were not destined to live together for any length of time in Berlin. Bakunin left for Dresden in 1842, Turgenev returned to St. Petersburg, Katkov to Moscow, his native city, where he immediately found work as a lecturer in an academy, and after his marriage with a Princess Shalikov became an influential member of society. Everybody is well acquainted with Katkov's future career. It is as well known in Western Europe as in Russia that the first two periods of his public life formed a striking contrast to the last one.

At the beginning of the 'fifties the Moscow professor of philosophy resigned the office, which he had filled with great credit, because he could not tolerate the pressure that was brought to bear by Prince Shikmatov[1] on the intellectual life and freedom of the universities.

[1] The then (1852) Minister of Popular Education.—ED.

In 1856, along with his friend Leontiev, he founded a monthly review (*Russky Vestnik*—"The Russian Messenger") in the learned and liberal pages of which a constant attack was kept up against the radical extravagances of the St. Petersburg journalism, and the fantastic ideas of the Moscow Slavophil press.

For six years Katkov was regarded as one of the most eminent representatives of the Liberal European tendency in Russia. Boris Chicherin, Korsh, Turgenev Pavlov, Bezobrasov, Filipov, and other excellent men reckoned him as one of their party; they supported the *Vestnik* as collaborateurs, and in all essential points held similar views to the editor.

Katkov's special merits consisted in the fact that he, in contradistinction to the supporters of the democratic party, was opposed to a constitution after the Belgian model. He favoured the establishment of self-government, as being the best means of attaining the full development of Russia. The follower of Gneist and Tocqueville urged decentralisation and the organisation of sound communal and provincial conditions; the pupil of Schelling, Werder, and Böckh preached the necessity of a classical education, and asserted that the talk of a purely national one was mere clap-trap; the master of European history and literature opposed to the dreams of Panslavism the reality of a historically developed Russian state. In the department of economies the *Russky Vestnik* advocated the doctrines of free trade; but his preference for English institutions was so well known that the comic papers always represented him as wearing a Scotch bonnet, and nicknamed him "The Englishman."

This continued till the spring of the dangerous year 1863, the date of the Polish-Lithuanian revolt, when a new phase in the development of Russia and in the history of Katkov (who shortly before had undertaken the editorship of the Moscow newspaper) began. His conduct during this last phase of his career, which embraced a period of twenty-five years, justified the opinion of his youthful friends, who had always maintained that Mikhail Nikoforovich's ambition, selfishness, and capriciousness would one day warp his good and estimable qualities and prove that he was wanting in the highest quality of all—moral character.

XIV.

ALEXANDER KOSHELEV'S MEMOIRS.

(From 1812 to 1882.)

THIS work on Russia, not only on account of the position of its author, but by reason of its contents, ranks as one of the most important contributions to recent memoir literature. A member of the Slavophil party, a zealous participator in the emancipation of the serfs, the champion of provincial institutions, and an indefatigable writer and agitator, Alexander Ivanovich Koshelev, who died in 1882, played no unimportant part during the last thirty years of Russian history. His literary remains are written with a fearless candour, and bring to the knowledge of the Russian public a multitude of facts which were hitherto imperfectly known, if known at all. Personal relations, private struggles and conflicts, are not passed over in silence, but are, almost without exception, summarily treated; in fact the vigorous author of these memoirs lived a life of action, with just sufficient margin for the development of his inner nature as appeared necessary to the maintenance of a certain moral balance. Koshelev fills the pages of his autobiography almost entirely with an immense number of his own experiences. The reader fares all the better on this account, inasmuch as the writer, for a party man and an official, retained the precious quality of independence. The zealous Slavophil remained free from the hatred of the nobility and the national narrowness of the party to which he belonged: the champion for the Russification of Poland became eventually the most determined opponent of his confederates and of their system; the high official of former days had no hesitation in criticising the government, of which he himself had at times been a member, in a large number of writings printed beyond the Russian frontier and forbidden by the Russian censorship.

From a man of so unusual a stamp a vast amount can be learned, even though disagreeing with him in many points and differing from his principles. His contribution to the knowledge of the newer Russian conditions can hardly be overestimated, since the facts brought to light are derived from first sources throughout.

I.

Alexander Ivanovich Koshelev was born in Moscow in 1806. His family were rich and originally Lithuanian: he was brought up with much care in the house of his parents, who had received a European education. His father had spent the most important years of his youth in London, where his uncle had been ambassador in the time of Catherine II: he studied at Oxford, and then for some years served as adjutant of Potenkin in the provinces. His first wife was Princess Menshikov: on her early death he married the daughter of a French emigrant, Desjardin; he retired as lieutenant-colonel and settled in the old capital of the Russian Empire. The first great event in the life of the son of these parents was the invasion of 1812; the second, the early death of his excellent father, who had been brought up in the traditions of the English nobility of the old school. His mother had the boy so successfully educated by the most celebrated teachers in Moscow (among them was Christian V. Schlöyer, who was later professor of politics in Bonn, and son of the famous historical investigator), that in his fifteenth year he could read Plato, Thucydides, and Xenophon in the original, and was in a position to devote himself to independent Russo-historical studies. At sixteen he attended the Moscow high school as a student of philosophy. Twelve months later the young man had his name struck off the list of students because he would not comply with the foolish order of the rector to attend the lectures of eight different professors at the same time.

Koshelev now devoted himself to private studies under the direction of Schlöyer: these included the philosophy of Schelling, and enabled the youth of eighteen to pass successfully his final academical examination, and to enter the government service as official of the Moscow Archives of the Ministry of Foreign Affairs.

The numerous leisure hours which this service left to him were almost exclusively devoted to intercourse with friends, who met together at social unions—a literary and a philosophical circle. Side by side with the study of Fichte, Kant, Oken, &c., they devoted their attention to Liberal politics with a special zeal. The revolutionary ideas which swayed St. Petersburg at that time, and drove the flower of the nobility, who were serving in the guards, to the Dekabrist revolt of 1825, had spread to Moscow. Koshelev makes no secret of it that several of his most intimate acquaintances were implicated in the conspiracy, that he looked upon it throughout sympathetically, and that it was generally matter for astonishment that he was not arrested in consequence of the catastrophe of December, and sent to the fortress of St. Peter and Paul.

The youthful members of the philosophical and literary union thought it advisable to burn their transactions, to suspend their regular meetings, and to observe strict silence—a silence which reigned over the whole Empire, and especially the Liberal aristocracy, for several years. Koshelev, although in his old age, expresses himself with respect to this period with the candour peculiar to him: "The terror and exasperation which filled all (*sic*) on the announcement of the execution of Pestel and of the four chief conspirators cannot be described in words; literally, every one felt as if he had lost a brother or a father. . . . For this reason the entry and coronation of the Emperor Nicholas bore the character of mere Court festivities. Very many (*sc.*, nobles) remained on their estates, and only those took part in the festivities who were obliged to do so by reason of their official position. The Emperor himself was extremely gloomy and unapproachable; gloomy also was the outlook."

In September of the year 1826, nine weeks after the conclusion of the coronation ceremonial, Koshelev, who was now twenty years of age, migrated to St. Petersburg in order to continue the career which he had begun as official in the *chancellerie* of Count Nesselrode, Minister of Foreign Affairs, and through his family connections to be introduced into society. The young Radical took his place at once in the brilliant society of the capital: he was in no way overburdened with his official duties, and like others enjoyed his leisure. But even then his youthful literary Moscow friends, Kiryeevsky and the poet Venevitinov, who had settled on the Neva, appealed more to the serious and cultured youth than the fashionable people, whose circles he frequented. At the death-bed of Venevitinov he became acquainted with Khomyakov, the retired lieutenant of the foot guards, who afterwards became so famous as the founder of the Slavophil theories, and of the doctrine of the universal mission of the Greek Orthodox Church. Khomyakov was a man whose religious enthusiasm made a great and lasting impression upon Koshelev. It was now that he began to feel the need of serving his country in a more practicable way than appeared possible in the *chancellerie* of foreign affairs. As Nesselrode withheld from him the desired position of secretary to the embassy at Constantinople, Koshelev, believing he had spoiled his chances with his *chef* through an inconsiderate arrogant remark, offered his services to Bludov, the Secretary of State, at that time head of the department of foreign confessions, resolving never again to return to the diplomatic career.

This change in Koshelev's official career was attended with important results, because it gave him his first actual insight into the inner working of the State machine. Bludov, a somewhat unexpected Liberal convert to the system of the Emperor Nicholas, was a man of intellect and sagacity, an excellent stylist, and so highly appreciated by the Emperor that he was consulted on all important matters of home politics, and participated in numerous vital questions—for example, the "reunion" of the Uniats with the Orthodox Church and the editing of the Canon Law of the Evangelical Lutheran Church. Our author, in common with other critics, estimates the most conspicuous of all non-military assistants of the Russian Emperor from 1825 to 1855 as a gifted man, benevolent at heart, but vacillating and "cowardly." On those days when he was obliged to have an audience with the Tsar, Bludov seemed distracted: he heard and understood nothing that was said to him, he was extremely restless, looked every minute at the clock, and regulated his watch early in the morning by that of the royal palace. If he returned from the audience without receiving a reprimand he was as happy as a child; he did not walk, but ran through the rooms, and was ready to fall on the neck of everybody who met him. It may here be incidentally remarked that Koshelev's criticisms on friendly and sympathetic persons (*e.g.*, the dreaded Count A. Orlov) are less reliable than are those on his opponents, to be just to whom he regarded as a duty. Harsh criticisms are clearly not in accordance with his kindly nature, and where he can see his way to praise and appreciate his judgments are sometimes wanting in proportion.

From the information we have with respect to Koshelev's official activity we learn that a proposal, made under the auspices of Bludov and Dashkov to ameliorate the lot of the serfs, remained a dead letter, in spite of the approval of the Emperor, and the knowledge, even at that time, of the common danger and the indefensibility of the existing situation. It may also be noted that Koshelev, as one of the secretaries of the commission for the administration of the law (published in 1832) with respect to the Evangelical Church of Russia, became aware of the stubbornness with which the representatives of the diets of Livonia, Esthonia, and Courland defended their rights and privileges. Koshelev was now five-and-twenty, and his head and heart were filled with quite other matters. About the same time that he learnt that intercepted letters had marked him out in the eyes of the Emperor as a dangerous man (" C'est un mauvais homme, et je vous conseille d'être sur vos gardes avec lui," his Majesty had said on one occasion to Count Bludov) Koshelev was seized with a violent passion for a beautiful fascinating lady of high position, who had also a *penchant* for him, but with whom he nevertheless broke off relations, because he had no sympathy with her inclinations and plans, which were mainly directed towards playing a fashionable part in society. During the days that followed the decisive letter the earnest lover was on the brink of madness; then he was seized with a serious illness, and on his recovery he was advised by his physician to go to Carlsbad and try the cure for the dyspepsia which had troubled him for years.

Since the outbreak of the Polish Revolution (1830)

passports had been exceptionally difficult to obtain, and it required the intervention of Bludov and a delay of several months before the traveller could proceed on his journey. This increased his impatience to the highest degree, and filled him with an enthusiasm for travel which the modern reader may well envy. German life, with which Koshelev became familiar when, after surmounting the difficulties of the cholera-quarantine, he left the vessel *Nicolai I.* and stepped on land at Travemünde, appeared to him in glowing colours. We have already quoted (p. 187) the description of the delightful impressions made on Koshelev by Travemünde, Lübeck, and Hamburg. Berlin had little attraction for Koshelev, nevertheless it seems to have interested him for a time on account of the lectures of its famous professors.

For an educated man—no matter whether he came from London, Moscow, or Rome—to have visited Germany, and not to have talked with Goethe, was like going to Rome and not seeing the Pope. As a matter of course, Koshelev, when he had finished his "cure" at Carlsbad, went to Weimar to be introduced by the princess (Mary Pavlovna) to the man whom he regarded as "the greatest of the living." The introduction of the distinguished Russian traveller was carried out in the usual way. The old man spoke of Weimar, of Her Royal Highness the Princess, of the fortune of the country in possessing so excellent a ruling house, and observed, when Koshelev mentioned the name of the poet Shukolovsky, "It will bring high honour to Shukolovsky to be entrusted with the honourable task of the education of His Imperial Highness, the successor to the Russian throne." The enthusiastic visitor retired somewhat disappointed; nothing but the eyes of his interlocutor had impressed him strongly. To his surprise Koshelev received in the meanwhile an invitation for the last evening before his departure. He met Heinrich Meyer and the Chancellor von Müller in Goethe's house, and this time the conversation turned neither on grand dukes, nor princes, nor royal highnesses. Goethe declared that "politics and realism threatened to stifle literature and art, and that since these could neither revolutionise mankind all at once, nor adapt themselves to the demands of the time, nothing was left to them but to take possession of the highest standpoint, and to show and open up to man a new world, and thus conquer him by the power of new ideas." The company left at half-past ten at a sign given by the chancellor.

Koshelev's stay in Germany seems to have been the most enjoyable period of his first travels, and to have moved him most strongly on account of the freshness of the impressions received. He spent the winter in Genoa. Revolutionary Paris was in the meantime interdicted to Russian subjects. At

Genoa he attended the lectures of Decandolle, De Larive, and Rossi, who afterwards became Count and Prime Minister to Pius IX., and often visited the house of Marie Naruishkin *née* Princess Chetvertinska, the former mistress of Alexander I. In spring he was at last able to set out for Paris. He had an introduction to Pozzo di Borgo, and made the acquaintance of Guizot, Thiers, Villemain, and Michelet. Then he went to London, where he had the good fortune to be present at the celebrated sitting of the House of Lords, at which the Reform Bill was passed on the 4th of June. In London Koshelev made the acquaintance of Count A. F. Orlov in a most peculiar manner. Orlov had been sent on an extraordinary mission to the Court of William IV. in connection with the Belgian question. The highly imperious confidant of the Emperor Nicholas had the habit of addressing those who were his subordinates as "thou," and also of imitating the humming and hawing of his master. Even officials so highly placed as the counsellor to the Embassy Kokochkin, who was afterwards envoy at Turin, submitted to this indignity. Koshelev therefore astonished everybody when at a dinner party by replying to the Count with the same contemptuous "thou." Contrary to his own expectations this did not bring about his ruin: the Count, who had the reputation of being highly irritable and irreconcilable, not only called the bold young man henceforth "you," but invited him to accompany him to Paris, and treated him on the journey and on future occasions with special kindness.

After his return home in August, 1832, Koshelev went first to Moscow, where he spent the winter at his mother's house, and it was not till the following spring that he went to St. Petersburg, which never seems to have had much charm for him. Here, however, he was not destined to remain. The then Governor of Moscow, Prince D. W. Galitsin, pressed him so strongly to accept the position of government councillor of the Moscow administration, that Koshelev felt himself obliged to do so, and to settle permanently in his native city in October, 1833.

Koshelev cannot praise his *chef* enough, and Prince Dmitri Galitsin, as we know from other sources, really deserves this praise. His own officials, as well as the inhabitants of Moscow, regarded the retirement of the old man who had been entrusted with the administration of their town for twenty years as a heavy loss. Yielding to an irresistible desire he resigned his office at the end of thirty years, in order to pass the remainder of his days in his beloved Paris. Koshelev had abandoned the service of the State before. As a characteristic of Galitsin, and of the difficult relations under which he administered his office, he relates the following noteworthy incident :—" In the year 1834 a terrible fire broke out in Moscow, which destroyed more than a thousand houses. It was generally believed that it was the work of incendiaries. A special commission of investigation was appointed, and, as the Emperor himself had come to Moscow, an inquiry was carried on day and night. On his departure the Emperor advised that the documents should be handed over to a military commission, which would have to pronounce a judgment within three days, and lay it before the governor for ratification. He desired an opinion from the Moscow government. As a member of the body I was dragged out of bed at two o'clock in the morning. I put on my uniform, hastened to the sitting, and there found the civil governor, Nebolssin, also in uniform. He put the case before me and my colleagues, and explained that we should have to give our opinion within twelve hours on the decision which he had read to us. This was impossible without previous knowledge of the contents of the documents: we refused to give an opinion on the judgment which had been arrived at, and asked for time in order to distribute the documents among those present and sift them to the bottom, promising at the same time not to leave the sitting before we had finished the task imposed upon us. The good Nebolssin, who had expected to lay the matter before Prince Galitsin in the morning and then to dispatch a courier to the Emperor, was in despair, but we remained firm to the resolution we had formed. At nine o'clock in the morning

Nebolssin went to the governor, who allowed us an extension of thirty-six hours. At last the real crisis began. The council of war had sentenced nine or ten of the accused to be flogged to death ; but we had the independence to maintain that the proofs were not conclusive, and that at most four of the accused should be left under suspicion. When Governor Nebolssin, who had been riveted to the president's chair for thirty-six hours, heard this decision, he fainted. Having been brought to, he exclaimed, 'Gentlemen, you will ruin both yourselves and me; consider well what you are doing!' We still held fast to our opinion, and our decision reached the hands of the general governor without the signal of the civil governor. Galitsin sent for us an hour later; he talked the matter over again, thanked us for the conscientious discharge of our duty, and promised to make use of the report as far as possible. He wrote to the Emperor that he could not consequently take upon himself the ratification of the judgment arrived at by the council of war. No one was sentenced to death, four of the accused received more or less severe punishment, the rest were simply placed under suspicion."

Some months later saw a decisive turning-point in Koshelev's life. On February 5, 1835, he married Olga Petrovna Soloveva, who had won his heart by reason of the serious earnestness of her character. In May of the same year he purchased from the imperial master of the horse, Prince W. W. Dolgoruky, and at his special request, 35,000 acres (Prussian) of arable land, and 11,666 acres of forest, including the neglected estate, Pessotchua, in the district of Sapochkov, for 725,000 roubles. Dolgoruky had never received any income from this rich property, and feared he would be completely ruined by it. Koshelev, when the bargain was completed, took his departure, and for the next twelve years of his life was exclusively landlord, distiller, and farmer of the Government monopoly on brandy for the different towns and districts of Riasan. Koshelev did not return to the transaction of public affairs until he had become a millionaire.

If these pages were meant for Russian readers it would be necessary to dwell with special care on this part of Koshelev's life.

Among the causes of the economic distress in which the Russian nobility and the Russian landlords were involved previous to the liberation of the serfs, absenteeism, extravagance, and the repugnance of the more highly educated and distinguished aristocrats to a landlord's life had for a long period been the most outstanding and dangerous. With relatively few exceptions the usual assumption was right, that the Russian noble who was exclusively occupied with the management of his estate must have taken up this calling on account of his incompetence for the service of the State or military life. A claim to social distinction could only be justified by those who had served several years in the guards, at the Court, or in the ministry, and who had only retired to the country in later years.

Along with their inferior position the landed aristocracy by profession were, as a rule, bad agriculturists, stupid and unmethodical, and entirely devoid of technical education. We know of no other Russian in recent times who can be compared with Koshelev as an eminent author and politician, and an effective and practical agriculturist. It appears no less remarkable that this exceptional man carried on for twelve years without loss the profitable but little respected employment of a farmer of the Government monopoly on brandy, which was abolished at the commencement of Alexander II.'s reign; that, side by side with the distillation of brandy, he successfully devoted himself to practical agriculture, and that he acquired the reputation of being at the same time a landlord who was a friend to the peasantry and a man who looked after his own interests. This unexampled position explains precisely how the influential and active leader of the Slavophil party was enabled to keep himself free from a host of the fatal blunders committed by his compatriots, and how he came to be recognised, both during and after the abolition of serfdom, as among the most competent and experienced critics of the state of Russia with regard to the condition of the land and the peasantry. All his numerous writings on this important matter reveal the practical man, who has got his knowledge at first hand, and is aware of all the points of importance.

In the summer of 1847 Koshelev had got his financial and agricultural affairs so well arranged that he could settle for the greatest part of the year in Moscow, and turn his attention to the scientific and political interests which corresponded with his inclinations and his intellectual interests. Two subjects especially claimed his attention during the following years: the distressing condition of the serf population and the study of the theology of the Greek Church, which had been stimulated by his friend Khomyakov. Koshelev's mind was drawn towards the state of the peasantry by his whole past life. He had repeatedly filled the office of a representative marshal in the district of Saposhkov, and had been obliged while in this position to take up the cause of the resident country population against their stupid and despotic masters, and in this way he had gained an insight into the abyss of the misery of serfdom which filled him with passionate hatred—a hatred which he could only slowly repress—against this " root of all our evils." We will spare the reader the reproduction of the reports with respect to the atrocities and villainies against which Koshelev had to contend. The amount of brutality, folly, depravity, and viciousness would, besides, appear incredible. It is enough that Koshelev, during the short period of his official duty, set to work with all the energy and superior power of the man of education and position, and made himself so thoroughly hated by the nobles of the old school through his behaviour towards the classes, that his re-election was not to be thought of. He looked upon it, therefore, as a patriotic duty to attack the subject from another side. Appealing to one of the many paragraphs of the ninth volume of the laws of the Empire, which had been designed to ameliorate the position of the peasants, Koshelev went to the Minister of the Interior, Count L. A. Perovsky, in October, 1847, to ask the Emperor to sanction a proposal directed towards the voluntary limitations of the right of proprietors—a proposal which he intended to lay before the assembly of nobles of the province of Riasan. Perovsky's reply was a refusal. "His Majesty fully recognised the good intention of the petitioner, and had himself long thought of taking measures for the reform of the agrarian situation; but the present time was not a suitable one for so important an undertaking. If Koshelev cherishes the wish to enter into agreements with his own people, which would ensure them a certain measure of freedom, no objection would be raised to his doing so." Nevertheless, Koshelev remained without any information from the Cabinet when he submitted proposals bearing on the same point in the years 1849 and 1850. The events of the revolutionary year 1848 had determined the Emperor to abandon his views on agrarian reform : his mind reverted to the subject again and again, but at the critical moment political considerations stood in the way of a solution.

Friendly intercourse within a small circle afforded the only consolation for the five years between 1848 and 1853, years which recalled the five following 1825. This was the circle of the Slavophils. Its origin, as is well known, dated back to the 'thirties, when a number of young enthusiasts met together, under the direction of Stankevich, to study the philosophy of Schelling and Hegel. The majority of these held at first the advanced Liberal ideas of the West. Subsequently a difference of opinion split up the friendly circle into two opposite camps. According to the Slavophils the only salvation for Russia—as for Europe—was to be found in a return to the principle of nationality and to the old ecclesiastical Byzantine tradition, as well as the only safety from the false heathen culture of the West.

The soul of this circle, as has been already mentioned, the intellectual and highly cultivated visionary, Khomyakov, succeeded at last in winning over to his side the cool-headed and practical Koshelev, who was now over forty. Koshelev gives no particulars as to this change in his inner nature, he contents himself by saying that Khomyakov had inspired him with a desire for the study of patristic literature and old Russian theology: that he had found in this complete satisfaction, and that he was convinced more and more of the necessity of an exclusively national development. Khomyakov's first acquisition in proselytism was Koshelev's intimate friend, the friend of his youth, Ivan Kiryeevsky, the earnest theological writer. Then followed Ivan Kiryeevsky's brother Peter, who made the collection and study of the songs and folklore of the Russian people his chief occupation, and the eccentric, high-spirited Constantine Aksakov, who was even then inclined to such grotesque exaggerations of the new doctrine, that his friends frequently found themselves compelled to restrain his zeal. Constantine's younger brother, Ivan Aksakov (later on a leader of the party), was then, to his brother's sorrow, so exclusively devoted to Western ideas that he was not reckoned one of the number. Juri Samarin (known in consequence of his odious polemical writings against Poland and the Baltic provinces) was regarded as the most distinguished dialectician of the school. The professors, Pogodin and Shefirev, represented the extreme right, while as Russians of the old school they inoculated Khomyakov with leanings towards Protestant Liberalism and an arbitrary conception of history.

As party agitation in the proper sense of the word

was out of the question on account of the pressure of outward circumstances, and as the new doctrine was treated chiefly as an interesting subject of conversation, members of the first Slavophil society felt themselves to be an exclusive body, and friendly relations and interminable discussions with the representatives of European Radicalism followed as a matter of course. The chief spokesman of the latter was Alexander Herzen, who often came into violent conflict with the other members. He left Moscow in 1847, and went abroad never to return. Granovsky, the professor of history, and Pavlov, the author, took Herzen's side, while Chadaev, who was many years older, stood opposed in a certain measure to both parties: he preferred Catholicism, and contended that Russian history was barren in substance and led to no results. This contention was regarded as epoch-making at the time. Chadaev's opposition to both parties roused intense excitement. A gradual breach, which afterwards became complete, was already beginning between Radicals and Slavophils. Koshelev, who had the good fortune to obtain a passport to visit the first London Exhibition in 1851, sent reports of the exhibition to the Slavophil periodical, *Moskovsky Sbornik;* but as his articles had to be sent to St. Petersburg to be submitted to the chief censorship bureau, and as they were never returned, he became disgusted and ceased writing.

This was the condition of things at Moscow—and Moscow was representative of a great part of Russia—when the war began in 1853, and with it a new chapter in Russian history. Koshelev's comments on this period are so characteristically frank that they deserve to be quoted verbatim. "After the outbreak of the war with Turkey a presentiment that a struggle with Europe was at hand pervaded all minds. The destruction of the Turkish fleet at Sinope roused society from its torpor, and the Government being occupied with war preparations and military operations, paid less and less attention to internal affairs. It looked as if we should at last be released from our dark and dreary prison-house and brought to a point of vantage, where, although we might not enjoy the free air of heaven, we might at least feel a refreshing breeze. The landing of the troops of the Western Powers in the Crimea, the battles of Alma and Inkerman, and the siege of Sebastopol caused us no great grief, for we were convinced that even a defeat would be more tolerable and useful to Russia than the duration of the position in which the Empire had found itself for years.[1]

Public opinion and even the opinion of the masses moved in the same direction. In this connection I must especially mention the calling out of the militia volunteers in 1854. Although wars against

[1] See Appendix, Note 27.

the Mahometans and in defence of kindred races and co-religionists always called forth the national sympathy of the Russians, yet the manifesto with regard to the militia was received by all classes not only with coldness, but with a feeling of displeasure. Melancholy processions followed the soldiers as if they were marching off to the other world (a thing which happened at other times only in the case of conscripts). There was no trace of enthusiasm visible, although the defence of the country was at stake. It was exactly the same when on the same occasion the nobles were called out. Only those nobles joined who on account of their position could not do otherwise. Any one who was relieved of the honour and duty of defending his country, whether from considerations of age, health, or family, made no secret of his joy. On the 20th of February, 1855, the announcement of the death of the Emperor Nicholas and of the accession of Alexander II. reached Moscow—an announcement which caused sincere sorrow only in the hearts of a few, since the three decades embraced by Nicholas's reign, especially since 1848, had been borne with difficulty. Suspicion and arbitrary power knew no bounds.

Koshelev (who assures us repeatedly that as a sincere nationalist he was always an advocate of absolute power) had had a memorial lying in his desk since the end of 1854, in which he advised the summoning of an assembly of the people for the purpose of strengthening the credit of the State, opening up new sources of revenue and transforming the war of the State into a war of the people. This memorial, originally destined for the heir to the throne, was transmitted to the Emperor in May, 1855, who (as the author was officially informed) handed it over to the Minister of Finance, but took no further notice of it. A little later Koshelev and his party obtained permission to publish a quarterly journal —*Russkaya Besseda* ("The Russian Discourses ")— which immediately acquired a certain influence, as being, so to say, the official organ of the Slavophil party, but on account of the continuance of the traditional difficulties of censorship only made headway gradually. Those of the old *régime* who still retained office regarded the Slavophil party as a variety of the dreaded revolutionists.

Prince W. A. Cherkasky, to whom frequent reference is made, was subsequently one of the collaborators of the *Besseda*. In spite of this Koshelev did not regard him as a genuine member of his party : he did not accept the orthodox view of the Church, he was an opponent of undivided common property, and a satirist of the idolatrous worship of nationality.

II.

The happiest and most prosperous period in the eventful reign of the Emperor Alexander II. was during the preparation and execution of the law abolishing serfdom (Feb. 19 (March 2), 1861).

"Friends are certain, fair are the promises, and our beginning is full of radiant hope," might be applied to the period of Russian development and Russian thankfulness which brought to fulfilment the wishes cherished for two generations by the best of the land, and which was regarded as the harbinger of a time such as the great Eastern monarchy had never hitherto experienced. The years 1857 to 1862 may likewise be looked upon as the most successful period in the career of Koshelev, who had attained the age of fifty when Alexander II. came to the throne. He had given his best years to the work of emancipation. This had been his first love, and as an old man he could look back upon it with undisguised if mingled feelings of satisfaction.

It is well known that the Emperor Alexander II. was devoted to his father's memory, and that he emphasised this feeling by retaining, during the first years of his reign, the chief representatives of the old system, although they were opposed to his own. The same ministers, Orlov, Panin, Dolgorukov, &c., who had been known in the preceding reign as opponents of every Liberal movement and of every idea of reform, were destined to be the chief instruments in the work of emancipation, which the new monarch wished to be treated as an inheritance from his father. Every day from 1857 to 1861, and especially the events connected with the commencement of the work, showed the impracticability of this arrangement. The first decisive step was taken November 20, 1857, by means of a rescript, in which the Emperor expressed his satisfaction to Nasimov, the Governor-General of the Lithuanian provinces, with respect to the emancipation proposals made by the representative nobles of his district. This rescript had to be circulated amongst all the governors and marshals of the Empire. It encountered, however, the determined opposition of Count Orlov, who tried to keep back the Emperor from this first step to revolution, and believed, after a long conversation which he had with the monarch, that he could boast of success. Alexander II., however, displayed on this occasion a firmness and resolution which did him the highest honour. No sooner had Orlov left the cabinet and given the comforting assurance to his friend, the elder Adlerberg, "He is shaken, and the rescript will not be sent," than Lanskoi, the Minister of the Interior, received orders to have the important document copied and sent without delay to all the provincial towns. Here it ought to be noted that the Emperor (although he made Orlov first president of the so-called Chief Committee[1]) displayed the same firmness during the whole time that emancipation was under discussion. At the critical moment he constantly took the side of the

[1] Dealing with the emancipation of the serfs.—ED.

friends of reform, and he succeeded in securing the adoption of the Bill, which afterwards became law in spite of the opposition of no less than six ministers of the Empire; but these ministers he left undisturbed in their offices.[1]

With the publication of the rescript of November 20, 1857, the Rubicon was crossed, and the abolition of serfdom took the form of a national event in which all sections of society believed they were bound to participate. Even at the beginning of the year 1858, proposals with respect to the principles to be applied to the great reform were presented to the Government from the most different quarters; reflections on the experiences of other countries were submitted in great numbers, and nothing else was talked of but emancipation. Koshelev thought that he too must produce his plan. In conjunction with his friends, Juri Samarin and Prince Cherkasky, he elaborated a scheme to be submitted to the Emperor, which proposed the redemption of the entire ground in the possession of the peasants: the operation to be brought to completion within a period of twelve years, and in the case of the proprietors a term of three years in consideration of entering into a contract of voluntary union with their peasants. The maximum price to be paid was to be settled by the Government, but after the expiry of the term of three years compul-

[1] See Appendix, Note 28.

sory sale was to be effected through the intermediary of Government officials. This proposal was put before the Chief Committee for examination, and afterwards before the Formulating Commission (to formulate the emancipation laws). It caused a certain sensation in Moscow and St. Petersburg society, on account of its Radicalism, until it was forced into the background by projects of a more radical nature.

At the beginning of the year 1858 all the Russian provincial assemblies of nobles received orders to elect deputies who should discuss in local committees the great project, in conjunction with men of trust named by the Government. Koshelev with Samarin and Cherkasky had begun to publish a brilliant journal—*The Country's Weal*. It advocated emancipation with such ardour, that neither he nor his friends could think of being elected. In order not to be excluded from all participation in the matter, he got himself nominated as Government delegate for the committee of Riasan (Cherkasky and Samarin entered the committee of the Tula province in a similar capacity), where he immediately took up a position hostile to the majority of the committee, and carried on the struggle with the greatest personal bitterness. At different times attempts were made to drive him from his position, and once they were very nearly successful. Cherkasky had expressed himself in one article in the journal referred to as being in favour of the provisional retention of corporal punishment, and in this way brought upon himself and his friend violent attacks from the St. Petersburg Radicals. When Ivan Aksakov took upon himself their defence, and said that it was foolish " to attack two men who as it was had to sustain hard battles against selfishness and ignorance," the majority of the members of the committee of Riasan declared that they desired the removal of Koshelev as satisfaction for the insults which he had heaped upon them. Koshelev eagerly accepted the challenge; he travelled to St. Petersburg, represented the case to Lanskoi, Minister of the Interior, and Count Rostovsov, president of the committee of supervision, and the latter issued a fulminating rescript, which administered a rebuke to Koshelev's opponents and declared all resolutions adopted in his absence null and void. The proceedings took their course, but an understanding was so little to be thought of, that at the end of the session three different schemes were proposed. Koshelev, who remained in the minority with his Liberal proposals, hastened once more to St. Petersburg, where his distinguished relations helped him to an exhaustive conversation with Count Rostovsov, whom he so completely converted to his views that he invited him along with Samarin and Cherkasky to join the Formulating Commission, that is, the most important central authority for the time being for the decision of questions relating to the law of emancipation. He accepted thankfully, but to his painful surprise, though both his friends were invited, he himself was left out. Count Panin, the ultra-Conservative, Minister of Justice, thought "that two leaders of the Slavophil party were enough," and struck out the name of Koshelev, which was especially obnoxious to him and his colleagues.

Deeply mortified, Koshelev procured a passport and went abroad for several months for the benefit of his health. From Carlsbad, where he underwent the usual course of treatment, he went to Prague for the purpose of discussing "the future of the Slavs and the Panslavist idea," with Hanka, Shaffarik, Shumovsky, &c. It was here he made the discovery that, with the exception of Hanka, there were in the Bohemian Prague only such Bohemians who expected to have the leading part in the hands of Bohemians themselves, not of the Russians. From Prague Koshelev went to Vienna, where he became more intimately acquainted with the most ardent Russian Panslavist agitator of recent times, M. Th. Rayevsky, the well-known priest to the embassy. From Vienna he went to Switzerland. In Domo d'Ossola he made the acquaintance of Cavour, who was there on a visit. Cavour received him very graciously, and on a later occasion, as they were travelling to Geneva, discussed the importance of the "Mir"—that is, a Russian community living in undivided possession of common land. Cavour expressed the opinion subsequently so often quoted, that he saw in the " Mir " a bulwark against the social dangers of the future such as no other country possessed, and for which Russia ought to be thankful. Koshelev assures us that the significance of the Russian commune was more thoroughly understood by Cavour than by any other foreigner he knew, the discoverer of this first principle of the development of the Russian state and society, Von Haxhausen, not excepted. After residing for some time in Geneva, Paris, Brussels, and Ostend, Koshelev suddenly returned to his own country. He was invited along with the representatives of numerous other provincial committees to come to St. Petersburg as a member of the local committee of Riasan, in order to discuss before the Formulating Commission the proposals he had brought forward with regard to emancipation, and to give his opinion of the resolutions arrived at by this central committee. At the same time he learned that the commission had gone far beyond the proposals made by him, and intended to grant to the peasant communities an extraordinarily large measure of independence, and to give the utmost scope to the bureaucratic tendency towards Government " regulation." Koshelev arrived in the Russian capital so opportunely that he was able to take part in the discussions and controversies which had just begun.

We cannot enter more fully into the position which Koshelev took up with regard to the Russian land question. This would necessitate a most minute examination of one of the most complicated, and for Western Europe one of the most difficult, laws of modern times. The reproduction of the numerous writings which our author has devoted to the subject would be necessary in order to make his views and the various modifications which they underwent in the course of time, at all intelligible.[1] According to his conception the peasants should be placed in the position of entering within the shortest possible time into the full possession of a portion of land sufficient for their independent existence; but at the same time the interests of the nobility should be safeguarded as much as possible, and all useless sacrifice avoided. At the commencement at least, a proprietorial control should be exercised over the administration of the communes, as the peasants, in his opinion, were totally devoid of all inclination and capacity for the independent management of their affairs. The Government organs entrusted with the regulation of the matter greatly differed from him in their opinions on that point. Immediately after he reached St. Petersburg, Koshelev learned that the Formulating Commission of supervision had

[1] Only a portion of Koshelev's work, "A Voice from the Country," published in 1869, has appeared in German.

adopted resolutions, making the present contributions of the peasants the standard of valuation of the estates to be redeemed, and discarding all special taxation with respect to these. It was further resolved that on determining the extent of the area belonging to the peasants, no account should be taken of the circumstances of individual provinces, but that general maximum and minimum standards should be applied, and that in future the large proprietors should have no influence in the administration of the present communes.[1] In order to anticipate the inevitable opposition of the representatives of the nobles, Count Rostovsov and Milyutin, the Secretary of State, drafted an instruction for the representatives of the local committees about to be elected, which excluded an actual discussion of the schemes elaborated on the part of the separate provincial committees. As a matter of form these schemes had to be presented to the so-called chief committee, while the invited deputies, in contradistinction to the Formulating Commission, had nothing to do but give advice with regard to the local administration of the resolutions already taken by the chief committee. Samarin and Prince Cherkasky, who belonged to the committee of supervision, and were essentially in accord with its views, urged Koshelev to keep quiet so as to expedite the despatch of the great work, and to re-

[1] See Appendix, Note 29.

frain from all opposition to the report of the commission; but their entreaties were in vain, for Koshelev resolutely refused to adopt this course. Without hesitation he entered into consultation with his opponents, the Conservative deputies, Count Shumalov, Ofrosimov, &c. : his chief object was to try and extend the rights which had been granted to the representatives of the local committees ; he wanted the proposals made by these committees to be substantially examined within the Formulating Commission; in other words, not to settle the question simply by a bureaucratic decision, but after its full discussion by representatives of those directly interested in its solution.[1] This undertaking failed so completely that Koshelev could not even succeed in getting an audience of Rostovsov, the President of the commission. Rostovsov, in conjunction with the influential Secretary of State, N. Milyutin, who was even then known as a determined opponent of the nobility, and who had declared Koshelev's criticisms of the report of the commission as the work of a mere pamphleteer, brought it about that the Emperor personally approved of the mode of discussion adopted by the Formulating Commission, and, as a consequence, all further opposition and all more detailed discussion of the opposition proposals of the provincial representatives became morally impossible.[2]

[1] See Appendix, Note 30.   [2] See Appendix, Note 31.

Koshelev returned to Moscow in November, 1859, deeply discouraged. Here he wrote a *brochure*, "The Deputies and the Formulating Commission," which was printed and published at Leipzig, but had no effect on public opinion.

This episode in Koshelev's life at which we have just glanced is extremely significant as showing his political leanings, and the opposition between his views and those of the other more influential leaders of the Slavophil party. It was composed of men who, standing aloof from the actual life of the people, were great enthusiasts for a peasantry which had remained unaffected by the evils of European civilisation. As the only practical man in the party, he predicted with true instinct that the hopes based upon the independent administrative talent and economic qualities of the Russian peasant would turn out a fiasco, and that the injury done to landed proprietors by the false friends of the peasants would be accompanied by dangerous consequences to the whole Empire. It is a moot point whether these consequences could have been generally avoided under the given circumstances, and whether Koshelev's special proposals would have been capable of arresting them. His prediction that the peasants would fail to manage their own affairs successfully, and that their economic condition would become worse, was unfortunately more than justified by subsequent events, and turned out to be even more correct than he himself could have expected. Proofs of this are to be found in such abundance in Koshelev's own later writings (especially in the *brochure*, " A Voice from the Land "), and in all more recent Russian literature, that nothing further need be said on the subject.[1] The emphasis with which he insisted on a participation of the representatives of the nobility in forming resolutions with regard to the law of emancipation, and the legislative measures connected with it, forms a second and no less prominent trait in his character. Unlike the majority of his party, Koshelev, in spite of all his earnestness for Liberal views, and his repugnance to antiquated gentry and nobility, had a preference for class organisations combined with aversion to the absolute power of the bureaucracy—a type of opinions which was peculiar to the strictest Russian Conservatives. Consequently he occupied a position midway between the two parties, which may be regarded as the chief reason of his failure to obtain an important place in the Government in spite of the unquestionable personal esteem in which he was held, his popularity with the leaders of the national movement, and his substantial agreement with their aims.

Koshelev's love of work and readiness to fill any honourable office were left unrewarded on account of his experience in 1859. Hardly a year after the

[1] See Appendix, Note 32.

defeat, which he suffered during his former residence in St. Petersburg,[1] he again returned to the capital in obedience to a summons from the Minister of Finance, inviting him to take part in the discussion with respect to a reform of the tax on brandy. Koshelev, who had farmed the Government monopoly on brandy in the Government of Riasan for many years, and who knew the demoralising effect of this system better than any one, had presented a memorial ten years before to the minister Vroutshenko, in which he pointed out that the farming of the monopoly was financially disadvantageous and politically destructive, since it degraded the police and administrative officials to mere assistants and pensioners of the farmers, and made them interested parties in the spread of debauchery. At last he had the satisfaction of seeing his idea accomplished, and in accordance with his proposals, a duty on the manufacture introduced, the amount of income derived from which exceeded all expectations. Within the commission the ardent nationalist and theoretical opponent of the Germans became intimately associated with the representative of the Baltic distillers, Heinrich von Hagemeister, but in the case of another German who belonged to the commission, and who was afterwards minister of finance, Von Reuter, he speaks in the most scornful and angry terms, and regards it as a grievous error

[1] See Appendix, Note 33.

to have reposed any confidence in him. This is the more remarkable as coming from a critic who is otherwise lenient in his judgments. The labours of the commission continued about six months, and brought Koshelev his first distinction from the State—the Vladimir order of the third class. His acceptance of the order caused a certain sensation, for a little before, his colleague, the stubborn and refractory Juri Samarin, refused the same order with the declaration that he could not accept a Government reward for a service rendered to the general community (the participation in the committee of supervision, which elaborated the law of emancipation).

The proclamation of the celebrated ukase with respect to the abolition of serfdom, February 19 (March 2), 1861, coincided with the time of the labours of the commission relating to the reform of the tax on brandy. Koshelev, whose Liberalism was always apparent, left St. Petersburg with the painful presentiment of a recoil, which would follow this great " step forwards." His dread that the adherents of the old order in alliance with the Court party would predominate was, however, not fulfilled; on the contrary, the activity for reform displayed by the Government continued unbroken for two years, and was not even checked by the incendiarism of 1862, and the ever more frequent excesses of the St. Petersburg Radical press. Meanwhile in the country the authorities were occupied exclusively with the administration of the law of emancipation and settlements between owners and former serfs. Koshelev was not successful in persuading his peasants to buy up their portions of land at once, for the most nonsensical reports were circulated with regard to a "new liberation by the Tsar"—a gratuitous partition of all the land in the immediate future.[1] It was at last possible to induce the ill-advised serfs at least to come to terms with respect to the change from forced to free labour. Koshelev bears exceedingly favourable testimony to the "mediators of peace," new officials, who were first chosen to superintend the change from the old to the new condition of things, and to examine and ratify all newly-made compacts, but he sorrowfully adds that the promising beginning lasted only a little while, and that the second generation of the "mediators of peace" were indolent and useless. The rich owner of Pessochna, who had had a long experience, did not escape the inevitable fate of others when the change took place from bondage to free labour with hired servants: the apprentice fee had to be paid, and losses incurred through waste, and the damage done to machines, horses, and cattle; but Koshelev appears to have emerged from this crisis more quickly and easily than the majority of his compeers. Embarrassments were so general

[1] See Appendix, Note 34.

that an absence of gaiety and sociability in Moscow marked the winter of 1862-3. Koshelev was at that time elected president of the Moscow Agricultural Society: in this capacity he had to maintain a violent conflict with the Government, which he took up with his usual ardour, and at last carried through victoriously. He settled some months in Dresden, and wrote a *brochure* (translated into German by Haxthausen), in which he proposed " no constitution," but the summoning of a "general land-assembly " with only consultative power (*Zémskaya Doúma*). Koshelev often returned subsequently to the same thought (entertained as far back as 1853) in order to repeat with greater emphasis that he was on principle an upholder of the unlimited power of the Tsar, but at the same time regarded a deliberative assembly " as was usual at a former time " (the seventeenth century is meant) as indispensable for the removal of the deeply rooted evils of the Russian State and administrative mechanism.

It can be easily understood that this last clause could not be omitted by a disciple of Khomyakov, and an adherent of the Slavophil doctrine. It appears all the more astonishing that a man of Koshelev's sobriety of judgment, experience, and lucidity of view should have remained all his life under the delusion (confessedly shared by many intelligent and well-meaning Russians) that a mere deliberative assembly of popular representatives was possible as a permanent institution, and reconcilable with absolute monarchy. It is apparent to the unprejudiced that all popular representation must have the natural tendency of gaining security for the carrying out of its "decrees" by the acquisition of definite political and financial powers, and that the summoning of a consultative body would accordingly be nothing more than the first step to constitutionalism. Another of Koshelev's cherished propositions appears entirely unjustified: his contention was that the specific peculiarities of the character of the Russian common people offered a satisfactory guarantee against any encroachments on the part of a deliberative assembly into the legislative and administrative domain, and that unlimited monarchy had nothing to fear from this side. The experience of the provincial assemblies established since 1864 has taught directly the contrary; they present a series of constantly recurring conflicts between the administration and the provinces, and numerous attempts to a forcible extension of the powers entrusted to the latter. Koshelev's insistence on this demand, which in spite of its palpable incompleteness and obscurity became rather popular, is to be attributed partly to the influence of those same Slavophil notions, which made him the champion of the undivided commune, partly to the discord which now exists between the different classes of Russian society. The education of the nobility is substantially Western and modern Liberal, while the bulk of the Russian people hold fast to the national ideas of the divine unlimited sovereignty of the Tsar. The classes in whose name Koshelev speaks were too clear-sighted to overlook the importance of this last factor. They believed, and believe, that a reconciliation between the two really mutually exclusive principles was to be found in a "deliberative assembly." This "reconciliation" is nothing more than self-deception. It ignores the fact, with almost incredible short-sightedness, that the Russian Empire, which had entered into the possession of Poland, Lithuania, the Caucasus, Finland, and the Baltic Provinces, cannot possibly be identified with the *Moscow* Russia of Michael and Alexis Romanov, and that the brother of Peter the Great, the Tsar Feodor Alexeyeevich, had reasons for no longer summoning the territorial assembly.

In September, 1862, Koshelev returned to Moscow, where he regularly spent the winter, from one of those journeys which took him almost every year to Germany. Six months later the Polish-Lithuanian insurrection, which was equally dangerous to both Poles and Russians, broke out, and in February, 1864, before it was completely quelled, Koshelev received, through Prince Cherkasky, a summons to go to Warsaw and undertake the chief direction of the financial department. He was a Polish minister in all but the name. Cherkasky was entrusted with the direction of the Interior. The conversion of Poland into a Russian province was definitely decided upon; the Government was in reality to be carried on by Russians, and there was to be an entirely new organisation of the agrarian relations favourable to the emancipated peasantry at the expense of the rebellious nobility. The Secretary of State, Milyutin, who, since the time of the emancipation law, had been well known for his extreme Radical views, was entrusted with the carrying out of these affairs, and a commission to which Koshelev's friend and opponent, Cherkasky, and Juri Samarin belonged, was found to look after the scheme. The executive was to be in the hands of the Warsaw Organisation Committee, consisting of Count Berg, the Viceroy (*Namésknik*) of Poland, and a small number of high Russian officials, including the director of the financial administration.

As the invitation proceeded from Milyutin, Koshelev was extremely doubtful as to how he should receive the offer, which was entirely unexpected. He writes as follows on the subject: "I read the draft of organisation; I perceived that the property of the Polish nobility was to be sacrificed for the sake of an improved position of the peasantry. I thought, however, in looking back to former oppressions, and the rebellion for which this nobility were responsible, that I could see no violation of justice in this sacrifice. Besides, I was obliged to recognise that it was absolutely necessary, in consideration of a complete subjection of the country under the Russian dominion, to gain over the affection of the Polish peasantry, and to limit the power and influence of the nobility. Accordingly the scheme of organisation appeared to me acceptable; but, as I knew Milyutin and Prince Cherkasky very intimately, I could not rid myself of the fear that in the hands of these men the law in question would not be so much the final measure for the suppression of the Polish revolt, as the starting-point for more sweeping measures aimed directly at the repression and ruin of the Polish nobility. I was an opponent of this nobility on principle, but, under the circumstances, I regarded them as incapable of being replaced, and as in need of a certain amount of consideration. Besides, oppression and acts of despotism were foreign to my whole nature. I could not doubt for a moment that the men who had called my positive objections to the draft scheme of the law of emancipation a '*pamphlet*,' would resort to violence and oppression. For these reasons I refused Milyutin's offer."

This reluctance to take office was in vain. Milyutin sent Koshelev an official note asking him to undertake the financial administration of Poland, and to enter the Warsaw Organisation Committee. He invited him to St. Petersburg, and so arranged matters that the Emperor commanded the "Court Councillor," A. Koshelev, to a private audience. Koshelev was received by his monarch in the Summer Palace at Tsarkoye Selo early in May, 1864; it was in the Emperor's study that the meeting took place.

" I know," said his Majesty, " it is hard for you to leave the private life to which you have been accustomed, but I beg you to make this sacrifice for your country, and to accept office as a member of the Organisation Committee and director of finance in the kingdom of Poland. I am convinced you will not decline that from *me*."

" These words " (so we read in the " Memoirs ") " decided me to go to Warsaw. I expressed my entire readiness to fulfil his Majesty's will, and only asked that I should be given a few months to make investigations before entering upon the duties of finance director. The Emperor consented to this, and allowed me four weeks' delay to arrange my private affairs. He shook me heartily by the hand at the termination of the very friendly audience."

Four weeks later, June 11, 1864, Koshelev reached Warsaw in company with a younger official, who joined him at Moscow. At first he was received in a very unfriendly spirit. Count Berg, the Viceroy of Poland, being a German and a Conservative, was a determined opponent of Milyutin's Radical politics. He had convinced himself that the new Minister of Finance was a tool in the hands of Milyutin, whose political power was constantly increasing. Accordingly, when Koshelev presented himself Berg kept him waiting half an hour, then received him standing, and neither shook hands with him nor offered him a chair. This first painful impression was, however, soon obliterated, as Berg apologised at their next meeting, and showed himself anxious to establish friendly relations. Berg was at that time seventy-four, but, in spite of his high position, had never become popular in Russia. Koshelev speaks of him as follows:—

"Count Berg was very judicious, extraordinarily active, moderately enlightened, courteous, and very ingratiating in his manners. . . . His power of work was unrivalled; he slept very little, showed himself always eager for work, and even when roused in the middle of the night rose fresh and active, without ever betraying a trace of weariness or fatigue. The sittings of the Organisation Committee began at nine o'clock in the evening, and frequently lasted till late in the night. On one occasion the debate on a motion brought forward by Prince Cherkasky was kept up till three o'clock in the morning. My motion was to follow, but I assumed that the sitting would be adjourned on account of the advanced hour. Berg, however, without further ado, called upon me to speak, and the matter was settled. It was the greatest pleasure to work with him; his quickness of apprehension was extraordinary; he always divined what was in the mind of another, and was ready at any time to give a decision." . . .

The Committee of Organisation for the reform of the administration and the agrarian affairs of Poland, over which Berg, the viceroy, presided, consisted at first of four, and later of five members, besides the president, Koshelev, and Prince Cherkasky. Side by side with this committee there existed an administrative council, which directed the current administration, and to which five other higher officials in addition to those already named were attached. Amongst their number were three Poles and one German, Witte, the director of education. The administration of finance was conducted temporarily by Baynevski, a Pole—that is, until Koshelev finally took it in his own hands. Koshelev perceived at the first glance that two hostile parties stood opposed to each other in both committees. Count Berg and the majority formed the moderate party, and were influenced not so much by political as practical administrative considerations; on the other hand, superior talent and greater influence were on the side of Cherkasky and Solovyev. They were supported by Milyutin from St. Petersburg. With the help of this ally they often carried out plans which remained in a minority in the committee; they frequently tyrannised over the majority, and "distinguished themselves by audacity and preconceived designs." Koshelev at first reserved his opinions, then he took up an intermediate position, but at last he felt himself compelled to throw in his lot with the majority, and make common cause with Berg, in spite of all his antipathies to the "bureaucrats" and "Germans." He offered the most determined opposition to Cherkasky on all the more important questions, although he was his "friend" and a fellow-member of the Slavophil party. The opposite camps tried to remain personally in friendly relations; professionally they carried on an almost uninterrupted war. The imperious Cherkasky attempted not only to exercise supreme control in questions of organisation, but even on occasions to encroach upon the province of the finance director, and so prepare difficulties for him with the aid of his allies in St. Petersburg. His policy was systematically directed—as Koshelev repeatedly shows—to the material ruin of the Polish nobility, to the sowing of dissension between them and the peasantry, to the uprooting of all the traditional institutions, and to the complete exclusion of the Polish element from the bureaucracy and the administration. Koshelev was diametrically opposed to all this, and was of opinion that the Government, if they rightly understood their own interests, ought never unnecessarily to persecute the already hard-hit Polish nobility and thus take up an unjustifiable position. The existing institutions ought to be altered only as far as was necessary for the unity of administration. The majority of Russian institutions were so imperfect, and so much in want of reform, that Koshelev regarded their extension to Poland as most impolitic. He was still more decidedly opposed to Cherkasky's scheme for the complete exclusion of the Polish element from the bureaucracy. Russia suffered from a want of upright, reliable, and properly equipped State officials; it would therefore, he contended, be just as senseless to drain the mother country of her best sons as to surrender the future of Poland at random to inexperienced immigrants from Russia, totally unacquainted with the local condition of the country. There was no lack of useful and competent Polish officials; it was only a question of finding them out and enlisting them in the service of the State. "A country that possesses a relatively high, even although unsound, civilisation" (so he writes), "and can look back upon a historical development of a thousand years, cannot as a rule be remodelled suddenly and all at once."

The limits of these pages prevent a complete enumeration of the controversies which took place between the two parties of the Warsaw Committee of Organisation. The first vigorous encounter occurred when Koshelev presented the list of those persons, whom he wished to admit to the commission over which he presided for the remodelling of the system of taxation in Poland. A still more vigorous conflict arose over the discussion of a bill relating to the regulation of the compulsory service of the peasantry and the commutation of their right of commonage and pasturage in the seignorial forests. It was recognised, on the one hand, that an eminently important question was presented for discussion, and that the destruction of forests caused by the peasants threatened a serious injury, not only to the nobility, but to the entire country; and, on the other, that the proposals brought forward were reasonable and just. For the rest, however, diametrically opposite opinions were held. Cherkasky said openly that he could give his assent to no commutation and regulation of such compulsory service, however reasonable, "because Russian interests of State demanded the continuance of hostile relations between the nobility and the peasantry of Poland." And he was able, with the help of Milyutin, to prevent the ratification at St. Petersburg of the bill, which had been accepted by the great majority of the committee.

These constantly recurring differences compelled Koshelev to go to St. Petersburg, where he requested an audience of the Emperor, and explained to him the discord between his opinions and those of Milyutin and Cherkasky. Without mentioning names, he emphasised the unanimity with which all desired the amalgamation of Poland with the

Russian Empire; and he pointed out that the means employed to that end, the suppression of the Polish nobility, the violation of existing rights of property, and the appointment of Russians of doubtful fitness to all important posts, seemed to him very questionable. In his opinion Poland could only be won by a furtherance of her real interests and of her material prosperity, and the attempt should be made to bring over to Russia the numerous reconcilable and intelligent elements of that country. If his Majesty did not approve of these views, then he (Koshelev) must send in his resignation. "The Emperor listened to my remarks, which went into numerous details, attentively and sympathetically. When I finished he embraced me, with the words: 'No; you carry out my wishes. I approve of your course of action, and request you to continue as heretofore.'" (Beginning of September, 1865.)

Koshelev returned joyfully to Warsaw. Shortly before, in spite of his humble rank, he had received the star and ribbon of the order of Stanislaus, of the first class. He was soon to discover that everything remained upon the old footing, and that the proposals to which he attached the greatest importance were met, now as formerly, with contradiction and obstruction at the centre of action. But little later his carefully-worked-out plan for the remodelling of the Polish system of taxation was similarly treated, and made no progress. His patience was now exhausted, and he sent in his resignation. The answer was his nomination as Actual Councillor of State (passing over two intermediate grades), and a letter from Count Adlerberg to the Viceroy in the name of his Majesty, which reiterated the wish that Koshelev might remain in the office he had directed with so much success. In obedience to the imperial suggestion, Koshelev restrained his wishes in the hope of better days. But, instead of improving, the position became constantly worse. The Budget proposals for the financial year 1866, which he had handed in in November, 1865, were returned to him only in March of the following year, in a condition from which he saw clearly "that the changes determined upon were made in complete ignorance of the subject, and solely with the intention of irritating me and the Viceroy." Four weeks later, Milyutin, who had long been the actual leader of Polish politics, was nominated in the place of Platonov, Secretary of State for the kingdom of Poland. Koshelev now definitely determined, after the completion of two of his most important labours (the project with regard to the reform of taxation, and the introduction of a duty upon brandy) to give up the hopeless struggle, and to resign on the ground of ill-health. To the surprise of Berg, he carried out his intention to return to private life three months later; the attempt on the life of the Tsar by Karakosov, and the fear that it should produce a departure from the policy of reform which had been hitherto followed, had strengthened him in the wish to leave the service of the State. On the 12th of July, 1866, twenty-five months after he had entered the Warsaw Committee of Organisation, he finally left Warsaw. In his "Memoirs" Koshelev is firmly of opinion that the Russification of Poland is an unavoidable necessity. He thought that he had successfully paved the way for the attainment of this object, and had done real service to the Russian interest in Poland. He had succeeded—in his opinion without compulsion or oppression—in introducing in his province the use of Russian language. He had induced the public institutions in relationship with the financial administration (among others the Polish Realeastate Banking Company) and numerous private institutions to present Russian documents. He had established friendly relations with a large part of the society of Warsaw, both male and female. "I have left in Warsaw" (he writes to a friend) "a pleasant recollection of myself, and have done better service to my fatherland than those who have done otherwise." A passing reference must here be made to M. Leroy Beaulieu's representation of the Polish "system" of Milyutin in his panegyric, *Un homme d'état russe*. The author of "*L'empire des Tsars et les Russes*," a laborious and deserving, but much overrated work, has here drawn an optimistic picture, which, in spite of its wealth of material, is thoroughly misleading. It is contradicted in all essential points by Koshelev's account of the work of the Warsaw commission, and of his relations to Milyutin and Cherkasky. Those familiar with the subject will understand from the above remarks that the learned Frenchman is upon the wrong track in his whole conception of the Russian agrarian question, and that he has been led into errors from which other and less accurately informed Frenchmen—for example, M. Leonce de Lavergne (who knew neither Russian nor Polish)—have, with an inborn instinct for the truth, contrived to keep free. Any one who studies the above-mentioned books of Leroy Beaulieu, comparing them with our "Memoirs," will recognise in them a scarcely credible dependence upon the more than partial representations of Samarin and Cherkasky, and will be confirmed in the frequently repeated experience, that he only is entitled to utter an opinion upon Russian affairs who can read *between* the lines of the Russian authorities and official accounts. This art, in which Koshelev was a master, has not been learned by M. Leroy Beaulieu, in spite of his researches into Russian legislation, for the reason that it can be learned by non-Russians only when they have grasped the fact that the preconceived opinions of Western Europe are once for all not applicable to the Russian situation. Of the circumstance that on the other side of the Weichsel quite other conceptions from those of the Germano-romance world are bound up with the same words and names, M. Leroy Beaulieu has either heard, or has wished to hear, nothing whatever.[1]

After a stay of several months in foreign countries Koshelev took up his residence for the latter part of the autumn of the year 1866 in Riasan, for the winter in Moscow, where he was especially intimate with Pogodin. The chief object of his activity and interest was henceforth the electoral provincial institutions (*zémstvo*) introduced in the year 1864, upon which he built great hopes, because he regarded them as forerunners of the convocation of the central representative body (*Zémskaya Doúma*), for which he had longed for ten years. He took on every occasion a lively interest in the proceedings of the assembly of the province of Riasan, and of the provincial board (*Zémskaya Oupráva*) chosen by it, but he was constantly forced to recognise that the efficiency of these bodies was very limited, the Government and the officials seeking as far as possible to curtail their power and narrow their sphere of action. He found that the greater number of the resolutions they made existed only upon paper, and there appeared to be not even a distant intention that the country should participate more actively in the ad-

[1] See Appendix, Note 35.

ministration and legislation of the State. Accustomed to persevere in the way upon which he had once set out, he did not lose his courage; he attempted to set at defiance the difficulties which the growing influence of the conservative body of officials, opposed as it was to every act of independence of the smaller circles, year by year heaped up. A large number of pamphlets, published in Berlin, and regularly forbidden by the censor, quickly followed each other. In these the unwearied Koshelev returned again and again to his most cherished ideas, and sought to prove the impossibility of any further healthy development in the purely bureaucratic path. Events appeared to prove that he was right. The prosperity of the peasantry, the achievements of the administrative authorities, and the development of national education were obviously on the decline; the public humour became more sombre, and the increase of nihilist and revolutionary activity weighed upon all the friends of law and progress. He felt, with the more regret, that this state of matters changed nothing in the decisions of the Government, which was driven into an ever more decided opposition to the parties of reform and of the people. Besides this condition of public affairs, Koshelev had also to undergo various painful personal experiences, which we pass over. We only mention that he decided upon the publication of a monthly political review. After two numbers had been burnt by order of the administration of the press, he was compelled to abandon the continuation of his enterprise.

The "Memoirs" do not linger over these events, of which they give a very summary account. But they had made upon Koshelev a deeper impression than he was willing to confess. That part of the "Memoirs" which refers to the history of his last years betrays a bitterness against all contemporary developments, which finally increases to an almost hopeless pessimism. He, who had formerly been so indefatigable, now limited his part in public affairs almost exclusively to attendance upon the provincial assemblies, which less and less realised his ideals, and became more and more divided and uninfluential. He therefore published in Berlin, almost every year, pamphlets which discussed from the most different sides the necessity of convoking a general assembly of the people. Because this wish remained unfulfilled, Koshelev became opposed to every influential personage in his country, and launched forth into attacks upon their entire line of policy. Valuev was for him a German in disguise, Katkov a coarse fanatic and blind advocate of reaction, Count Tolstoi[1] a danger to the community, an enemy of all education and of all progress. The war of 1877 he judged essentially from the stand-

[1] Demetrius Tolstoi, the Minister of Education, and afterwards of Internal Affairs.—ED.

point of the Slavophil party, which in other things incurred his censure ; and he gave his unconditional assent to the condemnation pronounced by Aksakov upon the results of the Congress of Berlin in 1878.

What he says of the events which followed, the era of attempted assassination and of exceptional enactments, shows an almost complete hopelessness. The author regards the fanaticism of the nihilist revolutionary party as the natural consequence of departure from the principles of the early reforming period of the previous Government. A ray of light appears to him to break during the last months of the rule of the Emperor Alexander II. In his foreign travels Koshelev had frequently met Count Loris Melikov, who had won his confidence, and shown himself a truly liberal-minded statesman. The Count had positively assured him that the Emperor waited only for the time when men's minds should be more calm and the peace of the Empire more stable, to return to the projects of earlier years and to commence the longed-for foundation of a central "assembly of the provincial councils" by the convocation of deputies of the provincial elective bodies. Koshelev knew that the decision on this point, prepared for a considerable time beforehand, would take place in March, 1881, and looked forward with eager impatience to that moment when his dearest wish should be realised. All the more violent was his indignation at the outrage which ended the earthly career of the "Tsar-Liberator" at the very moment when he was prepared to crown the great work of reform, and the more grief-stricken his lament, that with the dismissal of Loris Melikov, Abaza, and Count Milyutin,[1] all hope of further development in a Liberal sense appeared to be annihilated.

The nomination of the former Minister of Education, Count Tolstoi, as Minister of the Interior (May, 1882), affected him more painfully than anything else. To this he always returns with unconcealed bitterness. As Koshelev's death (November, 1882) was sudden—his varying health appeared to have improved after a course of treatment in the summer of his last year—the "Memoirs" cease in the middle of a bitter reflection upon the falling away of modern youth from all political and humane idealism. The result of this harmoniously constituted life, filled by unwearying activity, by ceaseless desire of work, appears to be a profound discord. The account of it will rank among the most important productions of the memoirs bearing upon recent Russian history, and will retain among them an enduring place.

[1] Minister of War, and brother to State-Secretary Nicholas Milyutin, so frequently mentioned in this chapter.—ED.

XV.

KRAYEEVSKY AND BYELINSKY.

IN the frivolous Berlin of the time of Frederick William II. a privy counsellor is said to have existed who often played cards with three ladies, each of whom had once upon a time been his wife. I was reminded of this strange individual when I made the acquaintance, about the middle of the 'sixties, of the now dead journalist, Krayeevsky, in the person of a stout and lively little gentleman. It was known of him that he had once edited each of the great St. Petersburg papers of his time (the *Russian Invalid*, the *St. Petersbourg Gazette*, the *Golos* ("The Voice"), the *Zapiski*, and the *Sovreménnik*), and that he had been very fortunate with each of them.[1]

It is not very long ago since this remarkable man ended a life of nearly eighty years. He had so close a connection with the history of recent Russian literature, that a few remarks upon the deceased master of the Russian press may not be inappropriate in this place.

[1] See Appendix, Note 36.

Krayeevsky was born in the year 1810. While he was still little more than a boy he obtained a position in the Government offices at Moscow, and acquired a taste for literature from occasional employment upon the review *Moskovski Vestnik*. About the beginning of the 'thirties he migrated to St. Petersburg, where he was put at the disposal of the Minister of Education, and employed alternately as tutor of the corps of pages and editor of the *Journal of the Ministry of Education*. He was versatile and, according to the standard of his time, highly accomplished. He had written, at the order of the Minister Uvarov, a dissertation upon the philosophy of a certain Abbé Bottin. These circumstances brought him into closer relations with the literary world of St. Petersburg, which was at that time divided into two hostile camps. On the one side, grouped round Pushkin and his fashionable friends, stood the *elite* of the literary circle, belonging, as nearly all the more prominent talent of the time, to the so-called *romantic* school (in opposition to the pseudo-classic); on the other, the party of literary hirelings and of vulgar taste, supported by Gretsch and Bulgarin, the editors of the *Northern Bee* and panegyrists of the existing system. Krayeevsky leagued himself at first with the latter party. He organised literary *matinées*, in which poets and *beaux esprits* of the second rank took part, and he published in the *Son of the Fatherland*—a journal of little repute, connected with the

Northern Bee—an article, which he had brought from Moscow, upon the Tsar Boris Godunov. His keen sense for what was the most advantageous for the moment then caused a sudden desertion to the opposite camp. There he became the friend of Pletnev (the confidant of Pushkin) and of Prince Odoyeevsky, and went so far in his veneration of the latter as to imitate the arrangement of his rooms and his working suit. He further attracted the attention of both parties by publishing an essay entitled "Thoughts upon Russia," in which he adopted the tone, new to St. Petersburg, of the Moscow Slavophil, and treated Russia as a world entirely different from the rest of Europe—as a "sixth division of the world."

This article, according to the testimony of Panaev, excited some attention, and for a few days the "sixth division of the world" was talked of both in and beyond the literary circle of St. Petersburg. Although he wrote no more than this trial essay, Krayeevsky had become so well known by it, that the *Literary Supplement to the Russian Invalid*, hitherto edited by Voinikov, soon fell into his hands. The *Invalid* was, and still is, the property and organ of the Ministry of War. The *Literary Supplement*, unfortunately not very consistent with the character of the paper, had been called into being because at that time the necessary permission from the authorities to publish new journals was extremely difficult to obtain. Once in possession of the *Supplement*, Krayeevsky managed it with so much skill, that after the death (in 1837) of Pushkin, who had founded the *Sovreménnik*, he was appointed joint-editor of that periodical. That his name could appear beside those of the celebrated and aristocratic friends of the great poet, so lately dead, meant for the young writer a success, the more marked that the actual conduct of the magazine shortly passed into his hands. Two of his colleagues, Prince Vyasemsky and the poet (and privy counsellor) Shukovsky, were distinguished men, whose appointment was merely honorary; Pletnev, the third (subsequently Rector of the University of St. Petersburg and Professor of the History of Literature), understood in his capacity of *bel-esprit* and poet practically nothing of the commercial side of journalism. Therein lay Krayeevsky's strength. The young editor produced little, and had still less desire to write, but he was always looked upon as an author, and was able in this way to associate as a colleague with his fellow-workers, to reckon with their weakness and their strength, to follow the taste of the public and to keep in touch with it. He quickly became acquainted with the manual and the pecuniary sides of his undertaking, and with his economy and regard to his own advantage soon saw that the surrender of Pushkin's organ to the aristocracy hindered its wider circulation. His reputation was assured him by the *Sovreménnik*, and he had numerous connections. These advantages enabled him, after a few years (1839), to farm from Svinin, the bookseller, for the sum of five thousand roubles (*banco*) per annum, his monthly review, the *Otéchestvenniya Zapiski*. After the death of Svinin the periodical became his exclusive property. He was thus raised to the first rank among the *littérateurs* of St. Petersburg, a position which he occupied for almost fifty years.

As, under the Emperor Nicholas, all discussion of political questions was interdicted, journals and reviews were limited exclusively to the publication of novels and poems, and to literary and theatrical criticism. Krayeevsky, who had married a daughter of the famous actor, Briansky, devoted himself during the first ten years of his journalistic career entirely to the interest of *belles lettres*. With exceptional tact he obtained for the first number of his *Zapiski* the services of the most popular poets and novelists. Many of the best-known poems of Lermontov appeared in its pages. The "folk-poet," Kolisov, contributed several charming songs, Count Sollohub his original and artistic novel, "A Pair of Goloshes"; Prince Vyasemsky his story of "Princess Sisi"; and the well-known poet-translator, Huber, the first Russian version of "Faust." Only a literary critic was wanting. He was the more necessary, since, in the absence of political and other public news, literary criticism took the place of a chronicle of events, was eagerly read even by the greater public, and hence played an important part. Krayeevsky was unfortunate in his first attempts to find among the writers of St. Petersburg a critic who should equal in merit even Senkovsky, the reviewer of the trivial and unprincipled type, who, in spite of his coarseness and vulgarity, was both witty and audacious. He turned to Moscow, and brought thence Meshevich, the critic of the *Telescope*—a review of that city which had recently been suppressed. He was no more successful than his predecessors. In despair Krayeevsky asked advice of a younger colleague on the *Zapiski*, Ivan Panaev, afterwards well known as a Radical writer. Panaev proposed to him a man, who soon after made an epoch in Russian literature, but at that time was in extreme destitution, and more feared than loved by those who knew him. He was the ex-student of medicine, Vissarion Byelinsky, and had been expelled from the University of Moscow "for incapacity."

Byelinsky was one of the most remarkable Russians of his time. Very incompletely educated, he could speak no foreign language, and knew mere fragments of the literature of Germany, England, and France. He possessed only two of the qualifications of a great critic, but these in a high degree: a brilliant talent for representation, and a fearless love of truth. "I was born for a (*sc.*, political) pamphleteer," he says himself. "That career I desire most keenly, and yet I am condemned to sing for ever the old litany of Lermontov, Pushkin, and Gogol, Gogol and Pushkin and Lermontov—æsthetics, æsthetics for ever and a day." In Moscow, Byelinsky had been content to wear these chains. He had taken his stand as a zealous disciple of Hegel upon " Art for Art's sake ; " he had shared the sovereign dislike of Goethe and Pushkin to the "influence of the rabble" in art, in the state, and in society; he had fought for his Conservative principles many a hard fight with the Young Hegelians of the school of Herzen. His standpoint was allied in one point only to that of these forerunners and originators of Russian Radicalism ; he was, in spite of an intimate personal relationship to Constantine Aksakov, an enthusiastic advocate of Western ideas, and a violent opponent of the Slavophil party and their worn-out old-Russian and Byzantine antiquities.

Byelinsky, who was then twenty-nine years old, received Krayecvsky's invitation to go to St. Petersburg as critic of the *Zapiski*, with a yearly salary of a thousand roubles, at the moment of a serious intellectual crisis. As he worked upon an essay, "Against Menzel, the critic of Goethe," serious doubts of the correctness of his standpoint attacked the apostle of " Art for Art's sake." A few months after his removal to St. Petersburg Saul had become Paul ; the enemy of Liberal and democratic ideas had espoused their cause. " A plague o' your lofty ideas !" he wrote to his friend Botkin at the beginning of 1841, "we live in evil days, and fate forces us to a vow of renunciation. We must suffer for our children's welfare. . . . My acquaintance with the society of to-day, in which rogues and mediocrities predominate, has been almost fatal to me. . . . All praise to Schiller, the noble defender of humanity, the liberator of society from inherited prejudice. For me the personality of man, the individual, stands higher now than society, than mankind itself. . . . As I review my past, two things distress me; . . . my wretched complaisance to a shameful reality. What abominable trivialities I used to write, and how fanatically I believed in them!"

This short introduction sufficiently characterises the man who in 1839 became the critic of the *Zapiski*, and for eight years held the post with brilliant though slowly recognised success. Under the thin mask of a critic persecuting false authority and bad taste in current literature—a mask impenetrable only to the shortsightedness of the censorship, he waged war against the existing order of things in society and the state. Under the form of a vigorous condemnation of the Slavophil party he attacked the hostility to education of the whole of retrograde Russia under Nicholas. His success was so remarkable, that Byelinsky was considered by his contemporaries and successors the greatest of all Russian critics. In recent memoirs his name occurs more frequently than any other. Turgenev, who called him the Russian Lessing, dedicated to him the greater part of his souvenirs; Alexander Herzen has covered with praise the opponent who afterwards became his ally; Constantine Aksakov was his close friend for years. The second part of Panaev's memoirs is devoted chiefly to Byelinsky, and Byelinsky is the fondest theme of the more recent works of Annenkas, the literary historian. Long before he became more widely known, the haughty Pushkin used secretly to send his journal to the poor ex-student in his garret in Moscow, and to value very highly a favourable judgment from his young critic. Gogol, whose pride, vanity, and weakness afterwards ended in insanity, received the destructive criticism with which a private letter of Byelinsky's visited his last book (the reactionary "Letters to my Friends") with a resignation which was almost a complete submission. Suspected as a Radical, and surrounded with spies by the political police, his favour was yet humbly courted by writing and scribbling generals and privy counsellors of the Emperor, anxious to propitiate his severity and to find favour in the eyes of the dreaded critic. When Byelinsky, weakly, shy, and awkward, came occasionally to his Saturday evening receptions, Prince Odoyeevsky regarded it as a great honour; and General Mikhailovsky-Danilevsky, the military writer, did not rest until the untitled civilian had accepted at least one of his Excellency's numerous invitations to dinner. Byelinsky gives a humorous description of the meal, and the unwearying attentions which the aristocratic giver lavished upon his modest guest. The General addressed him continually as "little father," ceremoniously requested permission to introduce his daughter, then eighteen years old, and desired her among other things to set the pipe of the "honoured little father" agoing with her own charming lips. Yet every one knew that Byelinsky could only with great difficulty be induced to accept invitations, and that in a large company he scarcely spoke a word.

Krayeevsky was undoubtedly aware of the tendency of his coadjutor's views, and of the danger to which he exposed himself in permitting his review to become the organ of so bold a revolutionary. This circumstance made his conduct the more praiseworthy, and the decision with which he refused attention to the complaints against Byelinsky of wounded vanities, great and small, of anxious friends, and of calumnious enemies, redounds the more to his credit. For himself it was a decidedly critical position, and it must be admitted that his famous colleague was not excessively accommodating. Commercially, Krayeevsky's magazine was certainly very prosperous, and gained steadily in repute and circulation, while he who was the cause of this success was, in spite of his poverty, very modest in his demands. The two men were perfectly polite, but they remained strangers to each other. Krayeevsky became rich, and Byelinsky famous. The former occupied, however, the more favourable position, so long as no one had the courage to enter into more intimate relations with the most feared and the most dangerous writer in Russia.

Nevertheless, a rupture came at last. In the summer of 1847 two warm friends of Byelinsky, and younger contributors to the *Zapiski*, Panaev, who has already been mentioned, and the poet, Nekrassov, obtained possession of the *Sovreménnik*. This periodical, of which the joint editorship had helped to create Krayeevsky's influence, belonged to the heirs of Pushkin, but was now more and more unsuccessful. Byelinsky abandoned his connection with the *Zapiski* and joined the staff of the journal taken over by his friends, the success of which seemed likely to depend mainly upon his contributions. But fortune once more favoured Krayeevsky; in May of 1848, the year of the Revolution, the famous critic died of consumption, before the commencement of any serious rivalry. It was perhaps fortunate for him, for a few weeks before his death the sick man was summoned before the Forum of the "third division," and there informed that the chief of the secret police, General Dubbelt, desired to make his "acquaintance." It was at all events fortunate for Krayeevsky and his review, for both were henceforth relieved from the dangerous rivalry of the *Sovreménnik*. Both magazines went on side by side, nor did the one seriously interfere with the circulation of the other. But Krayeevsky from a prosperous man became a rich one, and contrived to steer past all the rocks which threatened Russian journalism during the last years of the reign of the Emperor Nicholas. While the Government became from year to year more suspicious and more tyrannical, and the anxiety of the censorship finally outran all bounds, Liberal and Radical tendencies became increasingly strong among the educated public. It seemed an impossible problem to reckon with both factors with a like success; but Krayeevsky so successfully solved it, that the *Zapiski* survived the reign of Nicholas, and that its editor was yet, at the beginning of the new era, numbered among the most prominent of the influential Liberals in the journalistic world of St. Petersburg.

With his characteristic sharpsightedness Krayeevsky recognised that the predominance of reviews was past, and that the altered tendencies of the time favoured the rise of the daily press. The *Zapiski* still flourished,[1] and had begun actively to discuss the political questions of the day; but in the midst of the emotional movement which preceded the abolition of serfdom its editor farmed the *St. Petersbourg Gazette* (*Peterbourgskiya Viedomosti*), the property of the Academy of Sciences. It was easy for a man of his experience in journalism to make of this

[1] See Appendix, Note 37.

paper, the only one that circulated largely among the cultured classes of St. Petersburg of that period, an influential organ, to double in a short time its circulation and its income from advertisements, and to destroy the remaining reputation of servile journals of the character of the *Northern Bee*. His example was eagerly imitated. The *Journal of the Bourse* and the *Russian Invalid* were completely remodelled, as early as 1862 : their former size was doubled, and leaders appeared in them which attempted to excel in boldness and Liberal declarations those of the *St. Petersbourg Gazette*. But the last-mentioned paper preserved its dominant position. Some of its numbers were in themselves political events, and went the entire round of the Empire. We may instance the number of January 1, 1862, which published, under the title "862 to 1862," the talented historian Kostomarov's famous proclamation of the millennium. We quote a few sentences: "Russia has existed a thousand years. . . . The hour strikes, but it is not the knell of a dying race ; nay, it is the call to a new birth, to a new life of all the Slavonic peoples ! . . . Your hands, brothers ! with a new millennium begins a new existence !" and so forth. But Krayeevsky was not yet satisfied. The sum he had to pay to the Academy of Sciences for the possession of their paper was considerable, and the continuance of the relationship demanded a sacrifice which could be more profitably devoted to other purposes. Instead, therefore, of renewing the contract, which expired upon December 31, 1862, he obtained the proprietorship of a new paper. The academic daily was handed over to the well-known Liberal writer, V. Korsh, and Krayeevsky left it, after having secured for his new daily, the *Golos* (" The Voice"), which appeared in the same form as the *Viedomosti*, the collaboration of his most influential colleagues, and a large number of subscribers.

The new undertaking was crowned with a success yet greater than that of the *St. Petersbourg Gazette* and of the *Zapiski*. The *Golos* was favoured by the incessant demand for new political food, and by the feverish excitement which had seized upon Russian readers since the outbreak of the revolt in Poland and Lithuania. In the course of a few months it obtained a circulation which had been reached by other journals only after as many years. The experienced and enterprising editor bestowed equal care upon all the departments of his ambitious undertaking. The services of the most prominent literary and æsthetic critics of the Liberal party were secured for the *feuilleton* by high salaries. The chronicle of the day surpassed that of any similar enterprise, even the satirical *Whistle* (*Svistok*) of the Radical *Sovreménnik*, in audacity, wit, and combativeness.[1] The financial news gave daily evidence of Krayeevsky's intimate acquaintance with the trans-

[1] See Appendix, Note 38.

actions of the money market. The greater number of the political articles was written by Professor Bilbassov, the friend, and afterwards the son-in-law, of Krayeevsky, a man of high culture, and with a knowledge of all the details of Viennese journalism, which had then just begun to come to the front. It was chiefly due to his tact and flexibility that the *Golos* was able to surmount the difficulties which the condition of the Russian daily press had thrown in the way.[1] Since the spring of 1863 the Polish Revolution had been the chief object of public attention, and during the first half of that memorable year diametrically opposite views of the question prevailed in educated Russia. The Polish revolutionaries had wrongly counted upon direct support from those in Russia who espoused their cause. The attempts of the *émigrés* from London, notably Bakunin and Alexander Herzen, to bring the Varsovian rebels armed assistance, met with a pretty general condemnation. None the less did Liberal Russia regard Muraev's politics of Russification and oppression as imperilling the future of their fatherland; none the less did the still numerous Radical party sympathise more keenly with the secret government of Warsaw than with certain of the advisers of the Emperor Alexander II. Krayeevsky, himself of Polish origin, had yet, without prejudice to his Russian education

[1] See Appendix, Note 39.

and antecedents, espoused the plan of Vielopolsky, in accordance with which Poland was to be autonomous in matters of internal politics, a sister-kingdom of the great Russo-Slavonic world. His experience and cool insight told him that this plan was hopeless, and that the insurrection would result in the complete destruction and subsequent Russification of the unhappy country. Yet he was reluctant to take the side of the vulgar fanatics, who would destroy everything Polish, root and branch, and build up an empire of force upon the ruins of the order Vielopolsky had produced. On the other hand, the party of national fanaticism, led by the *Moscow Gazette,* and embodied in the person of Katkov, made such constant progress that open and direct opposition to it was surrounded with dangers. For some time the *Golos* took its stand by the side of the official opponents of the Moscow press dictator. It supported the timid attempts at moderation and tranquillity which were made by Valuev, the Minister of the Interior, and a man of Western ideas, and by Golovnin, the Minister of Education. It sought to give its polemic against Katkov the air of a struggle for St. Petersburg against Moscow, and as circumstances and the political humour changed, it adopted now a Liberal, now a national attitude. But this moderate position in time became untenable. The flood of nationalism rose daily higher, and began to burst its dams. The artillery of the *Moscow Gazette* was directed not only against Poland, but with a still hotter fire against Finland and the Baltic provinces. After the dismissal of Golovnin, Katkov's friend, Count Dmitri Tolstoi, the *oberprocouror* of the Synod, became Minister of Education. The *Golos* was thus compelled to make concession after concession to the ruling tendency, to join periodically in the outcry of the party in power, and to hide as carefully as possible the loopholes that it still kept open. It sought to disarm Katkov's blind fury of denunciation by occasional violent articles against Polish and German aristocrats, against Catholic and Protestant " hierarchs." It endeavoured to flatter the national feeling by animosity to the rising power of Germany; and it regarded with apparent cheerfulness the evident reactionary tendencies of those newly in power. But in everything, and particularly in the polemic against Poles and Germans, it remained more Liberal than national. Krayeevsky and Bilbassov never attempted to deny that their true politics were those of reform, and that they adhered to the Liberal traditions of the early years of the 'sixties. Wherever circumstances seemed to permit of it, whenever the authority of the national fanatics of Moscow diminished, the *Golos* attempted to return to its old standpoint, and to adopt the *rôle* of a Liberal opposition paper. The supporters of Golovnin's educational reforms were as much opposed to

Tolstoi's system of classical education as they were to the efforts to lessen the independence of the provincial assemblies, or to limit the absolute power of the tribunals in the interests of administrative omnipotence. Krayeevsky and Bilbassov had no sympathy with the partiality for Prussia and Germany of which the Court and those about the Emperor were accused in 1870 and 1871. Careful readers of the newspapers will still remember the furious diatribes which the *Golos* hurled at the victoriously advancing German army. They found classical expression, the day after the capitulation of Paris, in the article headed " Consummatum est." Hatred of the Prussians, which the champion of the Polish cause had never concealed, and a cool speculation on the national vanity and the party prejudice of the Russian public, contributed equally to an attitude by which the editor of the *Golos* desired, while flattering the racial fanaticisms of his readers, to secure for himself the right to hoist once more the flag of Liberalism.

As Russia began to look more calmly at the consequences of the power of Germany, the opinions of the *Golos* gradually underwent a change. Without disguising its preference for France, Krayeevsky's paper, as Katkov's had already done, declared itself in favour of the alliance between the three emperors; and when, shortly afterwards, the fires of the German *Kulturkampf* were kindled, Krayeevsky thought it due to his Liberal reputation to become a decided supporter of the Prussian cause. Questions of foreign policy were then for a time put in the background. Accordingly, after 1875 attention was increasingly directed to internal dissensions, and especially to the struggle between the representatives of reform and the reactionary school of Tolstoi. As the *Golos* had the most accurate information on the situation in Central Asia, and was supplied with news by the most talented political and financial correspondents in the capitals of Western Europe, it appeared to be indispensable to the commercial circles of St. Petersburg, Moscow, Odessa, &c., and its opinions and judgments were constantly quoted in the German, French, and English press. It began with increasing emphasis to represent the Liberal middle class, which during the last ten years had been forming in the larger towns of Russia, and which temporarily supplied the place of a genuine *bourgeoisie*. A shade of censure was discernible in the greater number of the articles, in which the most influential of the Russian daily papers expressed its views on questions of internal politics; but it abstained as carefully from overstepping the respect due to the authorities as from revolutionary paroxysms, or from stirring up the impulses of the mob.

The fateful days of the Turkish war began. True to its constant traditions, the *Golos* sought, immediately after the declaration of war, to turn the prevailing excitement to the profit of Liberal reform. The same number which published the manifesto expressed the hope, in an apparently harmless article in the *feuilleton*, "that society would be permitted some direct participation in deciding upon the measures to be taken in preparation for the war." In Russian terminology "participation of society" is a euphemism for the forbidden word "Constitution."[1] The sentence was so understood by the Government, and the answer was a decree of the overseers of the press suspending the *Golos* for three months. This decree was set aside in a few weeks, upon the intercession of influential friends, but Krayeevsky and Bilbassov were henceforth strictly watched, and treated with the same severity which at this time deposed V. Korsh from the management of the *St. Petersbourg Gazette*. For a time the *Golos* carefully restrained itself; but when in the spring of 1879 the indignation at the unhappy issue of the war and of the Congress of Berlin afforded an opportunity for new attacks upon the Government, it came into fresh contact with the censorship. To lag behind public opinion appeared to the veteran journalist at least as dangerous as to advance too far. When at the beginning of 1879 the jurors acquitted Vera Sassulich, who had attempted the

[1] The author of this *feuilleton* was a certain Markov, and was otherwise little known.

life of Trepov, the chief of the police, the *Golos* was one of the journals that approved of the acquittal. The number of those who lauded this outrageous breach of the law was so great that the Government did not consider it judicious to attempt to punish them.[1] A few weeks later the *Golos* remarked, apropos of an occurrence in Odessa, "that it was extraordinary that a boy of eleven years of age should be excluded from the Gymnasium[2] in that town on account of his political opinions." This drew down a warning severe enough to show that the last remaining organ of a quasi-European Liberalism in St. Petersburg had finally forfeited the favour of the chiefs of the censorship. The fact first became fully apparent after the death of Alexander II., when Count Loris Melikov resigned the post of Minister of the Interior. With his disappearance the last traces of consideration for the Liberal reform period and its traditions vanished. Up to 1881 the criticism of foreign affairs had been considered an open field, in the ordinary course of things unregarded by the censorship. Under the *régime* of Ignatiev all this was so completely altered that the *Golos* was suspended for six months, when it ventured to question the utility of the changes in the constitution of Bulgaria. Its fate was shared by the *Novaya Gazeta* ("The New Gazette"), which Krayeevsky had bought to supply the subscribers and

[1] See Appendix, Note 40.   [2] See Appendix, Note 41.

advertisers of the *Golos* during its suspension. The crime of the *Gazeta* was the expression of regret for the withdrawal (which was, it must be explained, voluntary only in form) of the Grand Duke Constantine from the administration of the marine.

When the six months' suspension was at an end the *Golos* once more appeared before the public, but for a short time only. Count Tolstoi, the former Minister of Education, took the place of Ignatiev in May, 1882. He was an old and sworn enemy of the tendencies of Krayeevsky, and had from the first decided to overthrow him on the earliest opportunity. In spite of all the vigilance of the management, this opportunity presented itself in February, 1883; and a ministerial decree commanded the complete suppression of the *Golos*, which was accused of systematic and malicious opposition to the Government. Krayeevsky, now nearly seventy-five years of age, laid down for ever the pen he had guided for more than half a century. Several years before he had sold the *Zapiski* to his former colleague and subsequent rival, Nekrassov,[1] and he had long possessed a fortune of over a million roubles. He retired from business, but remained president of the "Literary Fund" and the "Society for the Support of Needy Writers and Artists," both founded by him.[2] He was, besides, a member of the St. Petersburg town

[1] Later on this monthly has also been suppressed.
[2] See Appendix, Note 42.

assembly of deputies (*Gorodskáya Doúma*), to which he had belonged since 1870. In this capacity he gave his attention chiefly to educational improvement in St. Petersburg, it is said with a large amount of success. He died in his eightieth year, having survived his wife, his two sons, and several grandchildren His very extensive collection of letters and manuscripts, of great importance to Russian literary history, was bequeathed to the imperial public library in St. Petersburg.

The " Nestor of the Russian press " was neither a great writer nor a great character, but essentially a talented and industrious literary man of business. Sympathising at bottom with humane and Liberal ideas, he never made any real sacrifice for them. On the contrary, he more than once temporised in his personal interest. Yet it would be as unjust to refuse him the praise due to the intelligence and energy he employed in improving the Russian periodical press, as to deny his services to the cause of humanity in his fatherland. He pursued journalism as a business, but it was a decently conducted business. He never became the tool of obscurantism and the rule of might, nor allowed himself to be the plaything of the caprices of the rabble. Even where he followed a doubtful path he remained a gentleman, a "*homo liberalis*," who felt that he had once been the companion of such writers as Pushkin, Byelinsky, and Turgenev. It is perhaps not much to have to say in his praise, but it is incomparably more than can be said of nine-tenths of the present representatives of Russian journalism! Most of the journals with which the *Golos* had in its time to compete have long disappeared. The Radical monthlies, *The Russian Word* and *The Annals of the Fatherland*, the Slavophil *Day*, *Moscow*, and *The Citizen of Moscow* (*Moskvich*), the Retrograde *Tidings*, and the Liberal *Golos* rest in the grave dug for them all by the hands of the censorship. Repeatedly worried and injured by warnings, by suspensions and confiscations, Ivan Aksakov had lost the best part of his strength, when he founded his last paper, the *Rous*, shortly before his death. To escape the censorship, Aksakov's former friends, Samarin and Koshelev, had begun as early as the 'seventies to publish their Slavophil pamphlets in pagan Germany instead of in Holy Russia. Korsh died in Heidelberg, after he had been, by an arbitrary act of Tolstoi's, unjustly deprived of the editorship of the *St. Petersbourg Gazette*. Finally, Krayeevsky's paper was suppressed in 1883, and with it died the last European-Liberal journal of Russia.[1] The organ of brutal nationalism, the *Moscow Gazette*, was the last of the independent newspapers, and it lost the remainder of its interest at the death of Katkov.

The Russia of to-day possesses newspapers and

[1] See Appendix, Note 43.

reviews in considerable number. But there is not one among the many daily papers of St. Petersburg, some of them of very large size, that could justly claim to be dignified and independent—not one the contributors to which are notably talented. Such as *Novoya Vremya*, *Novosti*, *Svyet*, and *Grazhdanin*, represent nothing more than the frolics of weak-minded opportunism or Chauvinistic tendencies. They are all frothy; they have no kernel, no definite contents. How should it be otherwise? The questions that most interest the reading world must either not be discussed at all or discussed only as the Government wishes. Undesirable news is prosecuted like undesirable opinions, and only one province is open to independent discussion—that of foreign and international relations. Almost the half of a Russian newspaper, therefore, is filled with political chatter and conjecture, discussions *ad nauseam* of such favourite subjects as the villainous Kalnoky and the still more villainous Bismarck, or the imposing reserve of the great Tsar-governed and Tsar-blessed Russia. The remaining pages are occupied by speculations on the credulity of the Bourse, abstracts from official documents of Russia's material and military resources, lamentations over the increase of German influence, denunciations of Poles, Finns, Livonians, Armenians, Jews, &c.; and lastly, dissertations, friendly to-day, hostile to-morrow, upon France, " the ally of our future." At Court and in so-called "society" the *Grazhdanin*, edited by Prince Meshtchersky, has a recognised influence. That this miserable would-be aristocratic sheet, edited by a man of noble name and ignoble disposition, should obtain even a trace of credit, indicates the moral and intellectual condition of the governing classes. The reader of Turgeniev's *Smoke* will understand us if he will recall the political discussion in the tenth chapter in a company of Russian generals and fashionable women assembled at Baden-Baden. Meshtchersky's political judgment is on the level of this specimen of pretentious thoughtlessness. Colloquially written and larded with French phrases, the author's glosses upon current events appear to certain readers original and witty, while their real triviality surpasses anything that others would dare to print. Some importance has occasionally been attached, in Vienna and Berlin, to the fact that Meshtchersky will have nothing to do with France or the projects for a Franco-Russian alliance. The casual opinions of the princely writer have really no serious importance. They are the productions of a racial blindness which would reject the whole of Western civilisation, and would incidentally flatter, in the humblest manner, the fashionable aversion to a republican form of government. The *Grazhdanin* adopts the reactionary programme, formerly Tolstoi's, with regard to questions of internal policy. It struggles to show its aristocratic independence by occasional attacks upon the officials, the absolute power of the State, and so on.

The last light of educated and Liberal opinion in this journalistic morass is the monthly *Messenger of Europe* (edited by Spassovich, the literary historian, and the advocate, Stassulevich).[1] In the last ten years almost all the surviving witnesses of the Liberal period have formed a connection with this estimable review. The *Messenger of Europe* makes a decided protest against the existing system, but it is compelled to the greatest prudence and reserve, and hence it has not its due influence. The language employed by Stassulevich and Spassovich is, besides, too moderate and cultured to be understood and appreciated by the heroes of the market-place. For them the password will apparently still be for a time, "Ruere in servitium." The wind will then change once more, and what will prevail will be the very opposite of all that has been so long revered and practised.[2]

[1] See Appendix, Note 44.   [2] See Appendix, Note 45.

XVI.

RUSSIAN PIONEERS.

THERE are two kinds of missionaries in Russia, religious and political. The former labour chiefly among the Mahometans and Buddhists in the Eastern provinces of the Empire, in the Caucasus and in Siberia. Their success is, however, scanty; the converts frequently return to Islam, or to heathenism, and not seldom seduce the "true believers" to join their ranks, as is admitted even by Pobyedonostsev, the truest of true believers. In the "good old times" of the Emperor Nicholas and Count Protassov there was even talk of a project to form a "transitional religion," in view of the invincible sympathy for Judaism among the Buriates of Siberia, and it was intended to confer upon this first step on the road to orthodox Christianity the prestige of a governmental sanction.

The political missions of Russia are more important than the religious. Since 1864 it has become usual to give the name of missions to political and national propaganda. The emissaries of Russification (for the most part dismissed and disgraced Government officials), who were sent in large numbers into Poland and Lithuania, were called by the high-sounding title of "missionaries of our national cause," and were rewarded as an expression of the holiness of the cause with confiscated estates and highly-paid appointments.[1]

In spite of the lamentable failure of this enterprise, and the numberless scandals to which it gave birth, it is at present in process of revival. The reforms it is intended to introduce in the Baltic provinces are to be carried out with the help of national outcasts, and the German-Protestant districts of the Baltic shore are to be thus initiated into the secrets of the old Slavonic arts of bribery and extortion ("Lichoïmstvo" and "Msdoïmstvo.")

Older and more remarkable than this mission within the limits of the Empire is that to foreign countries, which is most active in the Slavonic districts of Austria and Turkey. Its first station was founded under Peter the Great, in Montenegro, the land of "our only true ally," and was much extended eighty years afterwards under the Emperor Paul.[2] Next in order came Servia, whither the bishop, Menadovich, of Belgrade, had, on his secret mission to St. Petersburg, invited his Rus-

[1] See Appendix, Note 46.
[2] Documents referring to its foundation were published by the *Allgemeine Zeitung*.

sian friends (1804). Thirty years later a Russian mission, composed at first of volunteers, began to work in Bohemia. The first messenger of the Eastern faith to reach the Moldau was a well-known savant, Professor Pogodin, a Slavophil of the old school of absolutism and reactionary principles. He formed a connection with many inquiring spirits in Prague, but he was too clumsy in his negotiations to obtain an enduring success. Instead of being satisfied with the propaganda which had then begun in favour of Bohemian literature, the author of " Russian Letters" wished at once to import a Russo-Slavonic policy, for which the time was not yet ripe. He was defeated by the circumstance that certain leaders of the national party, who had leanings towards Liberalism, did not appreciate the absolutism of the Emperor Nicholas which Pogodin preached. A change for the better took place twenty years later, when the Liberal reforms of Alexander II. began to attract the attention of the Slavonic world outside of Russia. About the same time the most capable and the most fanatical of all the Russian missionaries to Austria was sent to Vienna, in the person of M. Rayevsky, priest of the embassy. In spite of the extraordinary tact shown by this dangerous agitator during his thirty years' residence on the Danube, the cause progressed at first but slowly. It had become in the meanwhile so popular in Russia, that the well-known writer, Alexander Koshelev, who twenty years earlier had sworn by the land of Goethe and Schiller, volunteered in 1857 to go to Prague as inspector of the mission, that he might establish relations with Hanka, Schassarik, Schumavsky, Tomek, and others. To his regret Koshelev was able to discover only one "Russian Bohemian," Herr Hanka; the remaining nine of his acquaintances were content to be "Bohemian Bohemians." Schassarik explained this "discouraging circumstance" in a manner which elucidates the progress since made by the national party. The statement made by the famous scholar to his Russian friend was word for word as follows:—

"The national agitation has gained in extent in the last twenty years, but has lost in strength and courage. We have no funds, because our aristocracy belongs almost exclusively to the hostile party. Our nobility does not live in Prague; it wishes to be Austrian, not Bohemian, and it speaks German by preference. The money sent us from abroad injures rather than helps us. . . . You Russians, and particularly Pogodin, have designs in politics by which you do harm to us, to yourselves, and to the cause. Do not trouble yourselves about us. Sweep your own doorstep, do something creditable for yourselves, then we shall look to you, and try to promote at once our own and the Slavonic cause."

Koshelev travelled in the company of Hanka from Prague to Vienna, where he discussed the subject in detail with Rayevsky. The right reverend father complained of the indifference of the mass of the people, and of the Germanisation of the Slavonic nobility. He deplored the diplomacy of the Austrian Government, and its success in seducing Slavonic minds to the Austrian interest. The priest of the Russian Embassy was remarkable even then for the number and diversity of his connections with society. Kusmin, the dean of the Slavo-Lutheran College, the celebrated Miklovich, the Protestant preacher Urbar, Hurbak the Slovak, and Karadiez, the "esteemed apostle of Slavonic unity," belonged among others to the number of his friends. Among them also the lack of funds was generally deplored. They declared that the desertions to the German camp had made it a chronic evil. In the opinion of Krayeevsky only three of the five existing "matitsi," or literary clubs, those of Lemberg, Agram, and Prague, did their duty satisfactorily. Pesth and Klagenfurt were accused of a scandalous inactivity, and the Moravian union of a downright tendency to Catholicism.

It became manifest a few years later that the right reverend father had not lost heart, in spite of these unfavourable circumstances, but· had successfully continued his work. His cause, we grant, at first lost ground. After the ,year 1864 many of the revolutionaries fled from Russia and took refuge in Prague, Lemberg, Agram, Vienna, and other towns, where they spread dismal accounts of the despotism in Russia and Poland. They cautioned the Slavs against the government of St. Petersburg, and declared that their only hope of success lay in a general revolution. Basil Kelssiev, the most prominent apostle of this new doctrine, has described in a bulky volume his wanderings through Hungary, Galicia, and Bukovina, and his attempts to stir up a revolution among the Russian refugees and adherents of the old faith inhabiting these provinces.

"Ah! had I but money,
I'd soon find my wits,"

the unhappy man might have sung, when he was finally driven mad by privation, and returned to St. Petersburg praying for mercy. Krayeevsky, however, who did not lack money, retained full possession of his wits. With his co-operation the agrarian politics of conciliation of the peasantry, adopted in Russian Poland in 1864, were made the starting-point of a most successfully inaugurated agitation among the Ruthenian inhabitants of Galicia. At the same time a change "for the better" took place in Bohemia, which completely contradicted the pessimistic prophecies of Koshelev's guest. In June, 1868, a triple festival took place at Prague. The foundation-stone of the Bohemian theatre was laid, and the jubilee of the national museum at Prague (founded, as is well known, by a German) was celebrated at the same time as the seventieth birthday of Father Palacky. These events gave occasion to spectacular displays, which proved that the apparently Germanised nobility of Bohemia were good Bohemians, and that the Bohemians themselves had become good Russians. The first festival oration was delivered by an aristocrat, Count Clam-Martinitz; but the Universities of Moscow, Kiev, and St. Petersburg, the St. Petersburg Academy of Sciences, and the Rumianzow Museum at Moscow were much more numerously represented in the festival association than the scientific institutions of Vienna and German Austria. Rayevsky, adorned with the gold-embroidered robe of the high priest, was prominent in the foremost rank of the guests as honorary member of the jubilee institution. Rieger and a Count Anersperg were his neighbours, and of the honorary members chosen for the celebration of the day seven were Russian, and only one was German. The air was rent by Slav cries as the "glorious" names of Pogodin and Hilferding were mentioned among the number.

The "thorough Russian" who bore the German name of Hilferding was then Russian Consul in Seraievo, and was known far and wide as the mortal enemy of Austria. As was natural for this genuine patriot, Hilferding was a missionary in the first place, and only incidentally an official. He was a scholar, but in real life a man of little resource. He received the greater part of his instructions not from Prince Gorchakov, but from his friend Raievski, who, on this occasion as on others, played the part of counsellor to the Embassy.[1] The piping treble voice and the turgid Slavonic oratory of the loquacious consul were much ridiculed in Seraievo, while in St. Petersburg his achievements were highly estimated. The events of 1878 indicated for the first time, in the most humiliating way, that the successes of the great Russian were mere vapour and smoke. He removed in the meantime to St. Petersburg, where during the last years of his life he still played a not unimportant part as the scholar and orator of the Slavonic Benevolent Society. Rayevsky also has recently returned to the maternal lap of this society, in the desire to end his days in his native country.

The Slavonic Benevolent Society, originally called the Slavonic Committee, was founded in 1857 by Privy-Counsellor Bachmetiev, the curator of the University of Moscow. It was divided into a Moscow and a St. Petersburg section, and its ostensible object was the support of Slav reading clubs in foreign countries. But it announced from the first that its sympathies were political, and not literary or philanthropic. Bachmetiev's successor in the presidency of the Moscow section converted

[1] See Appendix, Note 47.

the committees into real nurseries for the mission to the Western Slavonic countries with such success that his successor, Ivan Aksakov, was able to secure the nomination in 1877 of Prince Vladimir Cherkasky, a member of the committee, since then called the "Benevolent Society," to the control of the civil administration of Bulgaria, at that time occupied by the Russian troops.

This apparent success proved in the sequel to be the worst possible mistake. Both the Russian mission in the Balkan peninsula and the Russian credit in Bulgaria received a blow from the election of Cherkasky, from which the politics of St. Petersburg have not yet recovered. The fêted friend of the people and leader of the Slavophil party had taken the knout across the border with him. He made so free a use of this national instrument of education, which he had learned to value in the days of his missionary activity in Poland, that the Bulgarians soon began to groan under its lashes, and to regard the new Muscovite Pasha as a Greek or a Turk in disguise. Although Cherkasky died upon the day when the peace of San Stefano was concluded, the unfavourable impression made by the first Russian Governor of Bulgaria long survived him. Its effects were subsequently still further strengthened. The majority of the civil officials and generals afterwards sent into the principality pursued Cherkasky's system of oppression with such conscientiousness and success that the final result of the Russian achievements in the cause of liberty in 1877 and 1878 has been the complete discredit of their name.

It was unavoidable that Bulgaria should be struck out of the list of Russian mission stations in foreign countries. For this reason the majority of our political missionaries have returned to their original occupations. Embittered by the ingratitude of their Western brethren, these excellent men have begun the liberal dispensation of their benevolence among the gagged dwellers by the Vistula, the Duna, and the Baltic Sea, as well as in Finland lately. There they undergo a practical preparation for the high calling that awaits them in the West.

APPENDIX.

NOTE 1, PAGE 1.

IT is difficult to guess whom the German author regards "the most competent of Russian historians," since he does not mean A. N. Pipin, ex-Professor of the St. Petersburg University, who is regarded in Russia as the authority on modern Russian history. In his excellent work, "The Movement in Russia under Alexander I.," he says of the "Decembrist" (*i.e.*, the participants of the mentioned conspiracy and rebellion in December, 1825): "History accords to them the credit of understanding the social and political problems so far as to advocate the liberation of the serfs, the reform of the Court, and some other points of Russian development, and of being the sole representatives of Liberal ideas at their period. They could do little towards putting their ideas into practice, but they prepared what came after, through calling attention to the wants of the people, through pointing out the best means towards general reform, and finally through the example of moral courage and of deep convictions which they showed in the sufferings they endured for their ideas." In fact the reaction began long before the outbreak of 1825, and there could be, and never was, any doubt that with the accession of Nicholas to the throne "autocracy would become the special aim" of the new reign, whether the rebellion had taken place or not. Even so early as 1818, when Alexander I. delivered the Liberal and constitutional speech in Warsaw, Nicholas—then heir to the crown—showed himself strongly in opposition to the Emperor, and, together with the State historiographer, Karamzín, a very influential person at the time, and many others, most decidedly condemned the Liberalism of Alexander I.—ED.

NOTE 2, PAGE 5.

Such a qualification of the May fires of 1862 is altogether unfounded. When those fires broke out throughout Russia, with, so to say, unusual persistence and fury, rumours of arson began to circulate, as is always the case on such occasions in Russia. M. N. Katkov (see chap. xiii.) introduced the matter into the press, insinuating that the malefactors were revolutionists. No single fact, however, has been produced in support of the calumny. On the contrary, those revolutionists, who afterwards were condemned, as Serno-Solovievich, Bené, and others, formed volunteer fire brigades and worked in their ranks. On the other hand, the Government undertook a series of inquiries into the matter, and persons like the Governor-General of St. Petersburg, Prince Souvórov, and Adjutant-General Den (personal adjutant of the Tsar), the latter, after his inquiry upon the subject made in Simbirsk, declared that the suspicion was void.—ED.

NOTE 3, PAGE 10.

It deserves to be noted that the manifesto calling the proposed assembly had been already signed by Alexander II., and would undoubtedly have been published had it not been that Ignatiev, thinking to gain supreme influence, regarded it as justifiable to cast suspicion on his colleagues in his first audience with the new monarch, and to express doubts with regard to the project for which he had formerly voted. The publication was stopped, and the Liberal ministers named above were soon dismissed. Ignatiev was master of the situation. So came the "father of lies" to be the founder of the present absolute *régime*.

NOTE 4, PAGE 11.

Official nationalism, as it is practised nowadays in Russia, is by no means a thing that "had not been tried" before. The Russian historian, Karamzín, when arguing, in his addresses to

Alexander I., against Liberalism, already used the formula (loyalty to), "orthodoxy, autocracy, nationality," as the basis of "sound" policy for Russia. This formula was repeated by Nicholas I., and became under him an official one, and his whole reign was nothing but a permanent attempt to carry it out in reality. The difference between the official nationalism of Alexander III. and that of Nicholas is only that the former is more Slavophil than the second, and that Alexander III. personally is more a man of convictions, while Nicholas was a man of position. Therefore so long as the Jews remained "loyal" to Nicholas, persecutions against them, such as the one we are now witnessing, were impossible under that monarch; they became possible only with the accession to the throne of an individual who is convinced that the Jews are obnoxious because they are neither of Russian origin, nor orthodox.—ED.

NOTE 5, PAGE 16.

His social nature shows itself in the free and easy musical evenings, which he holds in the most intimate circle, and in which he co-operates. How many a one, in the hope of gaining an entrance to these "beer-evenings," has taken pains to learn an out-of-the-way instrument, *e.g.*, the deep bassoon! Art has to serve the ambition of such people: it is not a question of bread and butter.

NOTE 6, PAGE 17.

This holds good of the persons who actually influence Alexander III.'s course of action, and who form his intimate *entourage*, but not of all the ministers who have to serve the Emperor's will. Everybody knows that Nabokov—formerly Minister of Justice—looked after his own interests without any fanaticism, and that Vuishnegradsky's calculating cunning was attributed to everything except fanaticism.

NOTE 7, PAGE 18.

Another circumstance must be noted. From his disinclination to persons who might influence him is explained the fact that Alexander III., when he is absent for a considerable time, as, *e.g.*, at Copenhagen, does not take with him such persons as the well-informed and skilled Count Adlerberg, but only those who are not accustomed to hold, or at least to profess opinions of their own. This circumstance attained supreme importance in the summer of 1886, when the sharp handling of Alexander of Battenberg brought about the political tension still felt in Europe.

NOTE 8, PAGE 22.

It is difficult to understand what our author means by the "popularity" of the present Empress. If there is any consideration for her among the masses it is a kind of awe inspired by her position, but not by her personal character, as the people know absolutely nothing about it. We readily admit that she may be popular on account of her personal character, but the sphere where she can be so is exceedingly narrow, as is the circle within which she is moving. The Court, a couple of privileged boarding schools for girls of the nobility, and those Gatchina policemen and soldiers of one or two regiments of the guards to whom she distributes red shirts and kerchiefs at Christmas, may admire her very much, but that is all. Her popularity as "Princess Dagmar" was very great and widely spread indeed. It can be explained partly by her being not a German princess, but mainly because of her fate being associated with the late heir to the crown, Nicholas (brother of the present Tsar), of whom great expectations were entertained. But since then the old halo has faded away, and no deeds have created a new one suited for the new position of the former Danish princess.—ED.

NOTE 9, PAGE 36.

Plenary sittings of the chamber take place only very seldom. The regular business of this high council, which is entrusted with the examination of the budget and the Bills elaborated in the ministries, is conducted in the sittings of its three departments and the justiciary. Only one part of the members of the *plenum*, and that the smallest, belongs to these departments. Of the five members of the imperial family who belong to the chamber, not one belongs (not even the president) to either of the departments, which have special presidents, and for the most part contain only five members : the same thing holds good of the ministers and superior directors, who by virtue of their office are members of the *plenum*. (It is hardly necessary to mention that none of the members of the Council of State are either elected or hereditary, but all are appointed by the Emperor.—ED.)

NOTE 10, PAGE 41.

So far as rumours go Vannovsky-is not liked in the army. It must be admitted that he did something to better the material position of the soldier, but, on the other hand, the rigid maintenance of unnecessary discipline among them, and the espionage introduced among the officers, make his administration hateful to many. On the other hand, the fact that "he has hardly anything in common with his predecessor" is not a very flattering recommendation, as Count Demetrius Milyutin (brother of Nicholas) was undoubtedly one of the most remarkable Russian statesmen. He reformed the whole army system, making it the duty of all citizens to serve, and reducing the term of service from twenty-five to four years, and he did more for education in Russia than any Minister of National Education, and was always on the side of Liberal reforms when he could.—ED.

NOTE 11, PAGE 41.

General Annenkov, the constructor of the Caspian Railway, also belongs to the category of those military men who have intimate relations with France and Parisian society. Annenkov is a brother-in-law of the ex-diplomatist and academician, Count Melchior de Bogné, who, as a widely-read author, has revealed modern Russia, and especially Russian romance literature, to France, and has helped to make Russia popular with the third republic.

NOTE 12, PAGE 46.

Ignatiev was subsequently the determined and bitter opponent of his former patron, whom he attempted to overthrow and to succeed during the twelve months that he had the direction of the Ministry of the Interior—attempts which contributed largely to the downfall of this revengeful man (May, 1882), and provoked the violent anger of the Tsar.

NOTE 13, PAGE 48.

The talents of Mr. Zinovyev were splendidly illustrated by the diplomatic documents printed by the Bulgarian press. It must be remarked, however, that both he and Von Giers are only executors of the Tsar's plans, the general direction of the external Russian policy being entirely in his hands. This information is derived from a personal friend of the Servian ex-Premier Pashich, a diplomatist who went to St. Petersburg on a diplomatic errand, and found that such was the real position of affairs.—ED.

NOTE 14, PAGE 62.

To be distinguished from the wealthy and distinguished ex-Governor of Moscow of the same name, who is president of the Slav committee, &c., and also from Privy Councillor Peter Dournovo, Director of the Police Department, who, though a subordinate of the minister, plays a rather prominent part, as he is the real chief of the political police, and a far more able, ambitious, and unscrupulous personage than his chief.—ED.

NOTE 15, PAGE 68.

The selection of these agents did not prove fortunate. The technical *chef* was very accommodating, but was too fond of getting money into his hands. A member of the official secret police at that time started a joke which became popular, saying that everything obligatory would soon become voluntary. The State navy could be dispensed with to make room for a "volunteer cruiser fleet," and lastly they would have a volunteer artillery, a volunteer cavalry, volunteer infantry, &c.

APPENDIX

NOTE 16, PAGE 84.

It is difficult to see how one could "open the eyes" of a sovereign who "wishes to avoid the discussion of subjects with which he is unacquainted," and who "never allows discussion of minute points, because he fears explanations which may lead to difficulties." Mind, this feature of the Tsar's character was officially stated by his Minister. In a circular addressed by Count Demetrius Tolstoi to all the governors of the different provinces of European and Asiatic Russia (and which, very naturally, greatly scandalised all the Tsar's most loyal subjects), that Minister informed them that some of them indulged in their yearly reports to the Emperor about the condition of their provinces in too many particulars, and that His Majesty wishes him (the Minister) to advise them to be shorter!—ED.

NOTE 17, PAGE 89.

It may be of interest to those who are unacquainted with Russian life, or who only know it from a distance, that as far as regards these holy wells, it is not a question of deep religious conviction, such as would rouse fanaticism or give an opportunity for the multiplication of sects, but simply one of those cases of orthodox deception which are so common in Russia, and which the law has tried to stop. (A law for their prevention was passed in the time of Nicholas I.). The simplest way to make such a deception (which might euphemistically be called a *pia fraus*) successful, is to throw a holy image, which may be bought for a few pence, into a well, and then to celebrate the finding of this image as a miracle. Russian literature is full of examples of these deceptions. It is sufficient in this place to recall a description by Dostoevsky. From this it is clear that such proceedings have nothing to do with religious motives: they are simply set on foot for the sake of gain. The holiness of the infirm father Sossima was celebrated by his cloister brothers as long as they speculated upon the fact of being able to exploit his bones as wonder-working relics. But after the death of the holy father, when the smell of corruption proceeding from his body could no longer be concealed, his cloister brothers defamed his memory, and branded him as a heretic who had disturbed them in their theological speculations. ("Die Brüder Karamazov," Leipzig, 1884.) These religionists are not ashamed to make use of such deceptions for ecclesiastical and political ends. At Püchlitz, in Esthonia, a holy well was created to lend a pretext for forbidding the completion of the neighbouring Lutheran affiliated church at Illuk (which building went to ruins in the meantime), and to instal a Greek orthodox priest at Püchlitz.

NOTE 18, PAGE 89.

One of the most enlightened men and accomplished officers of his time, Petr Yakovlevich Chadaev attempted to do so half a century ago : he was officially declared to be mad, was arrested and placed in charge of a doctor. No one has had the courage to follow his example.

NOTE 19, PAGE 92.

The so-called "Religious Union of Lithuania" (to Roman Catholicism) was effected on December 23, 1595, in Rome. It was altogether a sham business, concocted by the Jesuits, against the wishes of the Lithuanian and Oukraïnïen people, then under the rule of the Polish kings. Two dishonest bishops, Hypatius Potséy and Cyril Terletsky, treacherously acted as representatives of the Lithuanian and Oukraïnïen (orthodox) clergy and people, after which the Polish kings and magnates began to enforce the "Union" among the Lithuanians and Oukraïnïens. The misfortunes and miseries, together with the bloodiest civil wars that followed, were indescribable. The greater part of the orthodox population did not submit to the Union, but a small minority was forced into it, and as centuries went on they became as devoted Roman Catholics as their forefathers were Greek Catholics. In 1839 a "Uniat" bishop, Syemáshko by name, with some other persons of the same stamp, played, in an opposite direction, the same part which Potséy and Terletsky played centuries ago. They concocted a petition signed in the name of the "Uniats," asking for reunion with "Orthodoxy," and presented it to the Emperor Nicholas I. That petition never really represented the wishes of the bulk of the Uniat population. Nevertheless it was most graciously received by the Tsar, and the "Union" of 1595 annulled. Since then if the former Uniats do not choose to regard themselves as " Orthodox " they are treated like violators of the religious laws of the Empire, they are harassed, persecuted, and exiled.—ED.

NOTE 20, PAGE 98.

"Vart land är fattigt, kall so bli
För den, som guld begär ;
En främling far oss stolt förbi." . . .

(" Our country is poor, and will remain so
For him who desires gold ;
A stranger passes us proudly by." . . .)

NOTE 21, PAGE 101.

Dr. E. Mechelin, "Das Staatsrecht des Grossfürstentums Finnland," in " Handbuch des öffentlichen Rechts der Gegenwart," &c., edited by Dr. Heinrich Marquardsen, iv. 2, Freiburg im Breisgau, 1889, p. 245.

NOTE 22, PAGE 121.

The revolution had already been accomplished in Stockholm by a mere chance, even at the time when Sprengporten was going to embark with the Finnish troops, who had taken the oath of fidelity to the king.

NOTE 23, PAGE 126.

The following figures may give an idea of the importance of this development. About 1620 the number of inhabitants in Finland was estimated at scarcely 300,000. By the end of the seventeenth century it had increased to 700,000. The terrible years of bad crops and famine, 1674-1676, 1687-1688, and 1695-1697, in the last of which alone 100,000 people died, together with emigrations and the sufferings of the Northern war, reduced the population after the peace of Ngstädt (1721) to 200,000, or at most 250,000 The first census of 1749 (the first that was taken) showed for Swedish Finland about 420,000, and for Russian Finland about 100,000; in 1785, 680,000 + 177,000; and in 1809, 900,000 + 200,000. Of these, through the failure of crops and increased mortality, 103,260 people died in a single year. In the whole of Finland, in the years 1812, 1825, 1853, and 1865, the number of the inhabitants amounted to 883,832, 1,259,151, 1,698,101, and 1,843,000 respectively. After the terrible failure of crops and the autumn frosts of 1867-1868, the population in 1869 only numbered about 1,736,000, but in 1880 it rose to 2,060,782, and at the end of 1886 it was 2,232,378. Whereas during a long period of the Swedish rule trade and industry had been artificially kept down in Finland, in 1851 it possessed 148 manufactures with a produce value of about five million Finnish marks (or francs), and in 1876 this value reached the figure of 60 millions. In the year 1850 the total trade returns of Finland only amounted to 43 millions, but in 1882 it reached 286 millions (in 1881: imports, 154·8 millions; exports, 107·3 millions). In the year 1825 Finland possessed only 250 ships trading with foreign parts, in 1851 she had 539, together with 900 coasting vessels; although the number of Finnish merchant ships had been reduced by the Crimean war to 341, in 1882 the mercantile navy of Finland comprised 1980 vessels, among them 152 steamers. The state revenue which in former times did not exceed the value of 1,300,000 Finnish marks, represented in 1810, 1830, and 1860 the figures 6,700,000, 8,560,000, and 19,900,000 respectively, whereas in 1882 it reached the impressive total of 36,320,714. In 1880 Finland possessed a University with about 700 students, a polytechnic institution, two agricultural academies, a school of forestry, a cadet corps, and several naval and commercial schools, together with 17 grammar schools, and 7 higher schools for girls, as well as 570 national schools with some 27,000 scholars.

APPENDIX.

NOTE 24, PAGE 132.

" Yet this land we love ;
For us, with moors, fells, and scars,
A land of gold it is !

Thy blossom, enfolded as in a bud,
Will burst forth.
Behold, by our love will arise
Thy light, thy splendour, thy joy, thy hope :
Then louder let us sing once more
The song of our native home."

These lines are the immediate sequel to those given on page 295, note 20. The whole (11 strophes) is from the pen of John Louis Runeberg ; the tune to it was composed by Pacius.

NOTE 25, PAGE 136.

The first meeting between the two, and the cordial reception of Marie in the house of her father-in-law, are described in few and homely words, but with an incomparable depth of feeling. This passage may be confidently compared with the most beautiful passages in the literature of the world. The translation gives a flat and colourless rendering of it.

NOTE 26, PAGE 166.

Chadaev, a former officer of the guards, was a tragic figure in modern Russian history. A man of brilliant abilities and noble heart, he resented bitterly the degrading position in which the Russian nation was tyrannically kept under Nicholas I. One of the results of that patriotic resentment was an article, entitled "A Philosophical Letter," which he inserted (1836) in a Moscow review called *The Telescope*. In his essay Chadaev denounced the (then) present condition of the Russian people as a hopeless, blank desert, or rather a stagnant morass. His explanation of the fact was not very happy. He rightly sought it in Russia's deplorable past, but the conclusion derived by him from his researches was that the misfortune of the Russians was their not being Roman Catholics. His praise of Catholicism did not produce much effect, but his criticism of Russian life did. Unfortunately a mean individual, Vígel by name, called the attention of Count Benkendorf (the chief of the state police) to the article by sending him a vile insinuation against Chadaev. The latter was by order of the Tsar proclaimed a madman, and forbidden to write anything more, and everybody who had to do with the publication of Chadaev's "letter" was severely punished. Alexander Herzen afterwards stigmatised all that revolting episode thus : " The German, Vígel, took offence on account of offended Russia, the Protestant, and future Roman Catholic, Benkendorf, took offence on account of offended (Greek Catholic) Orthodoxy, and Chadaev, by virtue of His Imperial Majesty's public lie, was proclaimed insane, and a signed promise not to write any more was wrung from him."—ED.

NOTE 27, PAGE 212.

This is precisely the attitude of mind of the non-Chauvinist Russian patriots of to-day—*i.e.*, of those who find themselves debarred from giving expression to their opinions in the press. They desire nothing more ardently than a disaster to the Russian arms. This they regard as the entirely necessary preliminary condition for the more prosperous future of Russia. The eagerness of the Chauvinists for a war is in this way accentuated. This dangerous circumstance is unhappily too little regarded by Europe—politically rent asunder and therefore threatened.

NOTE 28, PAGE 217.

It is difficult for an unprejudiced outsider to see "firmness" on the part of Alexander II. in the fact of his conducting a conversation in a way which leads the interlocutor to believe that the Emperor was "shaken" while he all the time was determined to take a decisive step. Nor can we call "firmness" the method of appointing men opposed to reforms for their carrying out. In fact, Alexander II. was anything but a determined man, and facts which seem to the German author to prove his firmness, prove quite the contrary—that he was a "trimmer" and an insincere man, who always wavered in his decisions, never fully believed in his own plans, and therefore put obstacles in the way of fulfilling those very plans, thus preparing them to be a failure from the first ; and, having in his character a good deal of sentimentality (not real warmth) and indifference, tried, as the first thing, to keep peaceful and pleasant relations with everybody by means of seeming to agree with them (compare also pp. 240–241, and note 35, p. 302). It was a generally known fact that signs of increasing affection on the part of the Emperor were alarming to his ministers, meaning approaching dismissal, and when the latter finally happened Alexander II. embraced his "faithful servant," thanked him for his "good work," and sometimes even shed a few tears "of regret." His son and successor is said to have inherited his father's insincerity, without, however, any sentimentality. It is well known that, at his accession to the throne, when a manifesto about the event was discussed at the ministerial council, he showed to the then Prime Minister, Loris Melikov, all the tokens of his benevolence, and accordance with Melikov's, Milyutin's, and Abaza's constitutional views ; but Loris Melikov had not had time to make up a draught of the manifesto before another one was drawn by Pobyedonostsev in the diametrically opposite sense, and approved by the Emperor without Melikov knowing anything about it. The writer of these lines has learned from Chamberlain J. J. Krassovsky (and Governor of the Tomsk province)—quite a reliable source in that instance—a fact of minor significance, but of the same character. When the felonious squandering of national lands in the Oufá and Orenbóurg provinces (1859–1880), perpetrated by Governor-General Krizhanóvsky and others, came to light, that gentleman went to St. Petersburg to ask for a few months' leave. Not only was he admitted in the Emperor's presence, but the latter showed him no signs of displeasure, shook hands with him, and gave him the leave, while, in fact, the man was already a dismissed official, and the next morning informed of it. It must be remembered that the Governors-General are appointed and dismissed by the Tsar personally.—ED.

NOTE 29, PAGE 223.

It was theoretically supposed that the profit a serf-owner derived from his serfs was a kind of payment given by the latter for those portions of their master's land they tilled for themselves. Consequently it was decided in principle that the liberated serfs should have to pay their former masters for the land they were to be endowed with a sum which would compensate the landowners for the profits they were now going to lose, together with the souls and bodies of the peasants. In reality the overwhelming majority of the serf-owners got from them, not only the rent (for the land), but without comparison more, simply profiting by their power over the peasants, and making them work as much as they possibly could. Thus the adoption of the above principle of compensation for allotments meant in reality making the peasants pay not only for the land they got, but also—under that pretext—for their personal liberation. In other words, the obligatory price of the allotments was raised enormously. The projects of the Formulating Commission were finally brought before the Chief Committee, and here Alexander II.'s system—to put the bitterest enemies of a reform in those very institutions which had to carry out the reform—produced its bitter fruit, notwithstanding the Tsar's personal support of the Liberal party. The Chief Committee, which consisted of the most inveterate representatives of the slave-holding school, like Prince Orlov, Count Pánin, &c., curtailed the *norm* of the allotments, raised still higher the valuation, and introduced a very cunning new scheme (Gagárin's plan) : any serf, if he preferred to do so, could have, instead of his allotment, for which he had to pay, only one-fourth of it free of charge. This in reality meant the making of those unfortunate owners regular proletaires, and a large portion of the peasantry went into the trap. As for the valuation, it was proved many years later that, for example, in the Chernígov province the peasant allotments were valued *thirty times* higher than the market price of the land in those localities.—ED.

NOTE 30, PAGE 224.

Koshelev and his German eulogiser unfortunately forgot on

that occasion that the local committees consisted of representatives of only *one* of the parties interested—the nobility. As to the serfs, they had no representatives.

NOTE 31, PAGE 224.

The members of the local committee took part in the debates of the committee of supervision in two series. Koshelev belonged to the first series: a fruitless attempt was also made by the members of the second series to enlarge the powers of the deputies.

NOTE 32, PAGE 226.

The gradual impoverishment of the peasantry was to be easily predicted. But it would be a great mistake to believe that the explanation of the fact lies in "the peasants' failure to manage their own affairs." With the best abilities possible no one could prosper under conditions like the following : 1. The valuation of the land allotted to the peasants was so high that they had to pay away for years and years all the revenue which their lots yielded them, and to get some accessory income (by extra work, cattle-breeding, or the like) to pay the surplus ; 2. The budget of the State, which fell mostly upon the peasantry, increased year after year in an alarming proportion ; and 3. The movements of the people, and the spirit of enterprise, as also the popular education, were hindered at every step by the bureaucratic system of administration.—ED.

NOTE 33, PAGE 227.

For the sake of completeness it must be noted that Koshelev's friend, Khomyakov, and Constantine Aksakov, the principal founders of the Slavophil party, died about this time. Ivan Kiryeevsky predeceased them in 1856. From that time the authoritative influence of Ivan Aksakov and Samarin, to whom Koshelev was opposed, began.

NOTE 34, PAGE 229.

This shows that Koshelev did not know *everything* about

the Russian peasantry. And really the peasants were not at all so stupid and illogical as the German author believes them to have been. They were "serfs," *i.e.*, men "bound to the soil." Were the law strictly observed they ought not to be sold separately from the land they tilled. Consequently they regarded themselves as inseparable from the soil (and the idea was quite in accordance with history). They did not deny their being a kind of living property of the nobles, but a property inseparably combined with the land. Now that the Tsar, who, both according to law and public opinion, had all the right to restore them their liberty, did so—they understood they were liberated with the soil, of which they were always regarded as the attributes. They could not conceive what it was they had to pay for. And it was also as inconceivable to the Radicals. There was certainly not either much justice or logic in making the victims of a historical crime pay the expenses of its redemption. If, however, it was supposed that to compensate the serf-owners for their losses was practically unavoidable, it was a duty for the whole nation, not for the peasants alone. The Government ought to make a fair valuation of the lands allotted to the peasants and pay the value from the fisc. And such were the suggestions of the Radicals at the time.—ED.

NOTE 35, PAGE 245.

Koshelev has enlarged upon the difference between his conceptions and those of Cherkasky in a detailed record appended to his "Memoirs," which he sent to the Emperor in November, 1866, and of which the Emperor fully approved. The day after this record was sent in, Milyutin had an apoplectic seizure; Cherkasky hastened to St. Petersburg, received from the Emperor the assurance that the previous system would be adhered to, and already regarded himself as the successor of Milyutin in the Polish State secretaryship. Next day he learned that an opponent of his principles, the afterwards notorious minister of justice, Nabokov, had received this appointment. He was commanded to return immediately to his post at Warsaw. He replied by sending in his resignation, which was at once accepted. The Prince went to Moscow, where he was soon afterwards chosen Lord Mayor.

APPENDIX. 303

NOTE 36, PAGE 250.

The two latter periodicals were monthlies. Of these, Krayeevsky never either edited or published the *Sovreménnik* ("The Contemporary"). But when that Radical and socialistic magazine was suppressed by the Government, its chief editor, the poet Nekrassov, entered into an agreement with Krayeevsky, according to which Krayeevsky's monthly, *Otéchestverniya Zapiski* ("The Annals of the Fatherland"), which by this time had become altogether insignificant, and without any definite political and social platform, came into the hands of the *Sovreménnik* staff, now strengthened by some new and talented men, and continued the traditions of *Sovreménnik*, while Krayeevsky remained nominally its editor, and in fact its chief owner.—ED.

NOTE 37, PAGE 261.

Only comparatively, because by that time the *Sovreménnik* had acquired in the person of N. Chernishévsky a worthy successor to Byelinsky, and had taken up the lead among the better part of reading Russia.—ED.

NOTE 38, PAGE 263.

Never did any other satirical leaflet surpass in these qualities the *Svistók*, which at that time was conducted by a writer of first-class talent, equally skilful in prose and verse, Dobrolúbov by name, who was assisted by such brilliant stars as Saltikóv, Chernishévsky, Nekrassov, and Elisseëv. But the *Golos* had over the *Svistók* the advantage of being a *daily*, while *Svistók* (as a supplement, incorporated with the *Sovreménnik*) appeared only once a month.—ED.

NOTE 39, PAGE 264.

It must be plainly said that while this "flexibility" was inevitable for the existence and development of a paper with the circulation and resources of the *Golos*, it meant, on the other hand, unsteadiness in principle, and, by its practice, cultivated in the public the inclination to treat unflinching adherence to principles very lightly.—ED.

NOTE 40, PAGE 270.

It is only fair to remind the reader how really that "outrageous breach of the law" happened, and what it really meant. General Trepov, a personal favourite of the late Imperial couple, ordered a political prisoner, and former student of the St. Petersburg University, Bogolúbov by name, to be flogged in the so-called "House of Preliminary Detention," a model prison of the capital. This outrage was a breach of both the inner sense and the formal side of the law, as it was utterly unprovoked by Bogolúbov, and as the prison was under the rule of the Minister of Justice (Count Pálen), and Trepov had no right to give any orders there. Besides, it was the vilest insult to humanity, because the whole brutality was done to show openly and provokingly that Trepov in his position could defy any law and the so-called rights of man. People were already sick with the tendency of Russian officialdom to trample down the rights of citizens, and the general expectation was that this time insolence would be punished by the Government. It was bound to put Trepov to trial by the very laws it had proclaimed. But the Government preferred *to break the law*. Months passed, and it only tried to hush the case. Then a courageous young woman resolved to punish the offender in the name of insulted humanity, or rather, to bring the case before the tribunal of the conscience of the nation. And the verdict of the jury has shown that she acted in accordance with the imperative, though unoutspoken, requests of that conscience.—ED.

NOTE 41, PAGE 270.

A school corresponding, as to its place in the educational system, to an English high school or grammar school, but with a more encyclopædic course.—ED.

NOTE 42, PAGE 271.

Both titles belong really to the same association, the first being its colloquial, the second its official, name. It was founded by a well-known writer and translator of Shakespeare, Drouzhínin, but Krayeevsky was for a long time its president.—ED.

NOTE 43, PAGE 273.

The best Liberal daily paper ever published in Russia was the *Moscow Telegraph* (1881-83), edited by the barrister, Rodzevich (in Moscow), but it was suppressed very quickly.—ED.

NOTE 44, PAGE 276.

Here the German author makes again a mistake. Spassovich (who, by the way, is a lawyer) never edited the *Messenger of Europe*. Its joint editor is Pipin, formerly Professor of Universal Literature at the University of St. Petersburg, and later joint editor of the *Sovreménnik*. Stassulevich in former times was also Professor (of History) at the same University (but never a lawyer), and Lecturer on Universal History to Czarevich Nicholas (brother to the present Emperor), who died when heir-apparent.—ED.

NOTE 45, PAGE 276.

Besides the *Messenger of Europe* there are at present two other monthlies in Russia which try to be independent, honest, and advanced: the *Russian Thought* and the *Northern Messenger*. The former has secured the collaboration of the most noted and brilliant of Russian leading spirits in Russian literature, N. K. Mikhailovsky, the commentator, and opposer, in a certain sense, of H. Spencer and B. Darwin. The *Northern Messenger* tries to bring to the front the new generation of writers. Both, however, cannot speak openly on the most urgent questions, and their existence is a hard one in every way.—ED.

NOTE 46, PAGE 278.

Kamatscheiew, a Russian Governor of the province of Kovno, in 1866 wrote as follows on the subject of these missionary officials :—

"Our internal administration has always lacked capable and

trustworthy officers. When Muraev asked in 1864 that Russian officials should be sent to the territory under the Governor-General of Vilna, the chiefs of our administration took the opportunity to get rid of the pack with whom they could do nothing at home. These good-for-nothings flung themselves upon the Western (Lithuanian) provinces like vultures upon carrion. My predecessor was compelled to send them home by waggon loads, at the expense of the State. I could only follow his example, taking the greatest precautions to prevent the travellers from spending their journey-money upon drink. The Polish officials were incomparably more respectable and intelligent than those sent out to us, but they were politically unreliable," and so on.

NOTE 47, PAGE 284.

A part of the correspondence between Hilferding and Rayevsky fell in 1877 into the hands of the Turkish officials, by whom it was published. Little attention was paid to these important documents, which were soon forgotten in the turmoil of that year of war.

The Gresham Press,
UNWIN BROTHERS,
CHILWORTH AND LONDON.

www.ingramcontent.com/pod-product-compliance
Lightning Source LLC
Chambersburg PA
CBHW030003240426
43672CB00007B/808